THE EVERYTHING
WHOLE FOODS
COOKBOOK

Dear Reader,

Thank you so much for picking up *The Everything® Whole Foods Cookbook*. In this book I have striven to include a variety of recipes that not only utilize whole foods, but that taste great and are easy to prepare. Cooking with whole foods does not have to be daunting. It just means taking a step back from the freezer section, putting some boxed meals back on the shelf, and starting to cook with wholesome, fresh ingredients.

I am excited to share these recipes with you. I have always loved food and cooking from scratch. Cooking with fresh, local ingredients and whole foods is a passion of mine. There is nothing like eating the perfect tomato on a hot August day or making a dazzling dish with fresh-caught crab. Eating whole foods is not only good for you, it is also delicious. Please use this book as your guide to a new, exciting, tasty way to eat.

Rachel Rappaport

Welcome to the EVERYTHING® Series!

These handy, accessible books give you all you need to tackle a difficult project, gain a new hobby, comprehend a fascinating topic, prepare for an exam, or even brush up on something you learned back in school but have since forgotten.

You can choose to read an Everything® book from cover to cover or just pick out the information you want from our four useful boxes: e-questions, e-facts, e-alerts, and e-ssentials.

We give you everything you need to know on the subject, but throw in a lot of fun stuff along the way, too.

We now have more than 400 Everything® books in print, spanning such wide-ranging categories as weddings, pregnancy, cooking, music instruction, foreign language, crafts, pets, New Age, and so much more. When you're done reading them all, you can finally say you know Everything®!

QUESTION

Answers to
common questions

FACT

Important snippets
of information

ALERT

Urgent
warnings

ESSENTIAL

Quick
handy tips

PUBLISHER Karen Cooper

DIRECTOR OF ACQUISITIONS AND INNOVATION Paula Munier

MANAGING EDITOR, EVERYTHING® SERIES Lisa Laing

COPY CHIEF Casey Ebert

ASSISTANT PRODUCTION EDITOR Melanie Cordova

ACQUISITIONS EDITOR Lisa Laing

SENIOR DEVELOPMENT EDITOR Brett Palana-Shanahan

EDITORIAL ASSISTANT Matthew Kane

EVERYTHING® SERIES COVER DESIGNER Erin Alexander

LAYOUT DESIGNERS Erin Dawson, Michelle Roy Kelly, Elisabeth Lariviere, Denise Wallace

THE
EVERYTHING®
WHOLE FOODS
COOKBOOK

Rachel Rappaport

Adamsmedia
Avon, Massachusetts

To my husband, Matt, who loves food
as much as I do.

———————

An Everything® Series Book.
Everything® and everything.com® are registered trademarks of F+W Media, Inc.

Published by Adams Media, a division of F+W Media, Inc.
57 Littlefield Street, Avon, MA 02322 U.S.A.
www.adamsmedia.com

ISBN 10: 1-4405-3168-4
ISBN 13: 978-1-4405-3168-2
eISBN 10: 1-4405-3334-2
eISBN 13: 978-1-4405-3334-1

Printed in the United States of America.

10 9 8 7 6 5 4 3 2 1

Library of Congress Cataloging-in-Publication Data
is available from the publisher.

The information in this book should not be used for diagnosing or treating any health problem. Not all diet and exercise plans suit everyone. You should always consult a trained medical professional before starting a diet, taking any form of medication, or embarking on any fitness or weight-training program. The author and publisher disclaim any liability arising directly or indirectly from the use of this book.

Many of the designations used by manufacturers and sellers to distinguish their products are claimed as trademarks. Where those designations appear in this book and Adams Media was aware of a trademark claim, the designations have been printed with initial capital letters.

Nutritional statistics by Nicole Cormier, RD.

Contents

Acknowledgments

I would like to thank my friends and family for happily and enthusiastically taste testing many of the recipes contained within.

Introduction

EVER SINCE 1813 WHEN the first commercial canning factory opened in England, there has been tremendous interest in preserving food, not just at home but in mass, commercially viable ways. In 1923 Clarence Birdseye developed a method of flash freezing, which by 1930 meant that people could buy frozen seafood, fruit, meat, and vegetables at their local store. That was just the beginning.

In the years since, the processed food market has evolved from the simple preservation of whole ingredients to the era of convenience foods. By 1953 the TV dinner was on the market and the race to produce even more prefabricated meals, side dishes, and desserts had begun. Combined with a national obsession with modernity, people were excited by these inventions, which sought to free them from the long, laborious ways their parents and grandparents had to prepare meals. Anything that saved so much time must be good, right? Unfortunately, that is not the case.

Most frozen, canned, packaged, and otherwise processed foods are loaded with sweeteners, dyes, preservatives, and chemicals. These additives are to keep the product fresh, shelf-stable and attractive for as long as possible. Consumers have had negative reactions to these additives to varying degrees; for example, sensitivities or allergies to certain dyes.

Processing of food can have some negative effects on its nutritional value. Valuable vitamins and minerals can be lost entirely or diminished during processing. The food processing procedure itself also has drawbacks. Due to the large quantities of food being processed, there is a risk of contamination from bacteria or foreign objects.

Luckily, there is an alternative to processed food. Whole foods are foods that are minimally processed and that are in the purest, most natural form possible. Whole foods are preservative, dye, sweetener, and chemical free. Picture a pineapple fresh from the tree, not diced and stuffed into a can with maraschino cherries and heavy syrup. That is the sort of freshness and flavor whole foods provide.

Eating a diet full of whole foods like whole grains, fresh fruits and vegetables, unprocessed meats and seafood, and legumes helps promote a healthy immune system, leaving one less likely to fall victim to disease or chronic illness. Fiber-rich whole grains and legumes help maintain a high-functioning digestive track. Fresh, wholesome seafood is rich in heart-healthy omega-3 fatty acids and minerals. Fresh fruits and vegetables are not only delicious; they are also low in calories, high in vitamins and fiber. Combined with herbs, spices and a few sauces and vinegars, these foods become stars on the dinner table.

Eating whole foods does not mean giving up your favorite meals. It means putting down the box and making some food from scratch. In this book you will find new ways to use whole foods to create flavorful, tempting meals that the whole family will enjoy. There are recipes for everything from smoothies to tempting sauces to sandwiches to luscious desserts, which no one would guess were full of whole grains. The recipes reflect a wide range of cuisines and styles so there is something to fit every palate. Eating whole foods is anything but boring. The trick is to use the freshest ingredients possible in creative ways.

The included nutritional information makes it easy to choose a recipe based on your individual interest and need. All 300 recipes have the calorie, fat, protein, sodium, fiber, carbohydrate, and sugar content displayed.

CHAPTER 1

The Whole Foods Movement

The whole foods movement is gaining popularity across the globe. Now more than ever, people are interested in making changes to their diet to eliminate processed foods. They are choosing instead to consume foods that are as minimally processed as possible. In this book you will find all you need to become adept at making delicious, healthful meals with whole foods. Learn about the benefits of eating whole foods, sources for whole foods, commonly used ingredients, helpful kitchen equipment, and even a bit about canning your own in-season whole foods.

What Are Whole Foods?

Whole foods are foods that are as minimally processed as possible. Whole foods generally do not include foods with added ingredients. Whole foods are not necessarily organic, but the more unprocessed and natural the food is, the closer it is to being a whole food. Processed foods contain preservatives, stabilizers, sweeteners, and other food additives, which can have effects on the nutritional value of the product. For example, a fresh cut of meat is a whole food while a hot dog is not. Tomato ketchup is a heavily processed tomato product, not a whole food. Additionally, unlike processed foods, whole foods do not contain preservatives. A quick rule of thumb is that if it looks like it came straight out of the ground or off the tree, or is meat or seafood packaged with nothing else, it is a whole food. If it comes in a can, jar, or box, or the ingredient list is a mile long, it is not a whole food.

FACT

Slow Food International was founded in 1989 in Italy. It began as reaction to a McDonald's opening in Rome. The organization focuses on providing alternatives to fast food. In doing so, they promote eating local foods, knowing where your food comes from, preserving regional cuisines, and farming foods that are native to the region. There are now dozens of chapters around the globe and over 100,000 members.

Whole foods are healthful and provide maximum nutritional value for those who consume them. Whole foods can even help combat common illnesses and conditions, while processed foods are full of empty calories and for the most part, devoid of natural nutrition.

Why You Should Eat Whole Foods

With today's emphasis on quick and easy cooking, many people have fallen into the trap of relying on packaged foods and the microwave for their meals. Unfortunately, packaged meals are chock-full of preservatives and other chemicals. This is not how humans were supposed to eat!

Instead of indulging in pseudo foods that add calories and fat but not nutrition, we need to return to eating food as it was supposed to be, in the purest form possible. Whole foods are more nutritious. Whole foods are more likely to contain whole grains, which provide the much-needed fiber missing from most processed foods. Whole foods can help protect the body from disease and chronic illness by providing necessary vitamins, antioxidants, and other essentials for a healthy life.

Best Sources for Whole Foods

Luckily, it is not terribly difficult to find whole foods. There are websites and even apps for your phone that can tell you which fruits and vegetables are currently in-season in your area. Farmers' markets are a wonderful place to find these fruits and vegetables. Farmers' markets are good sources of fresh, high quality cheeses, butter, yogurt, meats and seafood. Best of all, the farmers that come to farmers' markets are nearly always local so the food is incredibly fresh. Look online or call your state department of agriculture to obtain a list of farmers' markets in your area.

ESSENTIAL

Storing vegetables and fruits properly is part of the whole foods lifestyle. Store fresh herbs in glasses of water to keep them fresh longer. Vegetables should be placed in the crisper away from fruits like apples, which give off a gas that causes vegetables to decay faster. Fruits should be kept on the counter to ripen fully, then be refrigerated if necessary.

Another great source for local whole foods is community supported agriculture (CSA). CSAs are a program where consumers pay a farm at the start of the season for regular fruit and vegetable delivery for the rest of the season. Occasionally, in addition to the fee participants are required to volunteer at the farm they are supporting. Volunteering at a farm is an excellent way to learn more about how food is produced and to earn a new respect for whole foods. Some CSAs also include locally sourced dairy, honey, and even baked goods. Participants either have the produce delivered to their door or it is delivered to a central location for pickup.

Food co-ops are another way to buy whole foods. Food co-ops are worker-owned stores whose goal is to provide high quality food to their members. Each member has a stake in the store and all decisions are made cooperatively. Members work in the store or pay an additional fee in exchange for the ability to shop at the co-op. Most co-ops' focus is on natural and whole foods.

ALERT

Vegetables can lose vital nutrients and vitamins if they are over-cooked. Steaming vegetables helps them retain vitamins. Sautéed vegetables retain a maximum amount of nutrients as well. Another option is to garnish dishes with raw or blanched vegetables.

When shopping at a conventional supermarket it is best to only shop the outer edges of the store. That is where the produce, meat, and dairy are located. The central aisles are nearly always where the sodas, canned foods, chips, and other processed foods are found. The areas that you should be visiting most are the produce and refrigerated sections.

Creating Meals Using Whole Foods

The first step to creating meals from whole foods is, as easy as it sounds, to start buying whole foods. Familiarize yourself with foods that may be unfamiliar to you. Go to your local farmers' market and pick one new-to-you fruit or vegetable a week to try. It is an easy way to not only expand your palate but to ease into eating more whole foods.

Eating whole foods does not mean dooming yourself to a lifetime of boring, bland foods. It means taking a new approach to eating. Start creating meals using whole ingredients instead of relying on prefabricated packaged goods.

Think about what kinds of packaged foods your family likes. Do they like frozen meals? Think about how you could make the same foods from scratch. Instead of buying frozen vegetables in heavy preservative-laden sauces, steam fresh vegetables and toss them with homemade vinaigrette. If you love the macaroni and cheese that comes with that bright orange powder, make macaroni and cheese with real cheese. Each little step will bring you closer to making meals entirely made with whole foods.

ALERT

Seafood safety is important. When shopping for seafood, look for a shop that follows proper food handling practices. Fish should smell fresh, not fishy. Whole fish should have clear, slightly bulgy eyes. Whole shellfish should be sold alive. Pack live seafood lightly in ice if traveling a distance after purchase.

Meal planning can help you incorporate more whole foods into your diet. Rather than wondering each day what is for dinner and picking up fast food or a frozen meal at the last minute, you will know. Each Sunday, draft a list of the meals you want to serve each day. Include meals that incorporate leftovers from other meals. For example if you make tuna steaks on Monday, cook extra so you can make tuna burgers on Wednesday. That will save you the time and energy it takes to make a whole meal from scratch each night. Write out a grocery list of all of the ingredients you need to make the meals for the week. If your pantry or spice cabinet is skimpy, add one or two new items to the list to have on hand that are not needed for this week's meals. Within no time, it will become second nature and your cabinets will be fully stocked.

Commonly Used Ingredients and Pantry Items

A fully stocked cabinet and refrigerator are key to becoming immune to the allure of processed foods and fast food. If you have food on hand, the urge to "just pick something up" is diminished. A full pantry also makes it easier to whip up a meal on a day when you did not get to shop or meal plan.

Spices

Keeping a well-stocked spice cabinet helps spice up all of those wonderful whole foods you are bringing home from the store. Sea salt and kosher salt are a cook's best weapons; they bring out the flavor of nearly every-thing they touch. Fine-grained sea salt is just right for everyday use; save the fancy ones for finishing dishes. Whole peppercorns, paprika (smoked, hot, and original), ground chipotle, ground cayenne, chili powder, ground jala-peño, and pepper flakes will spice up any meal. Chesapeake Bay Seasoning will make you think you are in the Delmarva and is perfect for seafood or even poultry. Dill seed, mustard seed, celery seed, and fennel seed are great for pickling, dry rubs, and adding concentrated flavor to other dishes. Gar-lic powder, mustard powder, and onion powder are great sources of flavor when wet ingredients wouldn't be appropriate.

Traditional baking spices like cocoa powder, nutmeg, allspice, cinna-mon, Saigon Cinnamon, and cloves actually can have both sweet and savory applications. Dried herbs are not quite as tasty as fresh but good in a pinch. Herbes de Provence adds a French flair to any dish, while chervil, basil, pars-ley, oregano, thyme, rosemary, and dill weed are tremendously adaptable.

The use of spices goes back to 50,000 B.C. The spice trade developed first in the Middle East and East Asia. Many cultures used spices not only for flavoring food but also as medicines. By the 1440s, the spice trade had become so important that people were risking their lives sailing to far-off countries in order to procure spices.

Vinegars and Oils

Even whole foods need a bit of flavoring help now and again. Dark and light soy sauce, chili-garlic sauce, rice vinegar, sesame oil, and fish sauce are all staples in Pan-Asian cuisine. Red and white wine vinegar, malt vinegar, champagne vinegar, tarragon vinegar, apple cider vinegar, and white vine-gar are all inexpensive and essential to making vinaigrette and other dress-ings. Olive and canola oil are essential to many recipes.

In the Pantry

Canned tomatoes are a great alternative when fresh tomatoes are unavailable. Look for tomatoes packed in juice with no added salt. Chipotles in adobo sauce add a lot of flavor and moisture to Mexican-inspired dishes. If homemade stock is unavailable, stock sold in cartons is fresher tasting than the canned variety. Buy no-sodium-added stock. Various sizes of pasta including spaghetti, farfalle, orzo, pastina, and linguine are essential for pasta dishes and many soups. Couscous and pearl couscous are great in salads or hot dishes. Whole grains including kasha, bulgur wheat, farro, cornmeal, polenta, barley, wheat berries, and old-fashioned rolled oats can be made into a myriad of dishes.

All-purpose flour, whole-wheat flour, buckwheat flour, baking soda, baking powder, vanilla extract, dried coconut, and white whole-wheat flour will take care of most of your baking needs. A variety of dried fruit is good to have on hand as well. Dijon and whole-grain mustards are the base of many dressings and sauces and are of course great on sandwiches.

On the Counter

Some fruits and vegetables do better on the counter than in the refrigerator. Tomatoes, avocados, potatoes, yellow onions, red onions, white onions, apples, and pears should all be kept unrefrigerated. Citrus fruit can go on the counter as well but if it ripens too quickly, refrigerating it will stop it from spoiling.

In the Refrigerator and Freezer

Keep your refrigerator well stocked. Chicken, turkey, duck, beef, lamb, bison, venison, seafood, and pork should of course all be kept refrigerated. Try different cuts of each kind. Milk, buttermilk, butter, sour cream, yogurt, Greek yogurt, and eggs are staples.

Homemade stocks can be kept frozen for up to a year. Nuts keep fresh longer frozen than in the cabinet. Stock up on meats and freeze them for up to six months. Freeze homemade ice pops, sorbets, granitas, and frozen yogurt in freezer-safe containers.

Kitchen Equipment

Assuming the absolute basics are in place like a refrigerator and a stove, there are some other kitchen items that can be very useful to the home cook.

Which ones you choose to have in your kitchen depends on your personal cooking style and needs.

Kitchen Appliances

Mixers come in two basic styles. Hand mixers can mix batters, soft dough, icings, and egg whites. Stand mixers have an attached bowl and are much more powerful. It is worth investing in one if you would like to be able to mix bread and other stiffer dough, or if you use a mixer a lot. Things mix much more quickly in the stand mixer and since it is hands-free, it enables you to multitask.

Blenders are essential for making things like smoothies and drinks. Look carefully at the description to make sure the blender does what you need it to do. If you need a blender that crushes ice, check that it is powerful enough to do that. Blender strength can vary greatly. Some are best at puréeing while some are strong enough to turn wheat berries into flour.

Immersion blenders are small, hand-held blenders that are used to purée. They are great for puréeing foods that would be awkward to blend in a traditional blender, such as hot soup or food that would have to be puréed in batches. You can use immersion blenders directly in a pot on the stove.

Mini choppers are food processors with a very small capacity. They are best used for puréeing or chopping small amounts of vegetables. They are also handy for small tasks like beating together ingredients for deviled eggs.

Food processors generally come in 7-, 12-, or 14-cup sizes. The size you need depends on what your needs are. Large ones are generally the most versatile because food processors do not need to be filled to a certain level to work. Some food processors come with juicer or slicer attachments.

Slow cookers are invaluable to busy cooks everywhere. Most slow cooker recipes cook for about eight hours which means one can get up in the morning, put some food in the slow cooker, and come home to a fully cooked meal. Slow cookers come in several sizes, ranging from 2 quarts (perfect for a couple) all the way up to 8 quarts, which could hold an entrée that would feed up to twelve people. Look for models that have low, high, and warm settings. The warm setting keeps the food at a safe temperature after it is done cooking.

Ice cream makers are certainly a nonessential piece of kitchen equipment. But if you are interested in making ice creams, sorbets, sherbets, or frozen yogurt, they are invaluable. Ice cream makers come in two types. The most affordable ice cream makers have a center insert that needs to be frozen, empty, before making a batch of ice cream. High-end models have a compressor that freezes the ice cream as it churns, eliminating the need for freezing an insert. That means one can make a frozen dessert on a whim.

Utensils and Tools

Must-haves include wooden and/or silicone spoons, spatulas, liquid measuring cups, dry measuring cups, measuring spoons, tongs, meat thermometer, reamer, can opener, potato masher, brush, slotted spoons, mixing bowls, colander, vegetable peeler, pepper grinder, sharp knives, and oven mitts.

Nonessential but helpful tools include a candy thermometer, a spider skimmer, ice cream scoop, cooking chopsticks, cherry pitter, offset spatula, meat fork, serving utensils, baster, metal sieves, cookie cutters, kitchen twine, cheesecloth, canning equipment, marinating container, and salad dressing shaker.

QUESTION

How important is it to sharpen my knives?
It is easy to forget to sharpen your knives. However, it is really important to do this regularly. Sharp knives not only cut better, they are safer. When you use a dull knife, you have to press harder on what you're cutting, which leads to greater risk of cutting yourself. Learn how to use a steel to sharpen your knives; it is easier than it looks!

Pots and Pans

Essential pots and pans include:

- Baking sheets
- Muffin tins
- Loaf pan
- 2-quart casserole
- 8" round cake pan

- 9" × 13" pan
- 8" × 8" pan
- 12" cast-iron skillet
- 10" or 12" nonstick skillet
- 8" skillet
- 2-quart saucepan
- Dutch oven
- Wok
- Roasting pan with rack
- Stockpot

Helpful but nonessential items include bundt pans, tube pans, lobster pot, omelet pan, crêpe pan, 4-quart saucepan, mini muffin tin, meatloaf pan, springform pan, and steamer baskets.

Canning In-Season Foods

Canning is having a revival right now and it is not a coincidence that it is happening at the same time as the whole foods movement. Both are focused on using whole foods and fresh, in-season fruits and vegetables. Can foods that are at the peak of their season and freshness. There is nothing more amazing than opening a can of peaches in December and having them taste exactly the same as they did in August. It is a wonderful way to have great-tasting whole foods all year long. Best of all, it is done without using the same sort of chemical preservatives as commercially canned or processed food. Once properly canned, food is shelf-stable for one year.

What to Can?

Deciding what to can is the hardest part of canning. High-acid foods (most fruits and pickles) can be canned using the hot water method. Low-acid foods like chicken stock and beans must be pressure canned.

Tomatoes are a classic choice for good reason; tomato season is short and out-of-season tomatoes are generally inedible. Tomatoes can be canned in their own juices either whole or diced. Tomato products like salsa, sauce, stewed tomatoes, and juice can be canned. Unripe, green tomatoes can be pickled. No preservatives needed.

Fruits like peaches, pears, and apples can be canned very successfully in very light syrup—much lighter than what is in commercially canned fruit or juice. Berries are better suited to jams, jellies, and preserves. Pectin, a natural, vegan gelling agent made from apples, can be added to jam, jelly, or preserves to help the product thicken so it is easily spreadable. Fruit butters can also be canned.

Virtually any fruit or vegetable one can think of can be pickled. Pickling is a centuries-old technique for preserving food for the winter.

ESSENTIAL

It is important to use established, tested recipes when canning. This will ensure a well-sealed, safe final product. The classic *Ball Blue Book Guide to Preserving* is an excellent guide to not only safe canning techniques, but step-by-step illustrated directions and dozens of recipes. Pickling makes a great first canning project; it is virtually foolproof.

Canning Equipment

Canning does not require much equipment. A large, lidded pot is needed for processing the jars using the hot water bath method. A rack or tea cloth for the bottom of the pot is essential to keep the jars from sitting flat on the bottom of the pot and possibly breaking. A jar lifter is helpful in removing the jars from the pot after processing. If canning low-acid foods, a pressure canner is required.

The food is canned in glass jars with rings and lids. The lids have an adhesive on them to help seal the jars. This means that the lids must be discarded after the jars are opened and used. However, the jars and rings can be used for many years.

CHAPTER 2

Smoothies and Drinks

Strawberry-Rhubarb Smoothie

Strawberries and rhubarb are a classic combination. The sweetness of the strawberries offsets the rhubarb's tartness.

INGREDIENTS | YIELDS 2 CUPS

1 cup milk

1½ cups frozen strawberries

½ cup diced rhubarb

½ cup fat-free plain Greek yogurt

Place all ingredients in a blender. Pulse until smooth.

PER SERVING Calories: 172 | Fat: 4 g | Protein: 11 g | Sodium: 80 mg | Fiber: 4 g | Carbohydrates: 25 g | Sugar: 16 g

Buying Rhubarb

Rhubarb can range in color from pinkish green to bright red. Look for stalks that are firm and not bruised. Discard the leaves, as they are poisonous.

Power Green Smoothie

Green smoothies are full of antioxidant-packed leafy greens.

INGREDIENTS | YIELDS 2 CUPS

1 apple, cubed

½ cup green grapes

1 banana

1 cup raw spinach

1½ cups ice

¼ cup fat-free plain Greek yogurt

Place all ingredients in a blender. Pulse until smooth.

PER SERVING Calories: 137 | Fat: 0.4 g | Protein: 5 g | Sodium: 25 mg | Fiber: 3 g | Carbohydrates: 33 g | Sugar: 22 g

Homemade Greek Yogurt

You can make Greek yogurt at home by simply straining plain yogurt through a cheesecloth-lined strainer into a bowl overnight. You need 2 cups of regular plain yogurt to make 1 cup of Greek yogurt.

Orangeade

A refreshing alternative to lemonade, orangeade is best when made with in-season oranges.

INGREDIENTS | SERVES 4

1½ cups freshly squeezed orange juice

3 tablespoons agave nectar

4 cups water

Pour all ingredients into a large pitcher. Stir until the agave nectar dissolves.

PER SERVING Calories: 94 | Fat: 0 g | Protein: 0.6 g | Sodium: 2.5 mg | Fiber: 0 g | Carbohydrates: 24 g | Sugar: 21 g

All about Oranges

While all oranges are high in vitamin C and low in calories, individual varieties are used in different ways. Valencia oranges are a sweet variety used most commonly for juicing in the United States. In Europe, the blood orange is preferred for juice. Navel oranges like the Cara Cara are seedless and mostly eaten out of hand.

Raspberry Banana Smoothie

Raspberries can be black, purple, red, and even yellow. Any color would be great in this smoothie.

INGREDIENTS | SERVES 1

½ cup raspberries

1 banana

½ cup skim milk

½ cup plain yogurt

1½ tablespoons flaxseed

Place all ingredients in a blender. Pulse until smooth.

PER SERVING Calories: 283 | Fat: 9 g | Protein: 12 g | Sodium: 111 mg | Fiber: 6.5 g | Carbohydrates: 42 g | Sugar: 26 g

Smooth Smoothies

If you make a lot of smoothies, consider investing in a very high-powered blender. Not only will your smoothies be super smooth, but they will be mixed together more quickly. Higher-powered blenders also crush ice more easily and efficiently than cheaper models.

Super Blueberry Smoothie

Antioxidant-rich blueberries turn this smoothie a shocking shade of purple.

INGREDIENTS | SERVES 1

1 frozen banana
¼ cup frozen blueberries
⅓ cup blueberry juice
¼ cup plain yogurt

Place all ingredients in a blender. Pulse until smooth.

PER SERVING Calories: 213 | Fat: 3 g | Protein: 4 g | Sodium: 34 mg | Fiber: 4 g | Carbohydrates: 47 g | Sugar: 33 g

Blueberries Are a Superfruit!

Blueberries are incredibly high in antioxidants. Antioxidants remove free radicals, which are atoms that are believed to contribute to some diseases. People who eat a lot of antioxidant-rich fruits and vegetables generally have a lower risk of heart disease.

Berry-Oatmeal Smoothie

Oats are a surprising ingredient in this refreshing smoothie.

INGREDIENTS | SERVES 1

¼ cup old-fashioned rolled oats
½ cup frozen mixed berries
½ frozen banana
½ teaspoon agave nectar
1 cup skim milk

1. Place the oats in a blender and pulse until powdery.

2. Add the remaining ingredients and pulse until smooth. Pour into a large cup and drink immediately.

PER SERVING Calories: 285 | Fat: 4 g | Protein: 12 g | Sodium: 110 mg | Fiber: 5 g | Carbohydrates: 53 g | Sugar: 30 g

How to Freeze Berries

Freezing berries when they are in-season means you can enjoy them all year. Simply place the berries in a single layer on a cookie sheet. Place in the freezer until frozen then transfer the berries to a freezer-safe container.

Watermelon-Mint Aqua Fresca

Literally "fresh water," aqua fresca is a water-based drink infused with fruit.

INGREDIENTS | SERVES 6

¾ cup sugar

2 cups water, divided use

½ cup fresh whole mint leaves

1 (6-pound) seedless watermelon, cubed

Make Watermelon "Ice Cubes"

Cut the watermelon into 1-inch cubes. Place on a baking sheet in a single layer. Freeze until solid. Use to cool down your drinks without watering them down.

1. In a small saucepan, bring the sugar, 1 cup water, and mint to a boil. Stir to dissolve the sugar.

2. Strain out the mint and discard. Allow the mixture to cool.

3. Place the watermelon and the sugar mixture into a food processor. Pulse until smooth.

4. Strain through a wide wire mesh sieve into a pitcher. Stir in the remaining water.

PER SERVING Calories: 238 | Fat: 0 g | Protein: 3 g | Sodium: 14 mg | Fiber: 2 g | Carbohydrates: 60 g | Sugar: 53 g

Ginger, Mint, and Lime Cooler

For a small amount of effort, you are rewarded with a spicy, refreshing drink.

INGREDIENTS | SERVES 4

2-inch knob ginger, cut into small chunks

3 tablespoons fresh whole mint leaves

¼ cup sugar

½ cup water

2 tablespoons lime zest

¼ cup lime juice

20 ounces club soda

1. Place the ginger, mint, sugar, water, and zest in a heavy saucepan. Bring to a boil. Continue to boil until the sugar is dissolved and the mixture thickens to light syrup.

2. Strain into a bowl. Discard solids. Allow to cool.

3. Spoon 2 tablespoons of the syrup into 4 glasses. Add 1 tablespoon of lime juice to each glass. Stir to combine. Evenly divide the club soda between the glasses.

PER SERVING Calories: 52 | Fat: 0 g | Protein: 0 g | Sodium: 34 mg | Fiber: 0 g | Carbohydrates: 13 g | Sugar: 13 g

Spicy Tomato Juice

Not only is this tomato juice wonderful fresh; it can be frozen for up to six months. Simply defrost it in your refrigerator overnight.

INGREDIENTS | YIELDS 2 QUARTS

10 large tomatoes, quartered
½ cup water
1 small onion, chopped
1 stalk celery, diced
½ teaspoon salt
½ teaspoon ground cayenne
½ teaspoon hot paprika
½ teaspoon red hot sauce

1. Place the tomatoes, water, onion, and celery in a large stockpot. Bring to a boil. Reduce heat and simmer 40 minutes.

2. Process the mixture through a food mill. Discard any solids.

3. Pour the liquid into a 2-quart pitcher. Stir in the spices and hot sauce. Refrigerate or freeze.

PER SERVING Calories: 7 | Fat: 0 g | Protein: 0 g | Sodium: 160 mg | Fiber: 0.4 g | Carbohydrates: 2 g | Sugar: 1 g

Mango Lemonade

Using naturally sweet mangoes eliminates the need to add much additional sweetener to this tasty lemonade.

INGREDIENTS | YIELDS 1½ QUARTS

1½ cups fresh-squeezed lemon juice
¼ cup puréed mango
3 tablespoons agave nectar
4 cups cold water

1. In a large pitcher, stir together the lemon juice, mango purée, and agave nectar until well combined.

2. Stir in the water. Refrigerate.

PER SERVING Calories: 37 | Fat: 0 g | Protein: 0 g | Sodium: 0.5 mg | Fiber: 0 g | Carbohydrates: 10 g | Sugar: 10 g

Avocado Milkshake

This might sound odd at first, but avocado drinks are popular all over the world, including countries like the Philippines, Vietnam, and Morocco.

INGREDIENTS | SERVES 1

1 avocado, peeled and pit removed
1 cup ice
1 cup milk
1 cup coconut milk

Place all ingredients in a blender. Pulse until smooth.

PER SERVING Calories: 601 | Fat: 42 g | Protein: 20 g | Sodium: 243 mg | Fiber: 15 g | Carbohydrates: 44 g | Sugar: 24 g

What Are Whole Foods?

Whole foods include foods that are either minimally refined, completely unrefined, minimally processed, or completely unprocessed. This includes fruits, vegetables, whole grains, and beans. Whole foods do not necessarily need to be organic.

Moroccan Almond Milkshake

These shakes are very popular in cafes in Morocco. Look for orange flower water in a well-stocked supermarket or Middle Eastern grocery.

INGREDIENTS | SERVES 2

½ cup peeled, blanched almonds
2 teaspoons orange flower water
2 cups milk
3 tablespoons sugar
¼ teaspoon cinnamon (optional)

1. Place the almonds in a blender. Pulse until very fine.

2. Add the orange flower water, milk, and sugar. Pulse until smooth.

3. Pour into 2 glasses and sprinkle with cinnamon.

PER SERVING Calories: 359 | Fat: 20 g | Protein: 13 g | Sodium: 106 mg | Fiber: 3 g | Carbohydrates: 36 g | Sugar: 33 g

Mango Lassi

Popular in India and Pakistan, mango lassis are easy to make at home. If your mango is very sweet, decrease the amount of sugar you use.

INGREDIENTS | SERVES 2

1 cup plain yogurt
1 cup peeled, cubed mango
½ cup 2% milk
3 tablespoons sugar
¼ teaspoon ground cardamom

1. Place the yogurt, mango, milk, and sugar into a blender. Pulse until smooth.

2. Pour into 2 glasses and sprinkle with cardamom.

   PER SERVING Calories: 228 | Fat: 5 g | Protein: 7 g | Sodium: 85 mg | Fiber: 2 g | Carbohydrates: 42 g | Sugar: 40 g

Date Shake

A Southern California coast favorite since the 1930s, the date shake is a fruity take on a classic milkshake.

INGREDIENTS | SERVES 2

1 cup pitted, diced Medjool dates
1 cup milk
2 cups vanilla ice cream or frozen yogurt

1. Place all ingredients in a blender and purée.

2. Divide mixture evenly between 2 glasses.

   PER SERVING Calories: 623 | Fat: 20 g | Protein: 11 g | Sodium: 169 mg | Fiber: 8 g | Carbohydrates: 107 g | Sugar: 93 g

Pomegranate Sparkler

This is wonderful at any time but it makes an especially good "mocktail" to serve at parties for the nondrinkers.

INGREDIENTS | SERVES 6

3 cups pomegranate juice

6 cups seltzer

¼ cup pomegranate arils

How to De-Seed a Pomegranate

To de-seed a pomegranate: fill a very large bowl with cool water. Use a knife to score the skin of the pomegranate. Place it in the bowl of water. Working underwater, break the pomegranate into pieces. Use your fingers to free the arils. Drain. Discard the skin and membranes.

1. Combine all the ingredients in a large pitcher.

2. Evenly divide the mixture among 6 glasses. Gently stir before serving.

PER SERVING Calories: 96 | Fat: 0 g | Protein: 1 g | Sodium: 5 mg | Fiber: 2 g | Carbohydrates: 24 g | Sugar: 22 g

Chai

For super authentic–tasting chai, buy the tea in your local Indian grocery.

INGREDIENTS | SERVES 4

2 cups 2% milk

2 cups water

¼ cup black leaf tea (also called green label tea)

2 teaspoons granular black tea (also called red label tea)

2 cinnamon sticks

2 whole cloves

8 black peppercorns

2 tablespoons crushed whole cardamom

1-inch knob fresh ginger

1 tablespoon sugar

1. In a large saucepan, bring the milk, water, both teas, cinnamon sticks, cloves, peppercorns, cardamom, and ginger to boil.

2. Reduce heat and simmer 15 minutes. Add sugar and stir.

3. Strain into 4 large mugs.

PER SERVING Calories: 140 | Fat: 7 g | Protein: 5 g | Sodium: 87 mg | Fiber: 5 g | Carbohydrates: 20 g | Sugar: 10 g

Raspberry Sorbet Chiller

Take care not to over-mix this fruity, icy drink. You don't want to turn sorbet into juice!

INGREDIENTS | SERVES 2

6 ounces pineapple juice

8 ounces Raspberry Sorbet (see Chapter 15)

½ cup pineapple chunks

1. Add all ingredients to a blender. Pulse 3 times.

2. Divide between 2 glasses and serve.

PER SERVING Calories: 226 | Fat: 2 g | Protein: 2 g | Sodium: 53 mg | Fiber: 2 g | Carbohydrates: 50 g | Sugar: 40 g

Apricot Fizz

Easy and festive, this drink is best served immediately.

INGREDIENTS | SERVES 8

4 cups apricot nectar

1 tablespoon ginger juice

1 tablespoon lime juice

4 cups sparkling water

1. In a large pitcher, stir together the apricot nectar, ginger juice, and lime juice.

2. Add the sparkling water. Stir very carefully to combine.

PER SERVING Calories: 70 | Fat: 0 g | Protein: 0 g | Sodium: 4 mg | Fiber: 1 g | Carbohydrates: 18 g | Sugar: 17 g

How to Make Ginger Juice

Ginger juice is available commercially but it is easy to make your own. Use a fine grater or specialty ginger grater to grate fresh ginger. Collect the juice. Save the pulp for another dish.

Kiwi-Tea Smoothie

Refreshing, antioxidant-rich green tea adds an herbal kick to this smoothie.

INGREDIENTS | SERVES 2

4 frozen kiwis, peeled
½ cup frozen yellow raspberries
½ cup plain yogurt
½ cup cooled brewed green tea
1 teaspoon agave nectar

1. Add all ingredients to a blender and pulse until smooth.

2. Divide evenly between 2 glasses.

PER SERVING Calories: 156 | Fat: 3 g | Protein: 4 g | Sodium: 36 mg | Fiber: 7 g | Carbohydrates: 32 g | Sugar: 7 g

What Does It Mean When Something Is Labeled Organic?

Organic fruits and vegetables are foods grown without pesticides, chemical fertilizers, or genetically modified organisms. Organic meats are not processed with irradiation nor are the animals allowed to have antibiotics. There is not a significant difference in the taste between organic and nonorganic foods.

Spiced Buttermilk Drink

This Indian-influenced drink is a great way to use up that last bit of buttermilk leftover from a baking recipe.

INGREDIENTS | SERVES 2

¾ cup buttermilk

½ cup water

½ teaspoon ground cumin

½ teaspoon ground ginger

¼ teaspoon salt

¼ teaspoon cinnamon

1. Stir together all ingredients in a bowl or pitcher.

2. Divide amount between 2 glasses.

PER SERVING Calories: 41 | Fat: 1 g | Protein: 3 g | Sodium: 392 mg | Fiber: 0 g | Carbohydrates: 5 g | Sugar: 4 g

What Is Buttermilk?

Buttermilk is the liquid leftover from churning butter. However, it is rare that an individual churns his or her own butter anymore so homemade buttermilk is generally unavailable. The buttermilk found at grocery stores is made by fermenting milk and can be used just as homemade buttermilk was in years past.

CHAPTER 3

Breakfast and Brunch

Banana-Black Walnut Muffins

The bananas for this recipe should be very, very, ripe; use ones with almost black peels!

INGREDIENTS | SERVES 18

⅔ cup dark brown sugar

2 teaspoons baking powder

1¼ cups flour

1 cup white whole-wheat flour

2 eggs, at room temperature

1½ cups mashed overripe banana

⅔ cup plain Greek yogurt

¼ cup canola oil

⅓ cup chopped black walnuts

2 bananas, sliced (optional)

What Is White Whole-Wheat Flour?

White whole-wheat flour is an excellent alternative to regular whole-wheat flour. It is closer to all-purpose flour in taste, texture, and appearance, yet has the health benefits of whole wheat. Ground from white wheat berries, it is milder tasting than traditional whole-wheat. It can be substituted for whole-wheat flour in a 1:1 ratio or for all-purpose in a recipe when the difference would go undetected.

1. Preheat oven to 350°F. Line or grease 18 wells in a muffin tin.

2. In a large bowl, whisk together brown sugar, baking powder, and both flours. Set aside.

3. In a medium bowl, beat together the eggs, mashed banana, yogurt, and oil until smooth.

4. Pour wet ingredients over the dry ingredients and mix until well incorporated. Fold in the nuts.

5. Divide the batter evenly among the wells. Top each muffin with a slice of banana if desired. Bake 20 minutes or until a toothpick inserted in the center of a muffin comes out with just a few dry crumbs.

6. Remove the muffins from the tin. Cool completely on a wire rack.

PER SERVING Calories: 138 | Fat: 4 g | Protein: 3 g | Sodium: 65 mg | Fiber: 1.5 g | Carbohydrates: 24 g | Sugar: 10 g

Carrot-Zucchini Cornmeal Muffins

Cornmeal gives these muffins a pleasant crunch.

INGREDIENTS | SERVES 12

¼ cup shredded carrot

¼ cup shredded zucchini

1 cup buttermilk

⅓ cup sugar

1 egg, beaten

2 tablespoons canola oil

⅛ teaspoon nutmeg

¼ teaspoon allspice

¼ teaspoon cinnamon

1½ cups flour

1 teaspoon baking powder

1 teaspoon baking soda

⅛ teaspoon salt

½ cup yellow cornmeal

1. Preheat oven to 350°F. Grease or line 12 wells in a muffin tin. Set aside.

2. In a large bowl, mix together the carrot, zucchini, buttermilk, sugar, egg, and oil until the sugar dissolves.

3. In a separate bowl, whisk together the spices, flour, baking powder, baking soda, salt, and cornmeal.

4. Add the dry ingredients to the wet ingredients. Mix until just combined.

5. Fill each well ⅔ full. Bake for 15 minutes or until a toothpick inserted into the center of the center muffin comes out clean. Cool in the pan for 2 minutes then invert to a wire rack to cool completely.

PER SERVING Calories: 136 | Fat: 3 g | Protein: 3 g | Sodium: 200 mg | Fiber: 1 g | Carbohydrates: 24 g | Sugar: 7 g

Baking Soda Versus Baking Powder

Baking soda is pure sodium bicarbonate, which when combined with an acidic ingredient like buttermilk or lemon juice and dissolved in liquid creates a chemical reaction that allows leavening to occur. If you used baking soda without adding an acidic ingredient, your baked good would not rise. Baking powder does not need the addition of an acidic ingredient for it to work, as it includes both a powdered acid and sodium bicarbonate. Once you add a liquid to the baking powder, the acid and base dissolve and it acts as a leavening agent.

Oatmeal Blueberry Muffins

Oatmeal adds body and fiber to these fruity muffins.

INGREDIENTS | SERVES 12

¾ cup flour
¾ cup white whole-wheat flour
1 cup old-fashioned rolled oats
⅓ cup dark brown sugar
1 teaspoon baking soda
1 teaspoon baking powder
1 teaspoon ground ginger
½ teaspoon allspice
¼ teaspoon ground nutmeg
¼ teaspoon ground cloves
¼ teaspoon salt
⅓ cup canola oil
1 egg, beaten
1 cup buttermilk
1 cup blueberries

1. Preheat oven to 350°F. Grease or line 12 wells in a muffin tin.

2. In a large bowl, whisk together the flours, oats, brown sugar, baking soda, baking powder, ginger, allspice, nutmeg, cloves, and salt.

3. In a small bowl, whisk together the oil, egg, and buttermilk until smooth.

4. Pour the wet ingredients over the dry ingredients. Mix until just combined. Fold in the blueberries.

5. Divide the batter evenly among the wells in the muffin tin. Bake 15–20 minutes or until a toothpick inserted in the center of the center muffin comes out clean. Remove the muffins to a wire rack and cool completely.

PER SERVING Calories: 150 | Fat: 7 g | Protein: 3 g | Sodium: 225 mg | Fiber: 2 g | Carbohydrates: 19 g | Sugar: 8 g

Cranberry-Hazelnut Muffins

Frozen whole cranberries can be used in place of fresh in this festive muffin.

INGREDIENTS | SERVES 12

1 cup buttermilk
1 cup old-fashioned rolled oats
⅓ cup canola oil
1 egg, beaten
⅓ cup light brown sugar
1¼ cups flour
2 teaspoons baking soda
¼ teaspoon salt
1 cup fresh cranberries
⅓ cup chopped hazelnuts

Did You Know?

Every year the Cape Cod Cranberry Growers' Association sponsors a cranberry harvest celebration in Wareham, MA. The main attraction is the opportunity to visit a real cranberry bog and watch the harvest. It is quite a sight to see! Visit *www.cranberries.org* for more information.

1. Preheat oven to 350°F. Grease or line 12 wells in a muffin tin.

2. In a large bowl, stir together the buttermilk, oats, oil, egg, and brown sugar until the sugar dissolves. Set aside for 10 minutes.

3. Meanwhile, whisk together the flour, baking soda, and salt in a small bowl.

4. Pour the flour mixture over the buttermilk-oat mixture and stir until just combined. Fold in the cranberries and hazelnuts.

5. Divide the batter evenly among the wells in the muffin tin. Bake 15–20 minutes or until a toothpick inserted in the center of the center muffin comes out clean. Remove the muffins to a wire rack and cool completely.

PER SERVING Calories: 182 | Fat: 9 g | Protein: 3.4 g | Sodium: 283 mg | Fiber: 2 g | Carbohydrates: 23 g | Sugar: 7.5 g

Whole-Grain Pumpkin Muffins

Surprisingly light in texture, these muffins are packed with healthful, hearty ingredients.

INGREDIENTS | SERVES 12

1 egg, beaten
1 cup puréed pumpkin
½ cup plain Greek yogurt
¼ cup canola oil
½ teaspoon ground cloves
½ teaspoon ground nutmeg
½ teaspoon allspice
½ teaspoon salt
1 teaspoon baking powder
1½ cups white whole-wheat flour
⅓ cup flaxseed meal
¼ cup old-fashioned rolled oats
⅓ cup whole pepitas
⅔ cup demerara sugar

1. Preheat oven to 350°F. Grease or line 12 wells in a muffin tin.

2. In a large bowl, stir together the egg, pumpkin, yogurt, oil, cloves, nutmeg, allspice, and salt until smooth.

3. In a small bowl, whisk together the remaining ingredients. Add them to the pumpkin mixture and stir until just combined.

4. Divide the batter evenly among the wells in the muffin tin. Bake 15–20 minutes or until a toothpick inserted in the center of the center muffin comes out clean. Remove the muffins to a wire rack and cool completely.

PER SERVING Calories: 192 | Fat: 8 g | Protein: 6 g | Sodium: 150 mg | Fiber: 3 g | Carbohydrates: 30 g | Sugar: 12 g

Pepita Facts

Pepitas are pumpkin seeds. They can be whole or hulled. They are a good source of protein, fiber, and zinc.

Zucchini Bread

Try this walnut-studded classic spread with a thin layer of cream cheese.

INGREDIENTS | SERVES 12

2 eggs, beaten

½ cup canola oil

1½ cups grated zucchini

2 teaspoons vanilla

1½ cups white whole-wheat flour

1 teaspoon salt

1 teaspoon baking powder

1 teaspoon ground cardamom

½ cup sugar

1 teaspoon cinnamon

½ teaspoon ground cloves

½ teaspoon ground nutmeg

½ teaspoon ground ginger

1 cup chopped walnuts

1. Preheat oven to 350°F. Grease and flour 1 standard loaf pan.

2. In a large bowl, combine the eggs, oil, zucchini, and vanilla. Set aside.

3. In a small bowl, stir together the flour, salt, baking powder, sugar, and spices. Add to the zucchini mixture. Stir until just combined. Fold in walnuts.

4. Pour into the prepared loaf pan. Bake 1 hour until a toothpick inserted in the middle of the loaf comes out with just a few dry crumbs. Place the pan on a wire rack for 10 minutes. Invert the loaf onto the rack and cool fully.

PER SERVING Calories: 213 | Fat: 16 g | Protein: 5 g | Sodium: 251 mg | Fiber: 3 g | Carbohydrates: 13 g | Sugar: 1 g

Crab Scramble

This is a tasty way to use up leftover crab from steamed crabs or from making crab cakes.

INGREDIENTS | SERVES 2

4 eggs, beaten
½ cup blue crab meat
1 tablespoon sour cream
¼ teaspoon sea salt
¼ teaspoon white pepper
1 tablespoon unsalted butter

The Noble Blue Crab

Native to the Atlantic Ocean, Maryland blue crabs have blue legs and claws when alive and turn bright red when cooked. Blue crab is a relatively low-calorie food; one large crab is only 87 calories and provides 34 percent of the RDL of protein.

1. Whisk together the eggs, crab, sour cream, salt, and pepper until fluffy.

2. Meanwhile, melt the butter in a large skillet over medium heat. Pour in the egg mixture and use a spatula to move it around the skillet, forming curds. Continue to cook, stirring frequently, until the egg is fully cooked.

3. Divide into 2 portions and serve immediately.

PER SERVING Calories: 257 | Fat: 18 g | Protein: 23 g | Sodium: 900 mg | Fiber: 0 g | Carbohydrates: 1 g | Sugar: 1 g

Veggie Spaghetti Strata

Most stratas use bread and need to be refrigerated hours before making. But this version is ready to bake in less than 15 minutes and is a great way to use up leftover spaghetti.

INGREDIENTS | SERVES 8

8 eggs, beaten
¼ cup grated smoked Gouda cheese
½ cup fresh corn kernels
½ cup fresh or frozen peas
½ cup halved cherry tomatoes
¼ cup minced basil
1 tablespoon minced parsley
½ teaspoon sea salt
½ teaspoon freshly ground black pepper
3½ cups loosely packed cooked regular or whole-wheat spaghetti

1. Preheat oven to 425°F. Grease an 8" × 8" baking dish.

2. In a medium bowl, stir together the eggs, cheese, corn, peas, tomatoes, basil, parsley, salt, and pepper.

3. Place the spaghetti in the baking dish. Arrange the spaghetti to cover the bottom of the baking dish. Pour the egg mixture over the spaghetti.

4. Bake for 30 minutes. Cut into squares and serve immediately.

PER SERVING Calories: 298 | Fat: 8 g | Protein: 15 g | Sodium: 279 mg | Fiber: 2.5 g | Carbohydrates: 41 g | Sugar: 3 g

Butternut Squash Cinnamon Rolls

This light orange–hued treat is about as healthy as cinnamon rolls can get!

INGREDIENTS | SERVES 12

1 ounce dry yeast
⅓ cup lukewarm water
¼ cup unsalted butter, melted and cooled slightly
1 cup puréed cooked butternut squash
¼ cup light brown sugar
½ teaspoon salt
2 eggs, at room temperature
4 cups flour
¼ cup unsalted butter, softened
¾ cup dark brown sugar
2½ tablespoons Saigon Cinnamon

Easy Baked Winter Squash

Preheat oven to 375°F. Pierce the squash with a fork or slice it in half. Place on a baking sheet. Bake 40 minutes or until fork-tender. Remove seeds. Use a spoon to scoop out the flesh.

1. In a large mixing bowl, stir together the yeast and water. Allow to sit 5 minutes.

2. Add the melted butter, butternut squash, light brown sugar, salt, and eggs. Using an electric mixer with a dough hook attachment, mix until all ingredients are well distributed. Add the flour and mix on low until a smooth, slightly sticky dough forms.

3. Place the dough on a floured surface and knead until the dough is elastic and smooth. Form into a ball. Place in a buttered bowl and cover with a tea towel. Allow to rise until it doubles in size, about 45 minutes.

4. Remove the dough from the bowl and place on a clean, floured surface. Roll out the dough into a large rectangle, ⅓-inch thick. Spread evenly with the softened butter. Sprinkle with the dark brown sugar and cinnamon. Roll the dough into a tight log. Slice into 1-inch thick slices.

5. Grease 3 (9" round) cake pans. Place the slices in the pans, forming a circle with 1 roll in the center. Cover loosely with tea towels and allow to rise 40 minutes. Meanwhile, preheat the oven to 350°F.

6. Bake for 15 minutes or until fully cooked. Cool in the pan for 2 minutes then invert to a wire rack to cool completely.

PER SERVING Calories: 317 | Fat: 9 g | Protein: 6.5 g | Sodium: 119 mg | Fiber: 3 g | Carbohydrates: 53 g | Sugar: 18 g

Homemade Breakfast Sausage Patties

Fresh tasting and preservative free, homemade sausage is a real breakfast treat!

INGREDIENTS | SERVES 6

1 pound lean ground pork
1 shallot, grated
1 clove garlic, grated
2 teaspoons ground sage
1 teaspoon crushed red pepper flakes
1 teaspoon light brown sugar
½ teaspoon paprika
½ teaspoon fennel seed
¼ teaspoon ground rosemary
¼ teaspoon white pepper
¼ teaspoon ground mustard
¼ teaspoon kosher salt
⅛ teaspoon allspice
⅛ teaspoon cloves

1. Place all ingredients in a medium bowl. Stir to thoroughly combine all ingredients. Cover and refrigerate overnight.

2. Measure out ¼ cup of the mixture, form into a flat patty. Repeat until the mixture is gone.

3. Cook in a nonstick skillet over medium heat until brown on all sides and fully cooked.

PER SERVING Calories: 217 | Fat: 17 g | Protein: 13 g | Sodium: 55 mg | Fiber: 2 g | Carbohydrates: 4 g | Sugar: 16 g

Raspberry Waffles

Antioxidant-rich raspberries add a fruity punch to this light and fluffy waffle.

INGREDIENTS | SERVES 4

1 cup all purpose flour
1 cup white whole-wheat flour
1 tablespoon light brown sugar
1 tablespoon baking powder
¼ teaspoon kosher salt
1 teaspoon vanilla
2 tablespoons canola oil
1 egg, at room temperature
1 cup buttermilk, at room temperature
1 cup sour cream, at room temperature
1 cup fresh raspberries

1. In a large bowl, whisk together the flours, brown sugar, baking powder, and salt. Set aside.

2. In a small bowl, whisk together the vanilla, oil, egg, buttermilk, and sour cream until smooth. Pour into the dry ingredients and stir to combine. Fold in the raspberries.

3. Cook in a Belgian-style waffle maker according to manufacturer's instructions. Serve immediately or keep warm in a 200°F oven.

PER SERVING Calories: 463 | Fat: 21 g | Protein: 3 g | Sodium: 283 mg | Fiber: 2 g | Carbohydrates: 23 g | Sugar: 7 g

Overnight Oatmeal with Dried Figs

Slow-cooked oatmeal cooks while you sleep so you wake up to a creamy, delicious breakfast.

INGREDIENTS | SERVES 8

4½ cups water

3 cups old-fashioned rolled oats

1½ cups diced dried figs

¾ cup dark brown sugar

1 teaspoon ground cinnamon

1 teaspoon ground allspice

1 teaspoon ground ginger

¼ teaspoon nutmeg

¼ teaspoon kosher salt

Place all ingredients in a 4-quart slow cooker. Cook on low overnight, about 8 hours. Stir and serve.

PER SERVING Calories: 227 | Fat: 2 g | Protein: 4 g | Sodium: 86 mg | Fiber: 4.5 g | Carbohydrates: 49 g | Sugar: 27 g

Breakfast Made Easy

Oatmeal can be refrigerated up to one week. Make a big batch of slow-cooked oatmeal one day. Divide it into meal-sized portions and refrigerate. Microwave or heat on the stovetop when ready to eat. Stir and serve.

Buckwheat Pancakes

These pancakes are especially good when topped with sliced strawberries, kiwi, bananas, or raspberry syrup.

INGREDIENTS | SERVES 4–6

¾ cup buckwheat flour

¾ cup all-purpose flour

2½ tablespoons sugar

¼ teaspoon salt

1 teaspoon baking soda

½ teaspoon baking powder

1¾ cups buttermilk, at room temperature

3 tablespoons canola oil

1 egg, at room temperature

Raspberry Pancake Syrup

Bring ½ cup water and ½ cup sugar to boil in a small saucepan. Add ¾ cup mashed raspberries. Bring to a second boil. Reduce heat and simmer until thickened, 5–10 minutes.

1. Heat a small amount of oil in a cast-iron skillet over medium heat. Meanwhile, whisk together the flours, sugar, salt, baking soda, and baking powder.

2. In a separate bowl, beat together the buttermilk, oil, and egg until frothy. Pour into the dry ingredients and mix until just combined.

3. Ladle ¼ cup portions of batter into the skillet. Cook for 2 minutes or until bubbles start to appear. Flip and cook 2 additional minutes or until golden brown. Serve immediately.

PER SERVING Calories: 228 | Fat: 9 g | Protein: 7 g | Sodium: 437 mg | Fiber: 2 g | Carbohydrates: 31 g | Sugar: 9 g

Mushroom-Wild Rice Omelets

Wild rice adds a nutty flavor to this otherwise classic omelet.

INGREDIENTS | SERVES 4

½ tablespoon unsalted butter

½ tablespoon olive oil

1 onion, sliced

4 cloves minced garlic

⅔ cup cooked wild rice

8 ounces crimini mushrooms, sliced

8 eggs, beaten

¼ cup diced scallions

⅓ cup grated Gruyère cheese

½ teaspoon sea salt

½ teaspoon freshly ground black pepper

1. Heat the butter and oil in a large skillet over medium heat. Sauté the onion, garlic, wild rice, and mushrooms until the onions are soft and just starting to brown. Remove from heat. Cover.

2. Spray a nonstick pan with spray oil. Pour ¼ of the eggs into the pan and tilt with a circular motion to cover the surface with the egg. Cook until the egg is nearly set, about 2–3 minutes.

3. Sprinkle ¼ of the scallion and cheese on the middle of the egg. Top with ¼ of the cooked mushroom mixture. When the egg is fully set, slide onto a plate and fold it closed. Repeat for each omelet. Season with salt and pepper. Serve immediately.

PER SERVING Calories: 329 | Fat: 17 g | Protein: 21 g | Sodium: 500 mg | Fiber: 3 g | Carbohydrates: 26 g | Sugar: 4 g

Breakfast Tacos

Serve this Tex-Mex favorite with salsa and hot sauce.

INGREDIENTS | SERVES 3

½ tablespoon unsalted butter

½ tablespoon canola oil

2 shallots, minced

2 cloves garlic, minced

1 habanero chile, minced, seeds removed

1 cubanelle pepper, chopped

1 bunch scallions, chopped

1 small zucchini, diced

¾ cup halved cherry tomatoes

¾ cup cooked, cubed russet potatoes

½ teaspoon kosher salt

½ teaspoon freshly ground black pepper

½ teaspoon ground chipotle

4 eggs

6 whole-wheat, flour, or corn tortillas, warmed

⅓ cup extra sharp Cheddar cheese

1. Heat the butter and oil in a cast-iron skillet over medium heat. Add the shallots, garlic, habanero, and cubanelle and sauté until the shallots start to brown, about 3–7 minutes.

2. Add the scallions, zucchini, tomatoes, and potatoes. Sprinkle with salt, pepper, and chipotle. Sauté until the potatoes and tomatoes are warmed through, 3–5 minutes. Remove from heat and cover.

3. Whisk the eggs until frothy. Pour the eggs into a nonstick skillet and use a spatula to move the egg mixture round the skillet, forming curds. Continue to cook, stirring frequently, until the egg is fully cooked.

4. Evenly divide the egg and the potato mixture between the tortillas. Sprinkle with cheese. Serve immediately.

PER SERVING Calories: 156 | Fat: 5 g | Protein: 5 g | Sodium: 415 mg | Fiber: 2 g | Carbohydrates: 27 g | Sugar: 5 g

An Austin Staple

Tacos for breakfast might seem odd to a lot of the country but they are ubiquitous in Austin, TX. They can contain a variety of fillings from refried beans and chorizo, chorizo and egg, scrambled eggs and bacon, egg and refried beans, to carnitas or barbacoa spiked tacos. They are a cheap and filling breakfast.

Milk and Oat Bars

*This homemade version of popular breakfast or "energy" bars uses
whole grains and nuts to make the perfect portable breakfast.*

INGREDIENTS | YIELDS 12 BARS

14 ounces sweetened condensed milk

2⅓ cups old-fashioned rolled oats

1 cup raw almonds

¾ cup unsweetened dried cherries,
cranberries, or blueberries

¾ cup shredded unsweetened coconut

¼ teaspoon sea salt

¼ teaspoon ground ginger

1 teaspoon vanilla

1. Preheat oven to 250°F. Oil an 11" × 7" baking pan. Set aside.

2. In a medium saucepan, heat the condensed milk. Do not boil. Stir in the remaining ingredients.

3. Pour the mixture into the prepared pan. Flatten with the back of a spoon or spatula, taking care the mixture reaches all 4 corners of the pan.

4. Bake for 60–70 minutes or until the mixture looks dry but is not browned. The mixture should only be slightly sticky at this point. Remove the pan from the oven and place on a wire rack. Allow the mixture to cool completely in the pan.

5. Use a large, flat spatula to invert the contents of the pan on to a cutting board. Slice into 12 equal-sized bars. Store in an airtight container.

PER SERVING Calories: 192 | Fat: 9 g | Protein: 5 g |
Sodium: 92 mg | Fiber: 2 g | Carbohydrates: 25 g | Sugar: 20 g

Shakshuka

This North African dish is popular all over the Middle East, especially in Israel where there are shakshuka-only restaurants!

INGREDIENTS | SERVES 6

3 tablespoons olive oil

4 cloves garlic, minced

3 jalapeño peppers, minced, seeds removed

1 large shallot, minced

28 ounces canned crushed or ground tomatoes

1 tablespoon Harissa (see Chapter 10)

¼ teaspoon salt

½ teaspoon freshly ground black pepper

½ teaspoon roasted ground cumin

6 eggs

1½ tablespoons minced Italian parsley

Italian Parsley Versus Curly Parsley

Italian parsley is also known as flat leaf parsley. Italian parsley is used most often in cooking because it has a stronger flavor and better texture. Curly parsley is used mainly as a garnish.

1. Heat the oil in a 12-inch cast-iron skillet over medium heat. Add the garlic, peppers, and shallot and sauté until fragrant and golden, about 5–10 minutes.

2. Add the tomatoes, Harissa, salt, pepper, and cumin and stir.

3. Simmer until the tomato reduces slightly and is warmed through, about 10 minutes.

4. Crack the eggs into the pan, forming a single layer of egg on top of the tomato mixture. Cook until the yolks are barely set and the whites are fully cooked, about 5 minutes. Sprinkle with parsley. Serve immediately.

PER SERVING Calories: 173 | Fat: 12 g | Protein: 8 g | Sodium: 359 mg | Fiber: 1.6 g | Carbohydrates: 10 g | Sugar: 4 g

Coconut-Strawberry Pancakes

Coconut adds an interesting texture and great flavor to these fluffy pancakes.

INGREDIENTS | SERVES 4

1 cup all-purpose flour

1 cup white whole-wheat flour

1½ cups 2% milk

¼ cup shredded, unsweetened coconut

3 tablespoons melted unsalted butter, cooled slightly

2½ tablespoons sugar

1 teaspoon vanilla

½ teaspoon salt

½ teaspoon baking powder

2 eggs, beaten

⅔ cup sliced fresh strawberries

1. Whisk together the flours, milk, coconut, butter, sugar, vanilla, salt, baking powder, and eggs until just combined. Fold in the strawberries.

2. Butter or oil a hot griddle set to medium-high heat. Ladle ⅓ cup of batter on the griddle for each pancake. Cook for 2–3 minutes on one side or until just beginning to bubble. Flip and cook until golden. Repeat until the batter is gone. Serve immediately.

PER SERVING Calories: 333 | Fat: 16 g | Protein: 10 g | Sodium: 433 mg | Fiber: 1 g | Carbohydrates: 37 g | Sugar: 13.5 g

Pancake Variations

Substitute ⅔ cup sliced banana for the strawberries. Alternately, you could use 1 cup blueberries or raspberries. Swap the coconut for flaxseed meal.

Tex-Mex Migas

Serve this Texas favorite with extra warm corn tortillas on the side.

INGREDIENTS | SERVES 4

2 tablespoons canola oil

1 onion, chopped

4 cloves garlic, minced

1 jalapeño pepper, minced, seeds removed

1 habanero pepper, minced, seeds removed

¼ cup diced scallion

1 medium tomato, diced

4 soft corn tortillas, cut into 1-inch strips

2 tablespoons hot salsa

2 tablespoons milk

4 eggs

⅓ cup shredded sharp Cheddar cheese

1. Heat the oil in a skillet over medium heat. Add the onion, garlic, peppers, scallion, tomato, and tortillas and sauté until the onion is soft, about 3–8 minutes.

2. In a small bowl, whisk together the salsa, milk, eggs, and Cheddar. Pour into the pan over the tortilla mixture.

3. Cook, moving the mixture around continuously with a spatula, until the eggs are fully cooked, about 5–8 minutes. Serve immediately.

PER SERVING Calories: 298 | Fat: 17 g | Protein: 13 g | Sodium: 376 mg | Fiber: 2 g | Carbohydrates: 23 g | Sugar: 5 g

Skillet Frittata

Cast-iron skillets are amazing vessels for frittata making. They cook evenly and are oven-safe.

INGREDIENTS | SERVES 6

1 tablespoon unsalted butter

1 tablespoon olive oil

1 small onion, diced

1 pound asparagus, chopped

¼ cup fresh or frozen peas

1 cup crumbled feta cheese

1 tablespoon minced oregano

1 tablespoon minced fresh dill

1 tablespoon minced Italian parsley

½ tablespoon minced basil

½ teaspoon sea salt

½ teaspoon freshly ground black pepper

7 eggs

Why Use Butter and Oil in the Same Recipe?

While it seems counterintuitive to use two different kinds of fats to grease a pan, there is a good reason. Butter cannot stand up to the same high heat as oil, but adds flavor oil cannot produce. The oil allows one to use butter without fear of burning in recipes when the flavor of butter would be appreciated.

1. Preheat oven to 325°F.

2. Heat the butter and oil in a 12-inch cast-iron skillet. Add the onion, asparagus, and peas and sauté until the onions are soft.

3. Meanwhile, in a small bowl, whisk together the feta, oregano, dill, parsley, basil, salt, pepper, and eggs.

4. Pour the egg mixture over the vegetables in the skillet. Tilt the skillet slightly to coat all of the ingredients with the egg mixture. Cook over medium heat until the eggs are just beginning to set, about 8–12 minutes.

5. Place in the oven and bake for 10 minutes or until the mixture is cooked through and just beginning to brown.

6. Remove from the pan and slice. Serve immediately.

PER SERVING Calories: 215 | Fat: 15 g | Protein: 13 g | Sodium: 560 mg | Fiber: 2 g | Carbohydrates: 7 g | Sugar: 4 g

Chive Scramble

Scrambles are great weekday breakfasts because they are fast.
Chives add a subtle onion flavor to this one.

INGREDIENTS | SERVES 2

4 eggs, beaten

½ cup chopped chives

1 tablespoon milk

¼ teaspoon sea salt

¼ teaspoon white pepper

1 tablespoon unsalted butter

Eggs, Eggs, Eggs

Eggs only have 70 calories. Egg yolks contain the antioxidants lutein and zeaxanthin, which help prevent macular degeneration. Eggs contain 13 percent of the RDL of protein.

1. In a medium bowl, whisk together the eggs, chives, milk, salt, and pepper until fluffy.

2. Meanwhile, melt the butter in a large skillet over medium heat. Pour the egg mixture into the skillet and use a spatula to move the egg mixture around the skillet, forming curds. Continue to cook, stirring frequently, until the egg is fully cooked, about 3–8 minutes.

3. Divide into 2 portions and serve immediately.

PER SERVING Calories: 203 | Fat: 16 g | Protein: 13 g | Sodium: 439 mg | Fiber: 0 g | Carbohydrates: 2 g | Sugar: 1 g

Raspberry-Yogurt Muffins

Yogurt keeps these muffins moist while raspberries provide bursts of flavor.

INGREDIENTS | SERVES 12

⅔ cup sugar
2 teaspoons baking powder
2 cups all-purpose flour
2 tablespoons flaxseed meal
2 eggs, at room temperature
⅔ cup plain Greek yogurt
¼ cup canola oil
1½ cups fresh raspberries

1. Preheat oven to 350°F. Line or grease 12 wells in a muffin tin.

2. In a large bowl, whisk together sugar, baking powder, flour, and flaxmeal. Set aside.

3. In a medium bowl, beat together the eggs, yogurt, and oil until smooth. Pour over the dry ingredients and mix until well incorporated. Fold in the raspberries.

4. Bake for 15 minutes or until a toothpick inserted in the center muffin comes out clean. Cool on a wire rack.

PER SERVING Calories: 195 | Fat: 6 g | Protein: 5 g | Sodium: 100 mg | Fiber: 2 g | Carbohydrates: 30 g | Sugar: 13 g

Vegetarian

Broccoli-Basil Pesto and Pasta

A pleasant, veggie-packed change from your regular pesto.

INGREDIENTS | SERVES 8

3½ cups broccoli florets

3 (loose) cups fresh basil

3 cloves garlic

¼ teaspoon salt

½ teaspoon white pepper

3 tablespoons olive oil

¼ cup grated Parmesan cheese

3 tablespoons toasted pignoli nuts

1 tablespoon lemon juice

1 pound cooked pasta

1. Place the broccoli in a large pot of boiling water. Boil until tender, about 10–15 minutes. Use a slotted spoon to remove the broccoli into a bowl. Allow to cool briefly.

2. Place the broccoli in a blender or food processor. Add the remaining ingredients except the pasta. Pulse until smooth.

3. Pour pesto sauce over hot or cold pasta.

PER SERVING Calories: 193 | Fat: 10 g | Protein: 6 g | Sodium: 120 mg | Fiber: 3 g | Carbohydrates: 22 g | Sugar: 1 g

How to Toast Pignoli Nuts

Bring out the best flavor of pignoli nuts, also known as pine nuts, by toasting them. Simply add them to a dry skillet and warm them over low heat. Watch the nuts closely so they don't burn.

Mushroom Frittata

Look for an assortment of wild mushrooms at your local farmers' market.
They will likely have more variety than the supermarket.

INGREDIENTS | SERVES 6

1½ tablespoons canola oil

8 ounces assorted wild mushrooms, chopped

2 shallots, minced

½ cup minced Italian parsley

½ cup fresh or frozen peas

½ cup crumbled Stilton cheese

¼ cup sour cream, at room temperature

6 eggs, beaten

1. In a large oven-safe skillet, heat the oil over medium heat. When hot, add the mushrooms and shallots and sauté about 10 minutes or until the mushrooms are soft and the shallots are translucent.

2. Add parsley and peas, stir. Cook an additional 2 minutes.

3. Meanwhile, in a small bowl, stir together the cheese, sour cream, and eggs. Pour egg mixture over the ingredients in the skillet.

4. Tilt the skillet slightly to coat the ingredients in the skillet with the egg mixture. Keep on medium heat and cook about 10 minutes or nearly set.

5. Place under the broiler for 5 minutes or until the top is just beginning to brown. Remove from pan and slice.

PER SERVING Calories: 141 | Fat: 8 g | Protein: 9 g | Sodium: 87 mg | Fiber: 1 g | Carbohydrates: 10 g | Sugar: 2 g

Delicata Squash Burritos

The combination of squash and beans make these burritos hearty enough to be a meal in themselves.

INGREDIENTS | SERVES 4

1 tablespoon olive oil
2 delicata squash, peeled and diced
1 small red onion, diced
2 cloves garlic, minced
3 serrano peppers, minced
1 cup baby spinach
1½ cups cannellini beans
1¼ cups cooked brown or white rice
4 burrito-sized tortillas, warmed
¾ cup grated Mexican blend cheese
¼ cup sour cream or crema agria

Not-So-Delicate Delicata Squash

Though it is often referred to as a winter squash, delicata squash is actually more closely related to summer squashes like zucchini. It has a thin, easy-to-peel skin and a mild, nutty flavor. Try it baked, steamed, or sautéed.

1. Heat the oil in a nonstick skillet over medium heat. Add the squash, onion, garlic, and peppers. Cook about 15 minutes or until the squash is softened, stirring occasionally.

2. Add the spinach, beans, and rice. Sauté until the spinach wilts and the beans are warmed, about 2–3 minutes.

3. Divide the mixture evenly between the tortillas. Top with the cheese and sour cream or crema agria. Fold the burrito shut. Keep warm if needed by wrapping in foil and placing in a cold oven.

PER SERVING Calories: 430 | Fat: 17 g | Protein: 17 g | Sodium: 631 mg | Fiber: 9 g | Carbohydrates: 54 g | Sugar: 8 g

Creamy Macaroni and Cheese with Swiss Chard

*Adding greens to a classic comfort food is a wonderful way to turn it into
a main course or just add some extra vegetables to your diet.*

INGREDIENTS | SERVES 8

3 tablespoons unsalted butter

3 tablespoons flour

½ teaspoon ground cayenne

½ teaspoon paprika

½ teaspoon chipotle flakes

2 cups milk

1 cup shredded sharp Cheddar cheese

1 cup shredded fontina cheese

1 bunch Swiss chard, chopped

1 pound small pasta, cooked and drained

1. Preheat oven to 350°F.

2. In a medium pan, melt the butter over medium heat. Add the flour along with the spices and stir until smooth.

3. Add the milk and whisk together until slightly thickened, about 5–8 minutes.

4. Whisk in the cheeses. Stir in the Swiss chard.

5. Pour the pasta into a lightly greased 2-quart casserole dish. Pour the cheese mixture over the pasta and stir to evenly distribute.

6. Bake covered about 15 minutes, then uncover and cook until hot and bubbly, about 10–15 additional minutes.

PER SERVING Calories: 290 | Fat: 16 g | Protein: 13 g | Sodium: 217 mg | Fiber: 1 g | Carbohydrates: 23 g | Sugar: 4 g

Okra and Oyster Mushroom Risotto

Risotto requires specific types of rice to ensure a creamy, toothsome final product. Do not substitute other rice.

Arancini di Riso

Try the traditional Italian way to use up leftover risotto. Simply stir an egg into the rice and roll the mixture into small balls. Roll the balls in bread crumbs. Pan-fry until golden.

1. In a saucepan, bring the stock to a simmer.

2. Heat oil and butter in a large pot over medium heat. Add the mushrooms, salt, pepper, garlic, and shallots and sauté until lightly caramelized.

3. Add the rice and sauté for 2–3 minutes, stirring continually.

4. Add the broth ½ cup at a time, stirring continuously, and waiting until the liquid is absorbed before each addition.

5. When you are about half way through the broth, add the okra to the rice. Continue to add broth and stir.

6. When the risotto is creamy and the rice is al dente, remove from heat and stir in the Parmesan.

PER SERVING Calories: 329 | Fat: 5 g | Protein: 7 g | Sodium: 59 mg | Fiber: 5 g | Carbohydrates: 62 g | Sugar: 1 g

Eggplant-Spinach Calzones

Buy pizza dough in the refrigerated section of the supermarket, at your favorite pizzeria, or make your own.

INGREDIENTS | SERVES 8

2 pounds prepared pizza dough

2 Italian eggplants, sliced into ¼-inch rounds

1 cup ricotta

2 tablespoons minced basil

2 tablespoons minced oregano

2 tablespoons minced Italian parsley

½ teaspoon salt

¼ teaspoon freshly ground black pepper

¼ cup grated Parmesan cheese

12 ounces baby spinach, chopped

1 cup shredded mozzarella cheese

1 cup Fresh Tomato Marinara (see Chapter 10)

Make Some, Freeze Some

Make a double batch or just freeze the leftovers for a future quick meal. Freeze them either individually wrapped or place a batch on a baking sheet. Freeze until solid then transfer them to a freezer safe container. Reheat at 350°F for 25 minutes.

1. Follow the rising instructions for the pizza dough. Set aside.

2. Preheat oven to 350°F. Line a baking sheet with parchment paper.

3. Place the eggplant slices on the baking sheet in single layer. Bake for 10–15 minutes or until they are soft and cooked through but not browned. Allow to cool slightly.

4. Turn the oven up to 400°F.

5. In a medium bowl, mix together the ricotta, basil, oregano, parsley, salt, pepper, Parmesan, spinach, and mozzarella.

6. Divide the dough into 8 equal chunks. Roll each ball of dough into a 6–8-inch round.

7. Add a single layer of eggplant in ½ of each round, leaving a ¼-inch border. Evenly divide the cheese mixture among the calzones. Fold the dough over to form a half-moon shape and pinch shut. Repeat until all are filled and pinched shut.

8. Bake on a pizza stone or on baking sheets for about 20 minutes or until golden and hot all the way through. Serve immediately with marinara sauce for dipping.

PER SERVING Calories: 707 | Fat: 43 g | Protein: 16 g | Sodium: 989 mg | Fiber: 11 g | Carbohydrates: 65 g | Sugar: 8 g

Du Puy Lentils with Root Vegetables

Slightly soupy, this dish is a perfect main course when served with crusty bread for sopping up the juices.

INGREDIENTS | SERVES 6

2 tablespoons olive oil

4 cloves garlic, minced

1 onion, diced

1 carrot, diced

1 stalk celery, diced

1 parsnip, peeled and diced

1 small turnip, diced

1 shallot, minced

1 bay leaf

1 teaspoon sea salt

½ teaspoon freshly ground black pepper

1 cup du Puy lentils

3½ cups vegetable stock or water

2 tablespoons tarragon vinegar

2 tablespoons minced fresh Italian parsley

1 tablespoon fresh thyme leaves

1. Heat oil in a large saucepan over medium heat. Add the garlic, onion, carrot, celery, parsnip, turnip, and shallot. Sauté until the turnips start to soften and the onions are golden, about 10 minutes.

2. Add the bay leaf, salt, pepper, lentils, and stock. Cover and simmer for 40 minutes or until the lentils are soft.

3. Stir in the vinegar, parsley, and thyme. Serve immediately.

PER SERVING Calories: 158 | Fat: 1 g | Protein: 10 g | Sodium: 428 mg | Fiber: 12 g | Carbohydrates: 30 g | Sugar: 2 g

The Caviar of Lentils

Du Puy lentils are French lentils that hold their tiny, pearl-like shape even after cooking. This unique attribute makes them highly sought after. Grown in volcanic soil, they have a nutty taste and are less starchy than other varieties of lentils. When purchasing, check that the label says "du Puy" and not simply "French lentils" to make sure you get the real deal.

Roasted Tomato Soup

Using roasted tomatoes in this soup gives it a richer, more tomato-y flavor.

INGREDIENTS | SERVES 6

3 pounds heirloom tomatoes, halved

¼ cup olive oil

1 onion, diced

3 cloves garlic, minced

2 stalks celery, diced

1 carrot, diced

2 cups vegetable stock

1 teaspoon sea salt

1 teaspoon freshly ground black pepper

Easy Vegetable Stock

Bring a large pot of water to a boil. Add any favorite vegetables or vegetable scraps. Return to a boil until it is reduced by about ¼. Strain and use, freeze, or refrigerate.

1. Preheat oven to 375°F.

2. Place the tomatoes in a single layer on a baking sheet. Drizzle with 2 tablespoons of olive oil. Roast for 20 minutes.

3. Meanwhile, heat the remaining oil in a Dutch oven over medium heat. Add the onion, garlic, celery, and carrots and sauté until the vegetables are softened, about 5–10 minutes.

4. Add the stock and spices, bring to a boil. Add the tomatoes.

5. Use an immersion blender to blend until mostly smooth. Serve immediately.

PER SERVING Calories: 137 | Fat: 10 g | Protein: 3 g | Sodium: 424 mg | Fiber: 4 g | Carbohydrates: 13 g | Sugar: 7 g

Portobello Cheese "Burgers"

This family-friendly recipe is a tasty alternative to commercial veggie burgers.

INGREDIENTS | SERVES 4

1 cup shredded extra sharp Cheddar cheese

½ teaspoon smoked paprika

¼ teaspoon ground cayenne

¼ teaspoon freshly ground black pepper

⅛ teaspoon sea salt

1 tablespoon olive oil

4 portobello mushroom caps

4 whole-wheat hamburger rolls

1. In a small bowl, stir together the cheese and spices. Set aside.

2. Heat the oil in a nonstick pan over medium heat. Place the mushrooms smooth side down. Evenly divide the cheese mixture between the undersides of the mushroom caps. Heat until the mushroom is heated through and the cheese is melted.

3. Place mushrooms on hamburger rolls.

PER SERVING Calories: 241 | Fat: 15 g | Protein: 12 g | Sodium: 391 mg | Fiber: 2 g | Carbohydrates: 17 g | Sugar: 4 g

Zucchini au Gratin

Zucchini becomes velvety smooth when prepared this way.

INGREDIENTS | SERVES 4

4 zucchini, cut into ¼-inch thick coins

1 large onion, sliced thinly

1 cup sour cream

¼ cup milk

½ teaspoon sea salt

½ teaspoon white pepper

¼ teaspoon freshly ground nutmeg

¾ cup extra sharp Cheddar cheese

1. Preheat oven to 350°F. Grease an 8" × 8" baking dish.

2. Bring a large pot of water to boil. Add the zucchini and onion and boil until the zucchini is fork-tender, about 5–10 minutes. Drain thoroughly.

3. Mix together the sour cream, milk, salt, pepper, and nutmeg in a large bowl. Add the zucchini and onion and stir. Pour into prepared baking dish.

4. Sprinkle with cheese. Bake 20 minutes or until bubbly and hot.

PER SERVING Calories: 251 | Fat: 20 g | Protein: 10 g | Sodium: 496 mg | Fiber: 3 g | Carbohydrates: 12 g | Sugar: 9 g

Asparagus Quiche

Chose tender, thin spears of asparagus for this quiche; it will make slicing easier.

INGREDIENTS | SERVES 8

1 cup flour

⅓ cup cold unsalted butter, sliced

1 cup shredded extra sharp Cheddar cheese, divided use

2 tablespoons ice water

4 eggs

1½ cups milk

1 bunch scallions, chopped

½ pound asparagus, chopped

2 tablespoons white wine vinegar

½ teaspoon salt

1 teaspoon freshly ground black pepper

1. Preheat oven to 425°F. Place the flour, butter, ¼ cup Cheddar, and the ice water in a food processor. Pulse until the mixture sticks together.

2. Form the dough into a ball. Place on a floured surface and roll out into a 10-inch round. Press into a 9" pie plate. Bake 10 minutes. Set aside.

3. Meanwhile, thoroughly mix together the eggs, milk, scallions, asparagus, remaining ¼ cup Cheddar, vinegar, salt, and pepper. Pour into the baked crust.

4. Bake 45 minutes or until fully cooked through.

PER SERVING Calories: 253 | Fat: 16 g | Protein: 10 g | Sodium: 292 mg | Fiber: 1 g | Carbohydrates: 16 g | Sugar: 3 g

Eggplant Rollatini with Spinach and Goat Cheese

Meaty eggplant creates a shell for a creamy, goat cheese filling.

INGREDIENTS | SERVES 6

3 graffiti eggplants, sliced into ¼-inch thick vertical strips

2 tablespoons olive oil

½ cup softened goat cheese

¼ cup defrosted and drained chopped spinach

1 shallot, minced

½ teaspoon sea salt

½ teaspoon white pepper

How to Select an Eggplant

Perfectly ripe eggplants should have smooth skin and feel heavy for their size. Avoid eggplants that are heavily scarred, wrinkled, or bruised. The skin is edible.

1. Preheat oven to 300°F.

2. Brush the eggplant on both sides with olive oil and place on a baking sheet. Bake until softened, about 5 minutes.

3. Meanwhile, in a small bowl, mix together the goat cheese, spinach, shallot, salt, and pepper.

4. Allow the eggplant to cool slightly. Spread each strip with 1 tablespoon of the cheese mixture. Roll closed. Serve warm or at room temperature.

PER SERVING Calories: 162 | Fat: 8 g | Protein: 6 g | Sodium: 237 mg | Fiber: 9 g | Carbohydrates: 19 g | Sugar: 6 g

Baked Ziti with Rapini

This classic baked pasta dish is given a healthful addition of rapini.
Rapini is also known as broccoli raab or broccoli rabe.

INGREDIENTS | SERVES 8

2 tablespoons olive oil

1 onion, diced

1 shallot, minced

2 cloves garlic, minced

28 ounces crushed tomatoes

2 tablespoons minced basil

2 tablespoons minced Italian parsley

½ teaspoon salt

½ teaspoon freshly ground black pepper

15 ounces ricotta

⅓ cup shredded mozzarella cheese

1 bunch rapini, chopped and steamed

1 pound cooked ziti

Easy Steaming

If a recipe calls for both pasta and a steamed vegetable, you can cook both at once! Simply use a large pot filled ¾ with water. Boil the pasta, then toward the end of the cooking time, place the vegetables in a sieve on top of the pot for the last few minutes to steam. No need to dirty two pots!

1. Preheat oven to 350°F.

2. In a large pot, heat the oil. Add the onion, shallot, and garlic and sauté until the onion is translucent, about 5–10 minutes.

3. Add the tomatoes, basil, and parsley. Stir and heat through.

4. Meanwhile, mix together the salt, pepper, cheeses, and rapini in a medium bowl. Set aside.

5. Pour the pasta into the tomato sauce and mix. Pour into a 9" × 13" baking dish. Dot with tablespoons of the cheese mixture. Cover and bake for 30 minutes or until bubbly and hot.

PER SERVING Calories: 378 | Fat: 12 g | Protein: 16 g | Sodium: 232 mg | Fiber: 3 g | Carbohydrates: 51 g | Sugar: 5 g

Vegetable-Stuffed Poblano Peppers

Large, unwrinkled poblano peppers work best in this dish.

INGREDIENTS | SERVES 4

2 tablespoons olive oil

4 cloves garlic, minced

1 onion, minced

2 chipotle chiles in adobo sauce, minced

2 zucchini, cubed

1½ cups fresh corn kernels

¾ cup defrosted, drained chopped spinach

4 poblano peppers

28 ounces canned crushed tomatoes

1. Preheat oven to 350°F.

2. Heat oil in a skillet. Add the garlic and onion. Sauté until the onion is softened, then add the chipotle chiles, zucchini, and corn. Sauté until the zucchini begins to soften, about 5–10 minutes. Pour mixture into a bowl and stir in the spinach.

3. Slice the poblanos down the middle but not all the way through, to form a pocket. Fill each with the vegetable mixture.

4. Pour half of the tomatoes on the bottom of an 8" × 8" baking dish. Arrange the peppers, open side up in a single row. Drizzle with remaining tomatoes.

5. Bake for 20 minutes or until cooked through.

PER SERVING Calories: 221 | Fat: 8 g | Protein: 7 g | Sodium: 32 mg | Fiber: 8 g | Carbohydrates: 36 g | Sugar: 15 g

Artichoke and Olive Pasta

Olives add a briny savoriness to this rustic pasta dish.

INGREDIENTS | SERVES 4

2 tablespoons olive oil

3 cloves garlic, minced

2 shallots, minced

10 ounces frozen artichoke hearts, defrosted

1 cup halved large, oil-cured green olives

½ cup toasted fresh bread crumbs

⅓ cup grated Parmesan cheese

¼ cup chopped fresh Italian parsley

10 ounces hot cooked fresh linguine

1. In a saucepan, heat the oil over medium heat. Add the garlic and shallots and cook until fragrant, about 3–5 minutes.

2. Add the artichoke hearts and olives. Cook until the artichokes are cooked through, about 5 minutes.

3. Remove from heat and stir in the remaining ingredients. Serve immediately.

PER SERVING Calories: 507 | Fat: 14 g | Protein: 17 g | Sodium: 546 mg | Fiber: 8 g | Carbohydrates: 82 g | Sugar: 3 g

Umami

Umami, the taste of savoriness, is one of the five basic tastes. Food rich in umami include cured meats, mushrooms, spinach, cheese, soy sauce, shrimp paste, pickles, and shellfish.

Potatoes and Green Beans

This could be a side dish but it is so filling, it is better as the main event.

INGREDIENTS | SERVES 4

1 pound baby red-skin potatoes, halved

¾ pound green beans, halved

6 ounces baby spinach

½ cup diced green onion

1 shallot, minced

2 tablespoons minced Italian parsley

1 tablespoon minced oregano

1 teaspoon yellow mustard seeds

¼ cup apple cider vinegar

3 tablespoons olive oil

1 teaspoon Dijon mustard

Spinach Trivia

Ever wonder why dishes made with spinach are called "Florentine?" Catherine de Médici loved spinach so much; she had it at every meal. Her birthplace was Florence, Italy.

1. Bring a large pot of water to boil. Boil the potatoes until nearly fork-tender. Add the green beans to the pot and continue to cook until the potatoes are fork-tender and the green beans are cooked. Drain.

2. Return the green beans and potatoes to the pot and immediately add the spinach and green onion. Cover.

3. In a small bowl, whisk together the shallot, parsley, oregano, mustard seeds, vinegar, oil, and mustard. Drizzle over the potatoes. Toss to coat. Serve warm.

PER SERVING Calories: 216 | Fat: 11 g | Protein: 5 g | Sodium: 63 mg | Fiber: 6 g | Carbohydrates: 27 g | Sugar: 5 g

Portobello Tacos

Meaty portobellos cook up quickly, making this a great weeknight meal.

INGREDIENTS | SERVES 6

8 portobello mushroom caps

1 tablespoon olive oil

6 corn tortillas

1 pint cherry tomatoes, halved

1 cup chopped romaine lettuce

⅔ cup shredded red cabbage

¼ cup diced onion

1 avocado, sliced

½ cup sour cream

1. Brush each mushroom cap with oil. Heat a nonstick grill pan over medium heat. Grill the mushrooms until warmed through, about 3–5 minutes. Slice into ¼-inch thick slices.

2. Evenly divide the mushrooms and remaining ingredients among the tortillas. Serve immediately.

PER SERVING Calories: 211 | Fat: 12 g | Protein: 6 g | Sodium: 45 mg | Fiber: 7 g | Carbohydrates: 24 g | Sugar: 6 g

A Mushroom By Any Other Name

Agaricus bisporus when mature is the Portobello mushroom. However, before it reaches that point it is alternately called crimini, baby bella, champignon, button mushroom, Italian brown, Swiss brown, or Roman mushroom. The name generally depends on the color of the cap.

Sunshine Curried Vegetables

Turmeric gives this dish a distinctive yellow color.

INGREDIENTS | SERVES 4

2 tablespoons unsalted butter

1 onion, chopped

3 cloves garlic, minced

1 inch knob ginger, minced

½ cup water or vegetable stock

1½ pounds diced potatoes

1 head cauliflower florets

1 cup frozen peas

1 teaspoon curry powder

½ teaspoon garam masala

½ teaspoon ground turmeric

1 teaspoon yellow mustard seeds

1. Melt the butter in a Dutch oven over medium heat. Add the onion, garlic, and ginger and sauté until fragrant, about 2–5 minutes. Add vegetable stock.

2. Add the potatoes, cauliflower, and peas. Sauté until the potatoes soften, about 10–15 minutes.

3. Add the remaining ingredients and cover. Cook, stirring occasionally, until the vegetables are fork-tender, about 5–15 minutes.

PER SERVING Calories: 286 | Fat: 7 g | Protein: 9 g | Sodium: 60 mg | Fiber: 10 g | Carbohydrates: 46 g | Sugar: 8 g

Sautéed Patty Pan Squash Rings

The patty pan squash's distinctive ruffled edges give this dish a delicate look.

INGREDIENTS | SERVES 4

2 tablespoons olive oil

8 cups thinly sliced patty pan squash

1 onion, sliced

1 banana pepper, diced

½ cup water

2 tablespoons minced tarragon

1 tablespoon minced thyme

½ teaspoon sea salt

½ teaspoon freshly ground black pepper

1. Heat oil in a lidded skillet over medium heat. Add the squash, onion, and banana pepper. Sauté until the squash begins to soften, about 5–12 minutes.

2. Add the remaining ingredients. Cover and simmer until the squash is fork-tender, about 3–8 minutes.

PER SERVING Calories: 112 | Fat: 7 g | Protein: 3 g | Sodium: 301 mg | Fiber: 3 g | Carbohydrates: 11 g | Sugar: 6 g

Stir-Fried Watercress and Mushrooms

While it is most frequently used raw, watercress is also delicious stir-fried.

INGREDIENTS | SERVES 4

2 tablespoons sesame oil

8 ounces shiitake mushrooms, sliced

12 cups watercress

3 cloves garlic, minced

1-inch knob ginger, minced

2 Thai Bird's Eye peppers, diced

2 tablespoons dark soy sauce

Egg and Cress

Use up leftover watercress in the classic egg and cress sandwich. Mix together 4 chopped hardboiled eggs, 2–3 tablespoons mayonnaise, and ¼ cup chopped watercress. Serve on white or wheat bread.

1. Heat the oil in a wok over medium heat. Add the mushrooms and stir-fry for 1 minute.

2. Add the watercress in batches, stir-frying and adding more as it cooks down. With the last batch, add the garlic, ginger, and peppers. Stir-fry until fragrant, about 2–5 minutes.

3. Remove from heat and drizzle with soy sauce.

PER SERVING Calories: 94 | Fat: 7 g | Protein: 3 g | Sodium: 455 mg | Fiber: 1 g | Carbohydrates: 6 g | Sugar: 3 g

Sweet Potato Fritters

These fritters are a tasty way to use up leftover mashed or roasted sweet potatoes.

INGREDIENTS | SERVES 4

2½ cups mashed sweet potatoes

1 egg, beaten

1 onion, diced

1 jalapeño pepper, diced, seeds removed

1 teaspoon Cajun seasoning

1 teaspoon fresh thyme leaves

½ cup fresh bread crumbs

Oil, for frying

1. Mix together all ingredients until thoroughly combined. Form into patties.

2. Heat ¼-inch oil in a large skillet over medium heat. Add the fritters to the oil and cook each fritter until browned on both sides, about 8 minutes. Drain on paper towel–lined plates.

PER SERVING Calories: 155 | Fat: 2 g | Protein: 5 g | Sodium: 163 mg | Fiber: 4 g | Carbohydrates: 29 g | Sugar: 6 g

How to Roast a Sweet Potato

Roasting a sweet potato is easy and doesn't require much monitoring. First, preheat oven to 400°F. Pierce each sweet potato several times with the tines of a fork. Place on a parchment-lined baking sheet. Bake for 45 minutes.

CHAPTER 5

Vegan

Homemade Bean and Vegetable Burgers

Homemade bean burgers are much better than their frozen store-bought counterpart.

INGREDIENTS | SERVES 4

1 (15-ounce) can dark red kidney beans, drained

1 large Yukon Gold potato, peeled, cooked, and cooled

⅓ cup cornmeal

⅓ cup fresh or defrosted frozen peas

2 tablespoons minced onion

¼ teaspoon ground chipotle

¼ teaspoon paprika

¼ teaspoon freshly ground black pepper

¼ teaspoon sea salt

2 tablespoons apple cider vinegar

2 tablespoons canola oil

Red Kidney Bean Warning!

Raw kidney beans contain a toxin which can be fatal. Luckily, there is an easy solution. Boil the fresh beans for 10 minutes and the toxin is destroyed.

1. In a medium bowl, mash the beans and potato together using a potato masher. Add the remaining ingredients, except the oil. Mix and form into 4 patties.

2. Heat the oil in skillet. Cook the burgers, flipping once, until cooked through and browned on both sides, about 5 minutes per side.

PER SERVING Calories: 502 | Fat: 8 g | Protein: 27 g | Sodium: 177 mg | Fiber: 28 g | Carbohydrates: 82 g | Sugar: 4 g

Buddha Bowl

Full of vegetables, this hardy dish is perfect for lunch or dinner.

INGREDIENTS | SERVES 4

1 cup broccoli florets

1 small red onion, chopped

1 carrot, grated

1 avocado, diced

¼ cup sliced Kalamata olives

3 ounces extra-firm tofu, cubed

1 cooked beet, cubed

1 cup cooked chickpeas

2 tablespoons rice vinegar

1 teaspoon freshly ground black pepper

1 tablespoon avocado oil

2 cups hot or cold cooked brown rice

Place all ingredients in a large bowl. Toss to combine all ingredients.

PER SERVING Calories: 461 | Fat: 16 g | Protein: 16 g | Sodium: 135 mg | Fiber: 16 g | Carbohydrates: 67 g | Sugar: 10 g

Healthy Tofu

Tofu is low in calories yet high in protein and iron. Soy has been reported to help lower LDL, "bad" cholesterol.

Spicy Peanut Noodles

A classic takeout dish made at home.

INGREDIENTS | SERVES 4

⅔ cup water

¼ cup smooth peanut butter

1 tablespoon sesame oil

2 tablespoons chili garlic sauce

2 cloves garlic

10 ounces cooked soba noodles, cooled

¼ cup chopped garlic chives

3 tablespoons chopped peanuts

5 ounces extra-firm tofu, finely cubed

1. Place the water, peanut butter, sesame oil, chili garlic sauce, and garlic in a blender. Pulse until smooth.

2. Place the noodles in a large bowl. Drizzle with sauce and toss to coat.

3. Divide into 4 bowls. Sprinkle each with an equal amount of garlic chives, peanuts, and tofu. Serve immediately.

PER SERVING Calories: 576 | Fat: 37 g | Protein: 15 g | Sodium: 398 mg | Fiber: 5 g | Carbohydrates: 50 g | Sugar: 3 g

The Mighty Legume

Peanuts are approximately 25 percent protein and trans fat–free. They are also a source of resveratrol, which has been associated with reduced risk of cancer and cardiovascular disease. Peanuts are full of antioxidants.

Saag Tofu

Perhaps one of the most popular vegan dishes in Indian cuisine.

INGREDIENTS | SERVES 4

2 tablespoons canola oil

1 onion, thinly sliced

3 cloves garlic, minced

2 green chiles, diced

2-inch knob ginger, finely diced

2 teaspoons black mustard seeds

½ teaspoon turmeric

2 teaspoons garam masala

½ teaspoon asafetida

½ teaspoon ground cayenne

16 ounces mustard greens, chopped

1¼ cups extra-firm tofu

½ cup water

1. Heat the oil in a large skillet. Sauté the onion, garlic, chiles, and ginger until the onions are soft, about 5–10 minutes. Add the mustard seeds and cook until they begin to pop.

2. Add the remaining ingredients and cook until the mustard greens wilt and the tofu is warmed through, about 2–5 minutes.

PER SERVING Calories: 131 | Fat: 8 g | Protein: 4 g | Sodium: 34 mg | Fiber: 5 g | Carbohydrates: 14 g | Sugar: 5 g

Types of Tofu

Tofu comes in many forms. Moisture-rich silken tofu has a texture similar to panna cotta. Firm tofu has a springy texture and is rather dense. Extra-firm tofu is even firmer and has most of the water removed.

Eggplant in Ginger-Garlic-Soy Sauce

Ginger, garlic, and soy team up to create the perfect savory sauce for eggplant.

INGREDIENTS | SERVES 4

2 tablespoons canola oil
4 Japanese eggplants, sliced
3 cloves garlic, minced
1-inch knob ginger, minced
¼ cup water
¼ cup soy sauce
2 tablespoons rice vinegar
1½ tablespoons sesame oil

1. Heat the canola oil in a skillet and add the eggplant, garlic, and ginger. Sauté until the eggplant is just softened, about 5–12 minutes.

2. In a small bowl, whisk together the water, soy sauce, rice vinegar, and sesame oil. Pour mixture over the eggplant and cover. Cook until the eggplant is tender, about 3–10 minutes.

PER SERVING Calories: 219 | Fat: 10 g | Protein: 7 g | Sodium: 910 mg | Fiber: 19 g | Carbohydrates: 33 g | Sugar: 13 g

Curried Cabbage

Coconut adds a toothsome texture to this curry.

INGREDIENTS | SERVES 4

2 shallots
2 cloves garlic
1-inch knob ginger, sliced
2 Thai Bird's Eye chiles
2 tablespoons canola oil
2 teaspoons black mustard seeds
1 teaspoon cumin seeds
1 teaspoon garam masala
1 teaspoon turmeric
½ teaspoon asafetida
1 teaspoon kosher salt
2 tablespoons unsweetened shredded coconut
1 cup water
1 head cabbage, shredded

1. Place the shallots, garlic, ginger, and chiles in a blender and pulse until smooth.

2. Heat the oil in a skillet. Add the spices and coconut and cook, stirring occasionally, until the seeds begin to pop.

3. Add the remaining ingredients. Cover and cook, stirring occasionally, until the cabbage is soft, about 5–15 minutes.

PER SERVING Calories: 181 | Fat: 8 g | Protein: 5 g | Sodium: 641 mg | Fiber: 6 g | Carbohydrates: 27 g | Sugar: 9 g

Red Onion and Olive Focaccia

Red onions and olives perk up the flavor of this classic Italian bread.

INGREDIENTS | SERVES 12

1½ tablespoons active dry yeast
2½ cups lukewarm water, divided use
3½ cups flour
6 tablespoons olive oil, divided use
½ tablespoon kosher salt
⅓ cup sliced Spanish green olives
1 small red onion, thinly sliced

Variations on Focaccia

Pretty much anything can top focaccia. Some combinations include rosemary and sea salt, onions and garlic, or spinach and red pepper. Nonvegan versions often include meat and a sprinkle of Parmesan at the end of the cooking time.

1. In the bowl of a stand mixer, dissolve the yeast in ½ cup lukewarm water. Allow to sit about 10 minutes.

2. Add the flour, 4 tablespoons olive oil, remaining water and salt. Use a dough hook to mix the mixture until a soft dough forms.

3. Remove the dough from the bowl and form into a round. Grease a 9" × 13" baking pan. Place the dough in the pan. Cover with a tea cloth and allow to rise for 1½ hours.

4. Preheat the oven to 450°F. Press the dough into the pan, reaching all corners. Allow to rise an additional 15 minutes.

5. Poke the dough with the tip of your fingers to create dimples. Brush with remaining olive oil. Scatter the olives and onion over the top of the bread.

6. Bake for 15 minutes. Serve warm or at room temperature.

PER SERVING Calories: 202 | Fat: 8 g | Protein: 4 g | Sodium: 329 mg | Fiber: 1 g | Carbohydrates: 29 g | Sugar: 0 g

Cauliflower "Steaks" with Fennel

Pick the largest heads of cauliflower for this recipe to yield the largest "steaks."

INGREDIENTS | SERVES 4

2 tablespoons canola oil

1 large head cauliflower, sliced vertically into ¼-inch thick slices

2 cloves garlic, minced

1 bulb fennel, sliced

2 teaspoons fennel seeds

1 teaspoon rosemary

½ teaspoon sea salt

½ cup water

1. Heat the oil in a large skillet. Place the sliced cauliflower flat in the pan. Arrange the garlic and fennel around the cauliflower. Sprinkle with fennel seeds, rosemary, and salt.

2. Cook for 3 minutes. Add the water and cover. Cook until the cauliflower is fork-tender, about 5–15 minutes.

PER SERVING Calories: 103 | Fat: 7 g | Protein: 3 g | Sodium: 339 mg | Fiber: 3 g | Carbohydrates: 8 g | Sugar: 3 g

Watermelon-Cucumber Jumble

Cooling watermelon and cucumber form the base of this unusual summery side dish.

INGREDIENTS | SERVES 4

2 cucumbers, diced

4 cups diced watermelon

¼ cup lime juice

1 tablespoon lime zest

¼ cup torn peppermint leaves

1 tablespoon ginger juice

1 Thai Bird's Eye pepper, minced

Place all ingredients in a large bowl. Toss to combine. Serve immediately.

PER SERVING Calories: 80 | Fat: 1 g | Protein: 3 g | Sodium: 11 mg | Fiber: 2 g | Carbohydrates: 19 g | Sugar: 13 g

Medicinal Peppermint

Peppermint oil has been shown to reduce symptoms of Irritable Bowel Syndrome. It has also been used as aromatherapy in treating insomnia and to enhance memory.

Broiled Spiced Eggplant

Broiling is a technique that produces similar results to grilling eggplant but without the need to heat up the grill.

INGREDIENTS | SERVES 4

4 Japanese eggplants, unpeeled, halved
3 tablespoons chili garlic sauce
3 tablespoons red miso
1 Thai Bird's Eye pepper, minced
1 tablespoon canola oil
1 teaspoon Japanese rice vinegar

Rice Vinegar Facts

Made from rice or rice wine, rice vinegar is popular in many Asian cuisines. Japanese rice vinegar is relatively mild and is used in many pickled and vegetable dishes. Seasoned rice vinegar is used for flavoring rice.

1. Place the eggplants skin side down on a broiling pan.

2. In a small bowl, whisk together the chili garlic sauce, miso, pepper, canola oil, and vinegar. Brush over the eggplant.

3. Broil for 5 minutes.

PER SERVING Calories: 203 | Fat: 5 g | Protein: 8 g | Sodium: 494 mg | Fiber: 20 g | Carbohydrates: 38 g | Sugar: 14 g

Black Bean Tacos

A snap to make, these bean tacos get their zip from fresh salsa.

INGREDIENTS | SERVES 4

30 ounces canned black beans, undrained
3 tablespoons lime juice
3 tablespoons water
1 teaspoon ground cayenne
½ teaspoon ground cumin
½ teaspoon ground jalapeño
8 corn tortillas
1 small white onion, minced
¾ cup Chunky Salsa Verde (see Chapter 10)

1. Place the beans, lime juice, water, and spices in a small pot. Cover and heat through, about 5–10 minutes. Remove from heat and mash with a potato masher.

2. Evenly divide the mixture between the tortillas. Top with onion and salsa.

PER SERVING Calories: 390 | Fat: 6 g | Protein: 17 g | Sodium: 1,296 mg | Fiber: 14 g | Carbohydrates: 67 g | Sugar: 8 g

Roasted Delicata Squash

Roasting caramelizes the edges of the squash, a sweetness that is tempered by the spices.

INGREDIENTS | SERVES 4

4 delicata squash
3 tablespoons olive oil
1 teaspoon smoked sea salt
½ teaspoon smoked paprika
½ teaspoon ground cayenne
¼ teaspoon allspice

1. Preheat oven to 350°F.

2. Slice the squash into ½-inch rings. Scoop out the seeds. Arrange in a single layer on baking sheets. Brush with olive oil and sprinkle with spices.

3. Roast for 20–30 minutes or until fork-tender.

PER SERVING Calories: 122 | Fat: 11 g | Protein: 2 g | Sodium: 594 mg | Fiber: 2 g | Carbohydrates: 7 g | Sugar: 4 g

Winter Squash Facts

Winter squash grows over the summer and is ripe for the picking in the fall. The hard exterior allows winter squash to be stored successfully in a cool, dark space for many months. Winter squash is a low-calorie food.

Sautéed Beet Greens

Don't toss away those beet greens! They are tasty and full of nutrients.

INGREDIENTS | SERVES 4

2 tablespoons olive oil
2 cloves garlic, minced
1-inch knob ginger, minced
1½ pounds beet greens, blanched
1 teaspoon red pepper flakes

1. Heat the olive oil in a large skillet. Add the garlic and ginger and sauté until fragrant, about 3–5 minutes.

2. Add the beet greens and stir for 3 minutes. Sprinkle with red pepper flakes and serve.

PER SERVING Calories: 152 | Fat: 7 g | Protein: 3 g | Sodium: 134 mg | Fiber: 5 g | Carbohydrates: 21 g | Sugar: 12 g

How to Blanch

Bring a large pot of water to a boil. Add the vegetables and cook for 2 minutes. Transfer immediately to a bowl of ice water, then drain.

Bulgur Wheat with Pears and Pomegranate

Autumn favorites pears and pomegranates add a fresh, fruity flavor to earthy bulgur wheat.

INGREDIENTS | SERVES 4

1 cup bulgur wheat
1 cup vegetable stock
2 tablespoons olive oil
2 tablespoons pomegranate molasses
½ teaspoon freshly ground black pepper
1 red onion, diced
2 Bosc pears, diced
1 cup pomegranate arils
1 stalk celery, thinly sliced

1. Bring the bulgur wheat and stock to a boil in a small saucepan. Reduce heat and simmer for 15 minutes or until tender. Allow to cool to room temperature.

2. Meanwhile, in a small bowl, whisk together the olive oil, pomegranate molasses, and pepper. Set aside.

3. Place the cooled bulgur in a medium bowl. Stir in the onion, pears, pomegranate arils, and celery. Drizzle with dressing and toss.

PER SERVING Calories: 307 | Fat: 8 g | Protein: 6 g | Sodium: 21 mg | Fiber: 11 g | Carbohydrates: 58 g | Sugar: 21 g

Appealing Pears

Pears are high in fiber and are a good source of vitamin C. The fiber is insoluble for the most part and therefore can work as a natural laxative.

Summer Vegetable Tian

Tian is a French vegetable dish consisting of a variety of thinly sliced vegetables forming a casserole.

1. Heat the oil in a large skillet. Add the garlic and onion and sauté until the onion is translucent, about 5–10 minutes.

2. Scrape garlic and onion mixture into a large bowl and add the remaining ingredients. Stir until the ingredients are evenly distributed.

3. Preheat oven to 400°F.

4. Arrange the vegetables in a baking dish. Roast for 30 minutes. Serve immediately.

PER SERVING Calories: 172 | Fat: 8 g | Protein: 6 g | Sodium: 323 mg | Fiber: 7 g | Carbohydrates: 24 g | Sugar: 15 g

Variations on a Tian

Tians can be made with any variety of vegetables. Try using onion slices and eggplant. Or thinly sliced pieces of potato and winter squash for a winter version.

Roasted Tomatoes with White Beans and Marinated Artichokes

Cherry tomatoes roast more quickly than regular tomatoes but taste just as good!

INGREDIENTS | SERVES 4

3 tablespoons olive oil

2 pints cherry tomatoes

2 tablespoons minced oregano

2 tablespoons minced basil

1 tablespoon minced Italian parsley

1 teaspoon freshly ground black pepper

½ teaspoon sea salt

8 ounces marinated artichokes, drained

25 ounces cooked cannellini beans

Homemade Marinated Artichoke Hearts

Bring ¾ cup apple cider vinegar, ¾ cup water, 1 teaspoon pickling salt, and 1 tablespoon of minced garlic to a boil. Add 9 ounces of frozen artichoke hearts and simmer for 5 minutes. Drain and divide into jars. Fill jars with olive oil. Refrigerate up to 1 month.

1. Preheat oven to 425°F.

2. Toss the oil and tomatoes together in a medium bowl. Pour onto a 12-inch cast-iron skillet. Roast for 10–15 minutes or until the tomatoes are soft.

3. Place the skillet on the range and add the remaining ingredients. Sauté until the beans are heated through, about 5–10 minutes.

PER SERVING Calories: 295 | Fat: 12 g | Protein: 13 g | Sodium: 874 mg | Fiber: 15 g | Carbohydrates: 39 g | Sugar: 8 g

Kohlrabi and Swiss Chard

Crisp kohlrabi contrasts with silky Swiss chard to make this citrus-kissed dish.

INGREDIENTS | SERVES 4

2 tablespoons canola oil

1½ pounds kohlrabi, cubed

3 cloves garlic, minced

2 shallots, minced

2 bunches Swiss chard, chopped

¼ cup blood orange juice

2 tablespoons blood orange zest

1 teaspoon white pepper

1 teaspoon sea salt

¼ teaspoon celery seed

1. Heat the oil in a large skillet. Add the kohlrabi, garlic, and shallots and sauté until the kohlrabi is nearly fork-tender, about 8–20 minutes depending on thickness of kohlrabi.

2. Add the remaining ingredients and sauté until the Swiss chard is wilted, about 2–3 minutes.

PER SERVING Calories: 164 | Fat: 7 g | Protein: 5 g | Sodium: 690 mg | Fiber: 7 g | Carbohydrates: 24 g | Sugar: 6 g

Why Use Shallots?

Shallots have a milder flavor than onions and a slightly garlic scent. They add a depth of flavor to many dishes either alone or in conjunction with onions.

Tofu Summer Rolls

Summer rolls are so named because they are served cold, perfect for the hot summer months.

INGREDIENTS | SERVES 6

1 pound extra-firm tofu, cut into ¼-inch × 3-inch slices

3 tablespoons soy sauce

2 teaspoons rice vinegar

2 teaspoons ginger juice

2 cloves garlic, grated

½ pound rice stick noodles

6 rice paper wrappers

½ cup steamed, chopped rainbow chard

¾ cup loosely packed Thai basil

Firmer Tofu

If you would like an even firmer, meatier texture to your tofu, it is easy. Simply wrap the tofu in a paper towel. Place a brick or heavy cans on the tofu. Allow to sit for at least an hour before use.

1. Place the tofu in a resealable plastic bag. Add the soy sauce, rice vinegar, ginger juice, and garlic. Refrigerate overnight.

2. The next day, prepare the rice stick noodles and rice paper wrappers according to the package instructions.

3. Add ¼ cup of noodles toward the middle of each wrapper.

4. Equally divide the chard, slices of tofu, and basil among the wrappers.

5. Fold the rice paper from both sides in toward the middle, then tightly roll the end away from you until the spring roll is closed. Serve immediately.

PER SERVING Calories: 211 | Fat: 2 g | Protein: 8 g | Sodium: 297 mg | Fiber: 1 g | Carbohydrates: 38 g | Sugar: 1 g

Thai Tofu Kabobs

Take care to use extra-firm tofu in these kabobs; softer tofu may fall off the skewers.

INGREDIENTS | SERVES 4

2 pounds extra-firm tofu
6 Thai eggplants, halved
2 red onions, cut into wedges
½ cup chopped Thai basil
¼ cup olive oil
⅓ cup lime juice
¼ cup Thai thick soy sauce
2 tablespoons minced lemongrass
2 tablespoons minced galangal
2 tablespoons minced fresh ginger
2 tablespoons palm sugar
2 Thai Bird's Eye peppers, minced

1. Place all ingredients in a resealable plastic bag. Shake to evenly distribute. Refrigerate 4 hours.

2. Thread the tofu, eggplant, and onion wedges alternately on 8–10 bamboo skewers.

3. Place the skewers on a nonstick grill pan and grill on each side until the tofu is golden, about 5–10 minutes.

PER SERVING Calories: 508 | Fat: 21 g | Protein: 26 g | Sodium: 1,000 mg | Fiber: 31 g | Carbohydrates: 63 g | Sugar: 26 g

Thai Basil Versus Italian Sweet Basil

Though relatives, Thai basil has a different flavor profile than Italian sweet basil. Thai basil has a licorice-esque flavor which is very strong, even after cooking. It is what gives many Thai dishes their distinctive flavor.

Butternut Squash Rice

In this dish, the squash cooks with the rice, infusing the rice with its sweet flavor.

INGREDIENTS | SERVES 4

2 tablespoons grapeseed oil

3 cloves garlic, minced

2 shallots, minced

1 cubanelle pepper, diced

2 cups rice (long grain or jasmine would work well)

1 pound cubed butternut squash

1 tablespoon thyme leaves

½ teaspoon sea salt

½ teaspoon freshly ground black pepper

½ teaspoon smoked paprika

3 cups water

1. Heat the oil in a Dutch oven. Add the garlic, shallot, and pepper and sauté until the shallots are soft, about 2–5 minutes.

2. Add the rice and sauté for 2 minutes.

3. Add the remaining ingredients and bring to a boil. Reduce heat and simmer until the rice is tender, about 15–30 minutes. Stir. Serve immediately.

PER SERVING Calories: 515 | Fat: 8 g | Protein: 10 g | Sodium: 308 mg | Fiber: 5 g | Carbohydrates: 103 g | Sugar: 4 g

CHAPTER 6

Seafood

Roasted Bay Scallops with Swiss Chard

Roasting brings out the naturally sweet flavor of the scallops.

INGREDIENTS | SERVES 4

1½ pounds bay scallops
¾ cup steamed chopped Swiss chard
⅓ cup seafood stock
2 tablespoons lemon juice
½ tablespoon lemon zest
2 cloves garlic, minced
1 small onion, minced
1 tablespoon minced Italian parsley
¼ teaspoon sea salt
¾ cup panko
1 teaspoon minced basil
1 shallot, minced
¼ teaspoon freshly ground black pepper
¼ teaspoon celery seed

1. Preheat oven to 350°F.

2. In a medium bowl, combine scallops, chard, stock, lemon juice, lemon zest, garlic, onion, parsley, and salt. Pour into an oiled 1½-quart baking dish. Use the back of a spoon to spread the mixture into a smooth, even layer.

3. In a small bowl, whisk together the panko, basil, shallot, pepper, and celery seed. Sprinkle over the scallop mixture.

4. Bake for 30 minutes or until the scallops are just cooked through and the panko is golden.

PER SERVING Calories: 237 | Fat: 2 g | Protein: 31 g | Sodium: 537 mg | Fiber: 1 g | Carbohydrates: 22 g | Sugar: 2 g

Herbed Salmon Cakes

The next time you make salmon, make an extra portion and use it to make these moist, flavorful, omega-3–rich fish cakes.

INGREDIENTS | SERVES 8

14 ounces cooked fresh salmon

½ cup fresh bread crumbs

⅓ cup mayonnaise

1½ tablespoons tarragon mustard

¼ cup minced onion

¼ cup diced celery

1 tablespoon fresh thyme leaves

1 tablespoon minced fresh Italian parsley

DIY Bread Crumbs

Making your own bread crumbs is not only thrifty but tasty. Simply cube leftover fresh bread (homemade or bakery loaves work best) and place in a food processor. Pulse until crumbs form. Add dried herbs and spices that complement the dish you plan to use them in if desired. Store in an airtight container.

1. In a medium bowl, mash the salmon with a potato masher until fairly smooth. Add the remaining ingredients. Stir to evenly distribute all ingredients.

2. Form into 8 patties.

3. Spray a skillet with cooking spray. Cook each patty for 3–5 minutes on each side or until golden and heated through.

PER SERVING Calories: 101 | Fat: 4 g | Protein: 11 g | Sodium: 75 mg | Fiber: 0.6 g | Carbohydrates: 6 g | Sugar: 1 g

Shrimp-Orange Kabobs

The citrus-soy sauce makes these shrimp kabobs sing.

INGREDIENTS | SERVES 4

1 navel orange, halved and cut into wedges

1 large red onion, cut into wedges

1 pound large shrimp, peeled and deveined

2 tablespoons orange juice

2 tablespoons soy sauce

Skewered

Choose skewers that have one pointy end. Skewer the food directly in the center. Each piece of food on the skewer should be of similar size for even grilling.

1. Heat grill to medium. Oil the grill rack.

2. Thread the orange wedges, onion, and shrimp on 4 skewers beginning and ended with oranges.

3. In a small bowl, whisk together the orange juice and soy sauce. Brush the sauce over the skewers.

4. Grill kabobs until the shrimp are fully cooked, about 5 minutes total.

PER SERVING Calories: 153 | Fat: 2 g | Protein: 24 g | Sodium: 616 mg | Fiber: 1 g | Carbohydrates: 9 g | Sugar: 5 g

Mussels in Fennel Caper Broth

Mussels are an excellent source of vitamin B$_{12}$ and a good source of zinc and folate.

INGREDIENTS | SERVES 6

1 tablespoon olive oil

1 large onion, diced

2 stalks celery, diced

2 bulbs fennel, diced

3 tablespoons capote capers

1¾ cups seafood stock or water

4 pounds fresh mussels

Mussel Tips

When buying mussels, ask for extra ice for the trip home. This helps keep the mussels cool and fresh. Rinse them off before cooking and discard any open mussels.

1. In a large stock pot with a lid, heat the oil. Add the onion, celery, and fennel. Sauté until the onion is soft and translucent, about 5–8 minutes.

2. Add the capers and stock. Add the mussels and steam until the mussels have all opened, can take from 5–20 minutes. Discard any mussels that do not open. Serve immediately.

PER SERVING Calories: 311 | Fat: 9 g | Protein: 37 g | Sodium: 1,033 mg | Fiber: 3 g | Carbohydrates: 19 g | Sugar: 1 g

Littleneck Clams with Zucchini

The zucchini in this recipe adds a light, fresh flavor.

INGREDIENTS | SERVES 4

1 tablespoon olive oil
1 tablespoon unsalted butter
2 zucchini, diced
1 onion, diced
1 stalk celery, diced
2 cups seafood stock
1 tablespoon red pepper flakes
½ teaspoon sea salt
½ teaspoon freshly ground black pepper
4 pounds littleneck clams

1. In a large, lidded pot, heat the oil and butter. Add the zucchini, onion, and celery. Sauté until the zucchini is beginning to soften, about 5–10 minutes.

2. Add the stock and spices. Stir.

3. Bring to a rolling boil. Add the clams. Cover and cook until the clams open, about 5–25 minutes. Discard any clams that do not open. Serve immediately.

PER SERVING Calories: 421 | Fat: 11 g | Protein: 59 g | Sodium: 563 mg | Fiber: 2 g | Carbohydrates: 18 g | Sugar: 4 g

Miso Sablefish

Sablefish is a naturally oily fish making it perfect for grilling; there is no need to add extra oils and there is little worry of sticking.

INGREDIENTS | SERVES 6

6 (5-ounce) sablefish filets
2½ tablespoons white miso
½ cup rice vinegar
½ cup mirin
2 tablespoons nori flakes

1. Place the fish in a marinating container or resealable bag. Whisk together the miso, vinegar, and mirin in a small bowl. Pour over the fish. Seal. Refrigerate 20 minutes.

2. Meanwhile, heat a cast-iron grill pan. Add the fish, skin side down, to the pan. Cook until nearly cooked through, about 10 minutes. Flip. Cook another 2–5 minutes or until the fish is fully cooked.

3. Remove to a platter. Sprinkle with nori. Serve.

PER SERVING Calories: 121 | Fat: 1 g | Protein: 25 g | Sodium: 119 mg | Fiber: 0 g | Carbohydrates: 0 g | Sugar: 6 g

Cedar Plank Salmon with Shallots

The cedar plank adds flavor and a stable cooking surface in this easy grill recipe.

INGREDIENTS | SERVES 4

1 pound salmon
3 shallots, thinly sliced
1 stalk celery, thinly sliced
2 tablespoons tarragon vinegar
1 tablespoon olive oil
1 tablespoon minced fresh tarragon
½ teaspoon freshly ground black pepper
¼ teaspoon sea salt

Using Cedar Planks

Cedar planks suitable for grilling are sold at many grocery and specialty stores. Most require soaking for up to an hour prior to use. After you are done cooking, they can be tossed on the coals and burned.

1. Place all ingredients in a marinating container or resealable bag. Refrigerate 2 hours.

2. Meanwhile, prepare your grill according to manufacturer's instructions. Place the salmon on a cedar plank designed for grilling. Pour the marinade over the salmon.

3. Grill, without flipping the salmon, until it is fully cooked, about 20 minutes.

PER SERVING Calories: 253 | Fat: 11 g | Protein: 24 g | Sodium: 215 mg | Fiber: 0.2 g | Carbohydrates: 15 g | Sugar: 0.2 g

Five-Spice Mahi-Mahi

This dish was inspired by the flavors of dishes popular in Hawaii.

INGREDIENTS | SERVES 4

4 mahi-mahi filets
1 tablespoon grapeseed oil
¼ cup lime juice
3 tablespoons Chinese five-spice powder
1 tablespoon smoked Hawaiian sea salt
½ teaspoon ground roasted ginger
½ teaspoon garlic powder
½ teaspoon freshly ground black pepper

Mahi-Mahi Name Game

Mahi-mahi has a bit of a name issue. In addition to its Hawaiian name, mahi-mahi, it is also called dolphinfish or dorado. Whatever you call it, U.S. Atlantic–caught mahi-mahi is a Best Choice when it comes to sustainability, according to the Monterey Bay Aquarium.

1. Preheat oven to 325°F.

2. Place the mahi-mahi on a baking sheet. Set aside.

3. In a small bowl, whisk together the oil, juice, and spices. Brush half of the mixture on the fish.

4. Place in the oven and bake for 10 minutes. Remove the fish from the oven. Brush again with the remaining mixture.

5. Return to oven and bake 5 additional minutes or until the fish is fully cooked.

PER SERVING Calories: 128 | Fat: 4 g | Protein: 21 g | Sodium: 1,867 mg | Fiber: 0.2 g | Carbohydrates: 1 g | Sugar: 0 g

Fish Tacos

A California favorite, fish tacos are a light, fresh meal which is welcome year-round.

INGREDIENTS | SERVES 4-6

6 tilapia filets

3 tablespoons apple cider vinegar

3 tablespoons lime juice

2 jalapeño peppers, minced, seeds removed

½ teaspoon cumin

1 teaspoon minced garlic

½ teaspoon freshly ground black pepper

¼ teaspoon sea salt

6 taco-sized corn tortillas, warmed

1 green onion, diced

¼ cup sour cream

½ pint cherry tomatoes, halved

¾ cup shredded red cabbage

1 avocado, sliced

2 tablespoons red hot sauce

1. Place the fish in a marinating container or resealable plastic bag. Add the vinegar, juice, peppers, cumin, garlic, pepper, and salt. Refrigerate for 30 minutes.

2. Add the contents of the container to a nonstick skillet. Sauté until the fish is fully cooked, about 5–15 minutes depending on thickness.

3. Divide the fish among the tortillas. Top each with green onion, sour cream, tomato, cabbage, and avocado. Drizzle with hot sauce. Serve immediately.

PER SERVING Calories: 417 | Fat: 15 g | Protein: 37 g | Sodium: 788 mg | Fiber: 6 g | Carbohydrates: 33 g | Sugar: 5 g

Shrimp Noodles with Chinese Chives

Chinese chives, occasionally labeled as garlic chives, look like chives but are flat and have a light, fresh-garlic scent.

INGREDIENTS | SERVES 4

8 ounces flat rice noodles

2 tablespoons canola oil

3 cloves garlic, minced

1 pound medium shrimp, peeled and deveined

1 tablespoon ginger juice

1 tablespoon fish sauce

1 pound Chinese chives, cut into 2-inch lengths

2 tablespoons dark soy sauce

Be a Wok Star

Buy a lightweight cast-iron wok for best results. Round bottom woks give you the most control over the food and flame. Use the smallest burner so the flame is concentrated on the bottom of the wok.

1. In a large bowl, soak the noodles in warm water for 15 minutes or until pliable.

2. Heat the oil in a large wok. Add the garlic and stir-fry until fragrant and just beginning to brown, about 2–5 minutes.

3. Add the shrimp, ginger juice, and fish sauce. Stir-fry until the shrimp is cooked, about 3–5 minutes. Add the chives. Stir fry for 2 more minutes or until the chives have wilted.

4. Add the noodles and soy sauce. Stir fry 5 additional minutes or until the noodles are soft. Serve immediately.

PER SERVING Calories: 426 | Fat: 9 g | Protein: 29 g | Sodium: 721 mg | Fiber: 4 g | Carbohydrates: 54 g | Sugar: 3 g

Southern-Style Fried Catfish

*Perhaps fried fish should only be an occasional treat but healthy,
sustainable catfish should be a part of anyone's diet.*

INGREDIENTS | SERVES 8

½ cup yellow cornmeal
½ cup super-fine flour
1 tablespoon Cajun seasoning
½ teaspoon celery seed
½ teaspoon freshly ground pepper
2 pounds catfish filets
⅓ cup lemon juice

Feeling Corny

Cornmeal is ground dried maize. In its coarsest forms it is used to make polenta, but finer grains can be used as a coating for food or in corn bread. It can also be used to keep pizza or bread dough from sticking to the pan or peel.

1. Mix together the cornmeal, flour, and spices in a large, shallow bowl. Set aside.

2. Arrange the fish in a single layer on a platter. Pour the lemon juice over the fish. Cover in foil and refrigerate 30 minutes.

3. Dredge both sides of the fish in the cornmeal mixture. Return the fish to the platter, cover and refrigerate for an additional 30 minutes.

4. Heat ½-inch of canola oil in a large skillet or cast-iron pan. Fry the fish in batches, cooking for about 5 minutes on each side, until golden.

5. Drain the fish on paper towel–lined plates. Serve immediately.

PER SERVING Calories: 153 | Fat: 1 g | Protein: 21 g | Sodium: 62 mg | Fiber: 1 g | Carbohydrates: 13 g | Sugar: 0 g

Shrimp Drunken Noodles

To make this restaurant favorite at home, it is important to use authentic ingredients. Look for them in well-stocked markets or stores specializing in Thai ingredients.

INGREDIENTS | SERVES 6

10 ounces dried flat wide rice noodles

¼ cup nam pla (Thai fish sauce)

¼ cup black soy sauce

¼ cup golden mountain sauce

1½ tablespoons palm sugar

5 cloves garlic, minced

4 Thai Bird's Eye peppers, minced

12 ounces medium shrimp, peeled and deveined

1 bunch gai lan (Chinese broccoli), chopped

⅔ cup shredded Thai or holy basil leaves

1. Prepare the dry noodles according to package instructions. Cover with a damp cloth or paper towel and set aside.

2. In a small bowl, whisk together the nam pla, black soy sauce, golden mountain sauce, and palm sugar. Set aside.

3. Heat a small amount of canola oil in a wok. Stir fry the garlic and peppers until fragrant, about 2–5 minutes.

4. Add the shrimp, gai lan, and the sauce. Stir-fry until the shrimp is bright pink and nearly cooked through. Add the noodles.

5. When the shrimp is thoroughly cooked, about 5–10 minutes, stir in the basil. Serve immediately.

PER SERVING Calories: 298 | Fat: 2 g | Protein: 17 g | Sodium: 803 mg | Fiber: 4 g | Carbohydrates: 54 g | Sugar: 7 g

Scallop Noodle Bowl

This is a surprisingly filling, homey dish. Fresh egg noodles ensure that it comes together in a flash.

INGREDIENTS | SERVES 4

1½ cups seafood stock

2-inch knob ginger, sliced

4 cloves garlic

2 stalks lemongrass

1 shallot, sliced

¼ cup light soy sauce

1½ pounds scallops

6 ounces fresh shiitake mushrooms

2 carrots, julienned

1 stalk celery, sliced thinly

2 baby bok choy, chopped

1 pound fresh egg noodles

1. In a small saucepan, bring the stock, ginger, garlic, lemongrass, shallot, and soy sauce to a boil. Boil until it reduces to 1¼ cup, about 10–15 minutes.

2. Meanwhile, heat a small amount of canola oil in a wok. Stir-fry the scallops, mushrooms, carrots, celery, and bok choy until the scallops are nearly fully cooked.

3. Add the noodles. Stir-fry until the scallops are cooked through, about 3–8 minutes. Serve immediately.

PER SERVING Calories: 680 | Fat: 3 g | Protein: 42 g | Sodium: 1,686 mg | Fiber: 8 g | Carbohydrates: 120 g | Sugar: 8 g

Great Ginger

Ginger is a rhizome that has been used to treat digestion for thousands of years. It has a spicy flavor and slightly woody texture. Look for it fresh, dried, candied, powdered, and as an extract.

Roasted Mahogany Clams

Mahogany clams, also known as ocean quahogs, have a robust, slightly briny flavor that is released into the dish as it cooks.

INGREDIENTS | SERVES 4

2 tablespoons olive oil

2 andouille sausages, cut into coins

1 onion, chopped

1 stalk celery, chopped

3 cloves garlic, minced

1 carrot, diced

1 shallot, minced

½ cup dry vermouth or water

4 pounds mahogany clams

How to Clean a Clam

Clams are frequently sandy and should always be rinsed with cold water before cooking. If you bought the clams at a grocery store this should be enough to ready them for cooking. If you dug them yourself or bought them dockside they may be sandy on the inside as well. Place them in a pot of salt water and refrigerate them overnight. They should expel the sand themselves.

1. Preheat oven to 350°F.

2. Heat the oil in a shallow, oven-safe Dutch oven. Add the sausage, onion, celery, garlic, carrot, and shallot. Sauté until the sausage is browned and the vegetables are fork-tender, about 8–12 minutes.

3. Add the vermouth or water and deglaze the pan. Add the clams.

4. Place in the oven and roast for 10 minutes or until the clams are open. Discard any clams that did not open and serve.

PER SERVING Calories: 480 | Fat: 15 g | Protein: 61 g | Sodium: 439 mg | Fiber: 1 g | Carbohydrates: 22 g | Sugar: 2 g

Rainbow Trout with Savoy Cabbage

Adding Savoy cabbage to the fish while it is cooking helps keep the fish moist.

INGREDIENTS | SERVES 4

1 pound rainbow trout filets

½ cup super-fine flour

3 teaspoons smoked paprika

1 teaspoon freshly ground black pepper

½ teaspoon sea salt

2 tablespoons olive oil

½ cup sliced onion

½ head Savoy cabbage, thinly sliced

2 tablespoons nonpareil capers

¼ cup lemon juice

¼ cup seafood stock

1. Place the rainbow trout on a platter. Sprinkle on both sides with flour, smoked paprika, pepper, and salt.

2. Heat the oil in a large skillet. Add the onion and filets, skin side down, in a single layer. Cook until the fish is halfway cooked and the skin is beginning to crisp, about 8 minutes.

3. Add the remaining ingredients and cover. Bring to a boil. Remove the cover and continue to cook until all of the liquid evaporates. Serve immediately.

PER SERVING Calories: 247 | Fat: 8 g | Protein: 23 g | Sodium: 505 mg | Fiber: 4 g | Carbohydrates: 21 g | Sugar: 5 g

What Is Pan-Frying?

Pan-frying is a method of frying that uses minimal oil; just enough to grease the pan. Pan-frying is best done in a skillet where there is maximum contact between the food and the pan. This maximizes browning.

Cod Poached in Tomato

This dish is wonderful served on a bed of warm polenta.

INGREDIENTS | SERVES 6

2 tablespoons olive oil

1 large onion, thinly sliced

¼ cup dry red wine

1½ pounds cod filets

28 ounces canned crushed tomatoes

2 tablespoons minced basil

2 tablespoons minced Italian parsley

2 tablespoons nonpareil capers

1 teaspoon freshly ground black pepper

½ teaspoon sea salt

1. Heat the oil in a Dutch oven. Add the onion and sauté until browned, about 10 minutes.

2. Deglaze the pan with red wine. Place the cod over the onions.

3. In a medium bowl, stir together the tomatoes, basil, parsley, capers, pepper, and salt. Pour over the cod. Cover and simmer for 20 minutes or until the cod is fully cooked.

PER SERVING Calories: 92 | Fat: 5 g | Protein: 4 g | Sodium: 479 mg | Fiber: 2 g | Carbohydrates: 8 g | Sugar: 4 g

Wasabi Tuna Tartar

Look for pungent, fresh wasabi at Japanese markets; it is better tasting than the green paste!

INGREDIENTS | SERVES 4

⅔ cup Japanese mayonnaise

1-inch knob fresh wasabi, grated

1 teaspoon sesame oil

1¼ pounds sushi-grade tuna, finely diced

¼ cup minced scallions

Carefully mix all of the ingredients in a small bowl. Chill 1 hour before serving.

PER SERVING Calories: 492 | Fat: 37 g | Protein: 34 g | Sodium: 267 mg | Fiber: 1 g | Carbohydrates: 5 g | Sugar: 0 g

Steamed Shrimp

Steamed shrimp is quick, easy, and low in calories—the perfect weeknight meal.

INGREDIENTS | SERVES 6

½ cup water

½ cup white wine

¼ cup diced red onion

1 clove garlic, minced

2 serrano peppers, minced

2 tablespoons yellow mustard seed

1 teaspoon ground cayenne

½ teaspoon celery seed

1 teaspoon freshly ground black pepper

2 pounds whole shrimp, peeled and deveined

1. Place the water, wine, onion, garlic, peppers, and spices in a large lidded pot. Bring to a boil.

2. Add the shrimp. Cover and steam until the shrimp turns bright pink and is fully cooked, about 5–10 minutes.

PER SERVING Calories: 198 | Fat: 4 g | Protein: 31 g | Sodium: 225 mg | Fiber: 1 g | Carbohydrates: 5 g | Sugar: 1 g

Shrimp Facts

Shrimp is an excellent source of protein. While shrimp is rather high in cholesterol, it is also very low in saturated fat. Shrimp is also a wonderful source of selenium, which has been reported to neutralize free radicals.

Pineapple Salmon

Try this Hawaiian-inspired dish over rice.

INGREDIENTS | SERVES 4

1 fresh pineapple, cut into ¼-inch rings
4 (5-ounce) salmon filets
¼ cup soy sauce
2 teaspoons sesame oil
2 teaspoons toasted sesame seeds
1 bunch scallions, chopped

Peppy Pineapple

Pineapple is an excellent source of vitamin C; one serving provides over 80 percent of your RDA. Pineapple contains bromides, which have been proven to reduce inflammation.

1. Preheat oven to 350°F.

2. Tear off 4 (2-foot) lengths of foil. Evenly divide the pineapple among the foil. Place 1 salmon filet on top of the pineapple in each packet.

3. In a small bowl, whisk together soy sauce, sesame oil, sesame seeds, and scallion. Spoon an even amount of sauce over each filet. Fold the foil shut.

4. Bake in the oven for 30 minutes or until the salmon is fully cooked.

PER SERVING Calories: 350 | Fat: 12 g | Protein: 30 g | Sodium: 963 mg | Fiber: 4 g | Carbohydrates: 31 g | Sugar: 23 g

Ouzo Orzo Scallops

Ouzo, the robust drink of Greece, adds an unusual, anise-like flavor to the dish.

INGREDIENTS | SERVES 4

2 tablespoons unsalted butter

2 cloves garlic, minced

1 shallot, minced

1 pound large sea scallops

2 tablespoons ouzo

2 tablespoons lemon juice

1 teaspoon lemon zest

1 pound baby spinach

2 cups hot cooked orzo

1. In a large skillet, melt the butter. Add the garlic and shallot and sauté until the shallot is translucent, about 5–8 minutes.

2. Add the scallops, ouzo, lemon juice, and zest. Sauté until the scallops are halfway cooked, about 3–5 minutes and add the spinach. Sauté until the spinach has wilted, about 2–3 minutes.

3. Serve over orzo.

PER SERVING Calories: 524 | Fat: 8 g | Protein: 34 g | Sodium: 283 mg | Fiber: 7 g | Carbohydrates: 79 g | Sugar: 4 g

Poultry

Chicken Meatballs with Spaghetti

Ground chicken absorbs flavor easily, which makes for an especially flavorful finished dish.

INGREDIENTS | SERVES 6

1 pound ground chicken

1 small onion, minced

4 cloves garlic, minced, divided use

1/3 cup fresh bread crumbs

1 tablespoon minced basil

1 tablespoon minced Italian parsley

1 tablespoon red wine vinegar

2 tablespoons olive oil

2 shallots, minced

30 ounces canned diced tomatoes

28 ounces canned crushed tomatoes

1 tablespoon minced oregano

1 teaspoon freshly ground black pepper

1 teaspoon sea salt

1 pound whole-wheat spaghetti, cooked

Making Mini Meatballs

Mini meatballs are easier than you would think. Simply roll the meat mixture into a 1/4–1/2-inch tube and cut into 1/4-inch slices. Toss in a sieve with some bread crumbs to make them round.

1. In a medium bowl, mix together the chicken, onion, 2 cloves garlic, bread crumbs, basil, parsley, and vinegar. Form into 2-inch meatballs.

2. Place the meatballs on a broiling pan and broil for 5 minutes or until they are starting to brown.

3. Meanwhile, heat the olive oil in a large skillet or Dutch oven. Add the shallot and remaining garlic and sauté until the shallot is softened, about 5 minutes.

4. Add the tomatoes, oregano, pepper, and salt. Add the meatballs to the sauce. Cook, stirring occasionally, until the meatballs are fully cooked and the sauce thickens, about 20 minutes.

5. Serve over hot spaghetti.

PER SERVING Calories: 583 | Fat: 18 g | Protein: 27 g | Sodium: 892 mg | Fiber: 6 g | Carbohydrates: 80 g | Sugar: 10 g

Chicken Potpie

What could be more comforting than chicken potpie? This one has extra vegetables for more nutrition.

INGREDIENTS | SERVES 6

1 tablespoon unsalted butter
1½ tablespoons olive oil
2 carrots, diced
2 parsnips, peeled and diced
1 turnip, diced
2 stalks celery, diced
1 onion, diced
1 shallot, minced
2 cloves garlic
3 Yukon Gold potatoes, diced
½ cup flour
2¾ cups chicken stock
1 bay leaf
1½ cups 2% milk
1 cup fresh or frozen peas
¾ cup fresh or frozen corn kernels
1 tablespoon minced sage
2 tablespoons minced Italian parsley
1 teaspoon sea salt
1 teaspoon ground white pepper
1½ pounds cooked, cubed chicken
1 sheet puff pastry
1 egg, beaten

1. Preheat oven to 350°F.

2. Heat the butter and oil in an oven-safe 2-quart casserole. Add the carrots, parsnips, turnip, celery, onion, shallot, garlic, and potato and sauté until the vegetables are beginning to soften and onions and shallot are translucent, about 5–8 minutes. Sprinkle with the flour and cook for 2 minutes, stirring occasionally.

3. Add stock, bay leaf, and milk and simmer until the mixture reduces and thickens, about 15 minutes. Discard the bay leaf.

4. Add the peas, corn, sage, parsley, salt, pepper, and chicken. Continue to simmer 5 minutes.

5. Top with puff pastry. Use a fork to pierce the pastry. Brush with beaten egg.

6. Bake for 30 minutes or until the filling is piping hot and the pastry is golden brown. Serve immediately.

PER SERVING Calories: 491 | Fat: 16 g | Protein: 35 g | Sodium: 606 mg | Fiber: 7 g | Carbohydrates: 53 g | Sugar: 12 g

Using Puff Pastry

Puff pastry can be made at home, bought refrigerated at the bakery, or bought frozen at the supermarket. If frozen, defrost overnight in the refrigerator before use. Look for organic versions; they often taste fresher than conventional puff pastry brands.

Tarragon Roasted Chicken

Classic roasted chicken gets a French twist with tarragon and Herbes de Provence.

INGREDIENTS | SERVES 8

1 (7-pound) chicken

3 tablespoons olive oil

½ cup loosely packed tarragon

2 tablespoons coarse sea salt

1 tablespoon coarsely ground black pepper

1 tablespoon Herbes de Provence

Herbes de Provence

Herbes de Provence sound fancy but they are really just a collection of dried herbs. The mix typically contains savory, fennel, basil, thyme, and lavender. Try them on chicken or wild rice.

1. Preheat oven to 325°F.

2. Place the chicken in roasting pan. Rub with olive oil. Place half of the tarragon in the cavity of the chicken.

3. In a small bowl, stir together the salt, pepper, remainder of the tarragon, and Herbes de Provence. Rub the mixture into the skin of the chicken.

4. Roast for 2 hours then turn the oven temperature up to 350°F.

5. Continue to roast for 30 minutes or until the chicken is fully cooked. Allow to sit 10 minutes before carving.

PER SERVING Calories: 691 | Fat: 23 g | Protein: 112 g | Sodium: 994 mg | Fiber: 0 g | Carbohydrates: 2 g | Sugar: 0 g

Korean-Inspired Chicken Burgers

While not a traditional Korean recipe, these burgers were inspired by spicy Korean fried chicken.

INGREDIENTS | SERVES 4

1 pound ground chicken

3 cloves garlic, grated

1-inch knob fresh ginger, grated

2 tablespoons soy sauce

2 tablespoons gojujang (Korean red chile paste)

1 tablespoon black sesame oil

1 tablespoon rice vinegar

¼ cup panko

1. Place all ingredients in a medium bowl. Mix until all ingredients are evenly distributed. Divide into 4 equal patties.

2. Spray a nonstick skillet with cooking spray. Cook the burgers for 5 minutes on each side or until fully cooked.

PER SERVING Calories: 204 | Fat: 7 g | Protein: 26 g | Sodium: 586 mg | Fiber: 1 g | Carbohydrates: 7 g | Sugar: 1 g

Nonstick Skillet FYI

Do not use metal or abrasive utensils on nonstick skillets. They may scrape off the surface, which then might end up in the cooked food. "Green" nonstick skillets have a coating that doesn't scratch off and is heat-safe.

Lime-Marinated Chicken Quesadillas

Using fresh lime juice makes the chicken incredibly tender.

INGREDIENTS | SERVES 4

2 tablespoons olive oil

⅓ cup lime juice

4 cloves garlic, sliced

1 onion, chopped

1 chipotle chile in adobo sauce, minced

1 tablespoon lime zest

1 teaspoon kosher salt

½ teaspoon freshly ground black pepper

1 pound boneless, skinless chicken breast, cut into ¼-inch wide strips

6 ounces frozen spinach, defrosted and drained

8 large whole-wheat or regular flour tortillas

⅔ cup extra-sharp Cheddar cheese

1. Place the olive oil, lime juice, garlic, onion, chipotle, lime zest, salt, pepper, and chicken in a marinating container or resealable bag. Refrigerate for at least 2 hours or up to 8 hours.

2. Add the contents of the marinating container to a nonstick skillet. Sauté until the chicken is almost fully cooked, about 5–8 minutes. Stir in the spinach.

3. Place a tortilla in a second nonstick pan. Heat the tortilla on both sides until warm and slightly browned. Repeat for remaining tortillas.

4. Evenly divide the chicken-spinach mixture between 4 tortillas in a single layer. Sprinkle evenly with cheese. Place a second tortilla on top of the cheese and return it to the pan. Cook until the cheese has melted. Repeat for the remaining quesadillas. Slice and serve.

PER SERVING Calories: 478 | Fat: 21 g | Protein: 35 g | Sodium: 1,250 mg | Fiber: 4 g | Carbohydrates: 37 g | Sugar: 3 g

Lemon-Thyme Roasted Capon

Lemon and thyme is a classic combination for a good reason; it is delicious!

INGREDIENTS | SERVES 8

1 (8-pound) capon

1 lemon, halved

1 small onion, quartered

4 cloves garlic

2 tablespoons olive oil

3 tablespoons kosher salt

1 tablespoon coarsely ground black pepper

1½ tablespoons chervil

1½ tablespoons marjoram

1½ tablespoons thyme leaves

1. Preheat oven to 450°F.

2. Place the capon on a roasting rack. Place the lemon, onion, and garlic in the cavity.

3. Rub the capon with olive oil then sprinkle with salt, pepper, chervil, marjoram, and thyme.

4. Roast for 2 hours then reduce heat to 350°F and cook an additional 20 minutes or until fully cooked.

PER SERVING Calories: 1,093 | Fat: 80 g | Protein: 85 g | Sodium: 2,856 mg | Fiber: 1 g | Carbohydrates: 4 g | Sugar: 1 g

What Are Capons?

Capons are castrated roosters. They are moister and have a more robust flavor than hens. They also have incredibly tender meat. Look for them at a poultry farm or well-stocked supermarket.

Chipotle Lime Duck with Chipotle Cherry Sauce

A spicy, Mexican-inspired riff on the classic duck with cherry sauce.

INGREDIENTS | SERVES 6

1 (6-pound) duck
¼ cup lime juice
½ tablespoon smoked sea salt
½ tablespoon dried minced onion
½ tablespoon ground chipotle
½ tablespoon ground ancho chile
½ tablespoon dried oregano
½ tablespoon thyme leaves
1 (6-inch) cinnamon stick
6 chipotle peppers in adobo sauce, divided use
¼ cup duck or chicken stock
2 cups halved, pitted cherries
2 cups red wine
1 tablespoon unsalted butter or liquid duck fat
¼ cup golden syrup
½ teaspoon kosher salt
½ teaspoon fresh ground black pepper

1. Preheat oven to 325°F.

2. Place the duck in a roasting pan with a rack. Pour the lime juice over the duck.

3. Mix the smoked sea salt, minced onion, ground chipotle, ground ancho, oregano, and thyme together in a small bowl. Rub the mixture into the skin of the duck.

4. Place the cinnamon stick and 3 chipotle chiles in adobo sauce in the cavity of the duck. Place in the oven and roast until the duck is fully cooked, about 2 hours.

5. Meanwhile, purée the remaining chipotles in adobo with the stock in a blender. Scrape the mixture into a small saucepan. Add the cherries, wine, butter or duck fat, golden syrup, kosher salt, and black pepper. Bring to a boil, stirring occasionally.

6. Reduce to a simmer and cook until it reduces by half, about 20 minutes. Use a potato masher to lightly mash the cherries.

7. Allow the duck to sit for 5 minutes before carving. Serve immediately, drizzled with sauce.

PER SERVING Calories: 786 | Fat: 29 g | Protein: 83 g | Sodium: 1,148 mg | Fiber: 2 g | Carbohydrates: 30 g | Sugar: 10 g

Slow Cooker Turkey Tacos

Dried and fresh peppers give these tacos an amazing depth of flavor.

INGREDIENTS | SERVES 8

2½ pounds boneless, skinless turkey thighs

6 ounces tomato paste

15 ounces canned fire-roasted tomatoes

1 onion, chopped

2 cloves garlic, sliced

Pulp from 1 fresh tamarind pod

1 shallot, chopped

1 dried poblano pepper, sliced

3 fresh poblano peppers, sliced

¼ cup lime juice

1 tablespoon agave nectar

1 teaspoon freshly ground black pepper

Place all ingredients in an oval, 4-quart slow cooker. Cook on high for 7–8 hours. Serve with fresh corn or flour tortillas.

PER SERVING Calories: 207 | Fat: 2 g | Protein: 33 g | Sodium: 329 mg | Fiber: 2 g | Carbohydrates: 13 g | Sugar: 1 g

Pesto Chicken Breasts

Bright, fresh pesto perks up the standard chicken breast.

INGREDIENTS | SERVES 4

3 cups basil, loosely packed

¼ cup olive oil

¼ cup finely grated Parmesan cheese

¼ cup pine nuts

1 teaspoon kosher salt

1 teaspoon freshly ground black pepper

4 boneless, skinless chicken breasts

Leftover Pesto?

Try stirring leftover pesto into potato salad or in the yolk of a deviled egg. Use it as a spread on sandwiches or bruschetta. Whisk it into eggs for a basil scramble.

1. Preheat oven to 350°F.

2. Place the basil, olive oil, Parmesan, pine nuts, salt, and pepper in a food processor. Pulse until a thick paste forms.

3. Line a baking sheet with foil. Rub both sides of each chicken breast with the pesto and place on baking sheet. Bake until the chicken is fully cooked, about 20 minutes.

PER SERVING Calories: 498 | Fat: 29 g | Protein: 54 g | Sodium: 931 mg | Fiber: 2 g | Carbohydrates: 4 g | Sugar: 2 g

Turkey Caper Cutlets

This turkey dish creates its own gravy, making it perfect to serve over egg noodles or mashed potatoes.

INGREDIENTS | SERVES 4

4 boneless, skinless turkey cutlets
2 tablespoons mixed Italian herbs
¼ cup instant flour
1 tablespoon olive oil
½ tablespoon unsalted butter
1 onion, quartered and sliced thinly
¾ cup turkey or chicken stock
2 tablespoons nonpareil capers

1. Sprinkle both sides of each cutlet with the Italian herbs. Pour the flour in a shallow bowl and dip both sides of each cutlet in the flour to coat.

2. Heat the oil and butter in a large skillet. Add the onion and sauté until it is soft and translucent, about 5–10 minutes. Add the turkey in a single layer. Brown the turkey cutlets on both sides, about 2–3 minutes.

3. Add the stock and capers and bring to a simmer. Continue to simmer until the turkey is fully cooked and the liquid has reduced slightly, about 10 minutes.

PER SERVING Calories: 223 | Fat: 7 g | Protein: 27 g | Sodium: 261 mg | Fiber: 1 g | Carbohydrates: 10 g | Sugar: 2 g

Marinated Grilled Turkey Cutlets

Grill corn alongside the turkey for an easy side dish; they cook in about the same amount of time.

INGREDIENTS | SERVES 6

6 thick-cut turkey breast cutlets

1 cup light coconut milk

1 onion, diced

4 cloves garlic, minced

1 Scotch bonnet pepper, minced, seeds removed

2 tablespoons canola oil

1 tablespoon Caribbean-style curry powder

1 teaspoon fresh thyme leaves

½ teaspoon ground cayenne

½ teaspoon hot paprika

¼ teaspoon freshly grated nutmeg

1 teaspoon sea salt

1. Place all ingredients in a marinating container or resealable plastic bag. Seal and shake to distribute the ingredients. Refrigerate at least 1 hour or up to 8 hours.

2. Prepare your grill according to the manufacturer's instructions. Grease the grill grate. Remove the turkey from the marinade. Discard the marinade.

3. Grill, flipping once, until fully cooked, about 10 minutes.

PER SERVING Calories: 255 | Fat: 14 g | Protein: 29 g | Sodium: 455 mg | Fiber: 1 g | Carbohydrates: 5 g | Sugar: 1 g

Why Use Fresh Herbs?

Fresh herbs have more of the original nutrients intact than dried. The flavor of fresh herbs is brighter than dried herbs. Fresh herbs also add dimension of flavor to recipes.

Chicken Tenders with Honey Mustard Dipping Sauce

Fried chicken is a bit of an indulgence when it comes to eating whole foods, but everyone needs a bit of indulgence some times.

INGREDIENTS | SERVES 6

2 pounds boneless, skinless chicken breasts

1 tablespoon freshly ground black pepper

½ tablespoon kosher salt

2 teaspoons garlic powder

1 teaspoon hot paprika

1½ teaspoons ground mustard powder

½ teaspoon chili powder

1 cup flour

2½ cups panko

3 eggs, beaten

Canola oil, for frying

¾ cup mayonnaise

2 tablespoons honey

2 tablespoons Dijon mustard

½ tablespoon lemon juice

1. Cut the chicken into 1-inch wide strips. Toss the strips with the pepper, salt, garlic powder, paprika, mustard powder, and chili powder. Set aside.

2. Place the flour, panko, and eggs in 3 separate shallow bowls. Dip the chicken in the flour, then the egg, and finally the panko.

3. Meanwhile, heat 2 inches of canola oil in a deep skillet or Dutch oven. Fry the chicken until golden brown, about 3–5 minutes. Drain on paper towel–lined plates.

4. In a small bowl, whisk together the mayonnaise, honey, mustard, and lemon juice. Serve the chicken immediately with dipping sauce.

PER SERVING Calories: 761 | Fat: 32 g | Protein: 46 g | Sodium: 1,491 mg | Fiber: 4 g | Carbohydrates: 70 g | Sugar: 10 g

Jerk Chicken

Add extra flavor by adding whole allspice berries to the charcoal as the chicken cooks.

INGREDIENTS | SERVES 8

8 whole chicken leg quarters

⅓ cup canola oil

⅓ cup lime juice

¼ cup light brown sugar

3 tablespoons apple cider vinegar

1½ tablespoons fresh thyme leaves

3 teaspoons allspice

½ teaspoon mace

1 teaspoon freshly ground black pepper

1½ teaspoons sea salt

1 teaspoon ground cinnamon

½ teaspoon cloves

¼ teaspoon freshly ground nutmeg

1 bunch scallions

6 cloves garlic

1 small onion, quartered

6 Scotch bonnet peppers

1-inch knob fresh ginger, sliced

1. Place the chicken in a marinating container or resealable plastic bag. Set aside. Place the remaining ingredients in a blender or food processor and pulse until smooth. Pour over the chicken. Refrigerate the chicken for 8–12 hours.

2. Prepare your charcoal grill according to manufacturer's instructions. Grill the chicken over high, direct heat until the skin begins to caramelize.

3. Reduce the heat and continue to cook, covered, until the chicken is fully cooked, about 30–40 minutes. If desired, use the remaining marinade to baste the chicken during the cooking process. Serve immediately.

PER SERVING Calories: 455 | Fat: 30 g | Protein: 31 g | Sodium: 199 mg | Fiber: 2 g | Carbohydrates: 15 g | Sugar: 10 g

Chicken Adobo

The unofficial national dish of the Philippines, chicken adobo is frequently served with garlic rice.

INGREDIENTS | SERVES 8

4 chicken thighs
4 chicken legs
20 cloves garlic, smashed
1¼ cups coconut vinegar
½ cup soy sauce
½ cup water
1 tablespoon whole black peppercorns
6 bay leaves

1. Place all of the ingredients in a Dutch oven. Bring to a boil, then reduce to a simmer. Simmer until the meat is fully cooked and most of the liquid has evaporated, about 45 minutes.

2. Increase the heat and cook an additional 5 minutes or until the chicken is browned. Serve immediately.

PER SERVING Calories: 217 | Fat: 12 g | Protein: 22 g | Sodium: 98 mg | Fiber: 0 g | Carbohydrates: 3 g | Sugar: 0 g

Garlic Rice

Ubiquitous in Filipino cuisine, garlic rice is both flavorful and easy to make. Stir together 4 cups of steamed rice and a pinch of salt. Brown 4 cloves of minced garlic in 1½ tablespoons of oil. Stir in the rice and cook until heated through.

Tea-Rubbed Duck

Try this aromatic duck with freshly steamed sugar snap peas drizzled with soy sauce.

INGREDIENTS | SERVES 6

1 (7-pound) duck
1 teaspoon Saigon Cinnamon
1½ teaspoons ground star anise
1½ teaspoons ground ginger
½ tablespoon sea salt
1 teaspoon white pepper
2 tablespoons green tea leaves
1 large shallot, quartered
1 satsuma, quartered
5 whole star anise

Duck Fat

Somewhat surprisingly, duck fat is considered by many to be a healthy alternative to cooking with butter. It is high in beneficial unsaturated fats. Studies have linked unsaturated fat consumption to lower blood cholesterol levels. Drain the fat from the bottom of the pan and refrigerate it for up to 6 months.

1. Preheat oven to 325°F.

2. Place the duck in a roasting pan with a rack.

3. Mix the cinnamon, ground star anise, ground ginger, salt, white pepper, and tea leaves together in a small bowl. Rub the mixture into the skin of the duck.

4. Place the shallot, satsuma, and whole star anise in the cavity of the duck. Roast for 2 hours then raise the temperature to 375°F for 20 minutes.

5. Allow the duck to sit 5 minutes prior to carving.

PER SERVING Calories: 722 | Fat: 31 g | Protein: 96 g | Sodium: 2,157 mg | Fiber: 0 g | Carbohydrates: 9 g | Sugar: 0 g

Garlic Rosemary Rock Cornish Game Hens

Rock Cornish Game Hens are tiny; each hen is a single serving.

INGREDIENTS | SERVES 4

4 (2-pound) Rock Cornish Game Hens

16 cloves garlic

16 sprigs fresh rosemary

3 tablespoons unsalted butter, at room temperature

1 tablespoon minced fresh rosemary

1 tablespoon lemon zest

1 tablespoon kosher salt

½ tablespoon freshly ground black pepper

Did You Know?

Rock Cornish Game Hens are simply a variety of very small chicken. The breed was developed in the 1950s and gained popularity in the '60s. It was bred to develop a large breast in a short period of time, so each tiny hen can be served as a single portion.

1. Preheat oven to 350°F.

2. Place the hens on a rack in a roasting pan. Evenly divide the garlic and rosemary sprigs among the cavities of the hens.

3. In a small bowl, mix together the butter, minced rosemary, and lemon zest.

4. Loosen the skin on the breasts of each hen. Rub in the butter mixture under the skin of each hen. Sprinkle the outside of the birds with salt and pepper.

5. Roast for 45 minutes or until fully cooked. Allow to sit for 5 minutes prior to serving.

PER SERVING Calories: 99 | Fat: 9 g | Protein: 1 g | Sodium: 1,772 mg | Fiber: 1 g | Carbohydrates: 5 g | Sugar: 0 g

Fresh Ricotta–Topped Crostini (Chapter 14)

Chicken Potpie (Chapter 7)

Smoky, Spicy Deviled Eggs (Chapter 14)

Sausage with Rapini and White Beans (Chapter 8)

Pear-Sage Meatloaf (Chapter 8)

Herbed Salmon Cakes (Chapter 6)

Red Onion and Olive Focaccia (Chapter 5)

Rosemary Wild Rice Pilaf (Chapter 13)

Shrimp Cocktail (Chapter 14)

Mango-Chile Paletas (Chapter 15)

Meyer Lemon–Marinated Olives and Feta (Chapter 12)

Cranberry-Walnut Cake (Chapter 16)

Pearl Couscous with Mixed Vegetables (Chapter 13)

Chicken Tenders with Honey Mustard Dipping Sauce (Chapter 7)

Potatoes and Green Beans (Chapter 4)

Mango Lassi (Chapter 2)

Espresso Granita (Chapter 15)

Breakfast Tacos (Chapter 3)

Pickled Asparagus (Chapter 12)

Herbed Chicken and Rice Soup (Chapter 11)

Orange Cranberry Sauce (Chapter 10)

Beet-Grapefruit Salad (Chapter 9)

Escarole, Spring Onion, and Rice Soup (Chapter 11)

Zucchini Bread (Chapter 3)

Oven-Baked Chicken Wings

Spicy and sticky from homemade barbecue sauce, these wings are a snap to make.

INGREDIENTS | SERVES 6

5 pounds chicken wings

1½ tablespoons hot paprika

1½ tablespoons chili powder

2 tablespoons ground mustard powder

1 teaspoon ground cayenne

1 teaspoon crushed chipotle pepper flakes

1 teaspoon garlic powder

1 teaspoon sea salt

1 teaspoon freshly ground black pepper

1 cup Homemade Peach Barbecue Sauce (see Chapter 10)

1. Preheat oven to 300°F.

2. Place the wings and spices in a large resealable plastic bag. Shake to coat.

3. Arrange the wings on broiling pans or wire rack–lined baking sheets. Bake for 25 minutes.

4. Raise the temperature to 450°F. Bake for 30–40 minutes or until the wings are crisp and golden.

5. Drain on paper towel–lined plates if needed. Place the wings in a large bowl. Drizzle with sauce and toss to coat. Serve immediately.

PER SERVING Calories: 81 | Fat: 1 g | Protein: 1 g | Sodium: 939 mg | Fiber: 2 g | Carbohydrates: 18 g | Sugar: 11 g

Red Cabbage Braised Chicken

The cabbage in this dish becomes incredibly tender due to the long cooking time.

INGREDIENTS | SERVES 6

2 tablespoons olive oil

2 tablespoons unsalted butter

1 onion, thinly sliced

3 cloves garlic, minced

4 cups finely shredded cabbage

½ cup chicken stock

1 (6-pound) whole chicken, cut into pieces

1 teaspoon caraway seeds

¼ teaspoon celery seed

½ teaspoon freshly ground black pepper

½ teaspoon salt

2 tablespoons balsamic vinegar

Caraway Seeds

Caraway seeds have been used for centuries in various ways as health treatments. They have been used as a tisane to treat digestive disorders. Caraway oil tablets are used to help relieve indigestion.

1. Heat the oil and butter in a 12-inch cast-iron skillet. Add the onion and garlic and sauté until the onion is translucent and soft.

2. Add the cabbage. Sauté until it starts to wilt. Pour in chicken stock. Cover and simmer until the cabbage is very tender, about 30 minutes.

3. In a nonstick skillet, quickly brown the chicken pieces, about 5–8 minutes. Transfer the chicken to the cast-iron skillet. Add the remaining ingredients. Cover the pan and simmer, turning the chicken occasionally. Cook until the chicken is cooked through, about 20–40 minutes.

4. Uncover the pan and continue to simmer another 10–15 minutes or until most of the liquid has evaporated. Serve immediately.

PER SERVING Calories: 635 | Fat: 22 g | Protein: 97 g | Sodium: 552 mg | Fiber: 2 g | Carbohydrates: 6 g | Sugar: 3 g

CHAPTER 8

Meat

Mustard Grilled Lamb Chops

Lamb loin chops are a wonderful, lean way to incorporate lamb into your diet.

INGREDIENTS | SERVES 4

4 lamb loin chops

1 lemon, sliced thinly

1 shallot, minced

4 cloves garlic, minced

2 tablespoons minced rosemary

¼ cup red wine vinegar

¼ cup olive oil

¼ cup Dijon mustard

½ teaspoon sea salt

1. Place all ingredients in a marinating container or resealable plastic bag. Refrigerate for 4 hours.

2. Prepare your grill according to manufacturer's instructions. Place the lamb chops on the grill and cook, turning once, until medium-rare, just a few minutes on each side.

PER SERVING Calories: 546 | Fat: 49 g | Protein: 19 g | Sodium: 543 mg | Fiber: 1 g | Carbohydrates: 8 g | Sugar: 0 g

Rosemary

A woody herb, rosemary may have some potential as a medical supplement. Rosemary is a source of carnosic acid, which in additional to having anti-inflammatory properties may also protect the brain from free radicals.

Herb-Rubbed Bison Steaks

Bison is an incredibly lean yet flavorful meat, making it an excellent alternative to beef.

INGREDIENTS | SERVES 2

1 teaspoon ground rosemary

1 teaspoon dried parsley

1 teaspoon dried oregano

1 teaspoon dried basil

½ teaspoon paprika

½ teaspoon ground mustard

½ teaspoon sea salt

2 (6-ounce) bison steaks

1½ tablespoons olive oil

1. In a small bowl, mix together the spices. Rub them into all sides of the bison steaks.

2. Heat the oil in a nonstick skillet. Pan-fry the bison, flipping once, until desired doneness.

PER SERVING Calories: 261 | Fat: 13 g | Protein: 35 g | Sodium: 694 mg | Fiber: 1 g | Carbohydrates: 1 g | Sugar: 0 g

Back to Bison

Once a rare meat on today's plate, bison is seeing a resurgence in popularity. Specialty bison farms specializing in organic and sustainable bison meat are popping up all over the country. In part, this is due to bison's high protein and relatively low fat ratio.

Pear-Sage Meatloaf

Look for a meatloaf pan at your local home goods store; it is made to help drain off any grease from meatloaf as it cooks.

INGREDIENTS | SERVES 8

1 pound 94% lean ground beef
1 egg, beaten
2 shallots, grated
¾ cup fresh bread crumbs
1 cup shredded Bosc pear
2 tablespoons grainy mustard
1½ tablespoons minced sage
1 teaspoon freshly ground black pepper
1 teaspoon sea salt
1 teaspoon smoked paprika
¼ teaspoon allspice

1. Preheat oven to 350°F.

2. Place all ingredients in a medium bowl. Mix together until all ingredients are evenly distributed.

3. Mold into a loaf and place in a loaf pan. Bake for 40 minutes or until fully cooked. Allow to sit for 5 minutes before serving.

PER SERVING Calories: 71 | Fat: 1 g | Protein: 3 g | Sodium: 381 mg | Fiber: 1 g | Carbohydrates: 12 g | Sugar: 1 g

Fruit-Glazed Pork Loin

The skins of the apricots are so soft, they nearly dissolve into the sauce.

INGREDIENTS | SERVES 6

1 pound apricots, pitted, unpeeled
¼ cup sugar
¼ cup water
½ teaspoon minced sage
½ teaspoon sea salt
1 (2-pound) pork loin

Buying Dutch Ovens

Dutch ovens are a wonderful tool in the kitchen. Able to go from stovetop to oven, they can be used for everything from stew to bread. Look for ones that have thick, sturdy bottoms and tight-fitting lids.

1. Preheat oven to 325°F.

2. In a Dutch oven, cook the apricots, sugar, water, sage, and sea salt until the apricots cook down, about 10–20 minutes. Mash them slightly with a potato masher.

3. Add the pork loin. Spoon the sauce over the pork.

4. Cover and roast for 30–40 minutes or until fully cooked. Allow to sit 5 minutes before slicing.

PER SERVING Calories: 482 | Fat: 35 g | Protein: 24 g | Sodium: 318 mg | Fiber: 2 g | Carbohydrates: 17 g | Sugar: 15 g

Venison Burgers

Venison has a distinctive, rich flavor yet is leaner than similar cuts of beef.

INGREDIENTS | SERVES 4

1 pound ground venison

1 tablespoon tomato paste

1 teaspoon minced fresh basil

1 teaspoon freshly ground black pepper

½ teaspoon ground cayenne

1½ tablespoons Worcestershire sauce

1 shallot, minced

1 clove garlic, minced

1 tablespoon canola oil

1. In a small bowl, mix together the venison, tomato paste, basil, pepper, cayenne, Worcestershire sauce, shallot, and garlic until well blended. Form into 4 patties.

2. Heat the oil in a skillet. Add the burgers and cook, turning once, until desired doneness is achieved and the burgers are browned on both sides, about 5–8 minutes.

PER SERVING Calories: 196 | Fat: 6 g | Protein: 27 g | Sodium: 156 mg | Fiber: 0 g | Carbohydrates: 7 g | Sugar: 1 g

Cooking with Venison

Venison is a very lean game meat. To keep it from tasting "gamey" it is best cook it only to medium-rare. Ground venison is the easiest kind of venison to find at the grocery store.

Roasted Pork with Pearl Onions and Pears

Bosc pears are the firmest of the pear varieties and hold their shape well in this dish.

INGREDIENTS | SERVES 6

2 pounds boneless pork roast

1 teaspoon sea salt

1 teaspoon freshly ground pepper

¼ teaspoon cinnamon

¼ teaspoon cloves

¼ teaspoon allspice

4 Bosc pears, sliced

½ pound pearl onions

½ cup pork or chicken stock

Peeling Pearl Onions

Peeling pearl onions can be tough but there is an easier way. First cut the pointy end off of the onion. Then boil it for 2 minutes. Drain and cool. Squeeze the root end of the onion to pop the onion out of the skin.

1. Preheat oven to 350°F.

2. Rub the pork on all sides with the spices. Place in a Dutch oven. Add the remaining ingredients and sauté until the onions and pork begin to brown, about 8–15 minutes.

3. Put the Dutch oven in the oven and roast for 45 minutes or until fully cooked.

PER SERVING Calories: 263 | Fat: 6 g | Protein: 34 g | Sodium: 496 mg | Fiber: 4 g | Carbohydrates: 18 g | Sugar: 11 g

Spicy Bison Burgers

Chipotle in adobo sauce keeps these burgers moist and adds a spicy kick.

INGREDIENTS | SERVES 4

1¼ pounds ground bison

2 tablespoons Worcestershire sauce

2 chipotles in adobo sauce, minced

1 shallot, minced

2 cloves garlic, minced

½ teaspoon sea salt

½ teaspoon hot paprika

½ teaspoon freshly ground black pepper

½ teaspoon dried oregano

2 tablespoons canola oil

1. In a medium bowl, mix together the bison, Worcestershire sauce, chipotles, shallot, garlic, sea salt, paprika, pepper, and oregano. Form into 4 patties.

2. Heat the oil in a skillet. Add the burgers and cook, turning once, until fully cooked and browned on both sides, about 5–8 minutes.

PER SERVING Calories: 229 | Fat: 9 g | Protein: 29 g | Sodium: 458 mg | Fiber: 0 g | Carbohydrates: 7 g | Sugar: 1 g

Shallot Tips

Shallots are in-season during spring and summer. When buying, look for dry bulbs with no sprouts or wrinkles. Store in a cool, dry place.

Shepherd's Pie

*Adding extra vegetables makes this classic dish even more
healthful and eliminates the need for a side dish.*

INGREDIENTS | SERVES 8

1½ pounds ground lamb

1 onion, diced

4 cloves garlic, minced

2 carrots, diced

2 parsnips, peeled and diced

1 stalk celery, diced

1½ cups lamb or chicken stock

1 tablespoon corn or tapioca starch

1 tablespoon Worcestershire sauce

1 cup frozen peas

½ tablespoon thyme leaves

1 teaspoon hot paprika

1 teaspoon summer savory

1 teaspoon sea salt

1 teaspoon freshly ground black pepper

2 pounds boiled potatoes

½ cup sour cream

¼ cup milk

1 egg, beaten

¼ teaspoon freshly ground nutmeg

Parsnip Power

Parsnips are a root vegetable related to the carrot. Like the carrot, they should be peeled before use and have a sweet taste. Parsnips are high in fiber and low in calories and fat.

1. Preheat oven to 350°F. Grease a 2-quart casserole. Set aside.

2. Brown the lamb in a large skillet, breaking up any large chunks, until it is browned, about 5–10 minutes. Drain off any excess fat.

3. Add the onion, garlic, carrot, parsnip, and celery. Sauté until the vegetables are soft, about 10–20 minutes.

4. Whisk together the stock, cornstarch, and Worcestershire sauce in a small bowl until the cornstarch dissolves. Add to the meat mixture.

5. Add the peas, thyme, paprika, savory, salt, and pepper. Simmer until the mixture is thick and nearly all of the liquid has evaporated, anywhere from 5–15 minutes.

6. Meanwhile, in a large bowl, mash the potatoes, sour cream, milk, egg, and nutmeg together.

7. Pour the meat mixture into the bottom of the prepared casserole pan. Spoon the mashed potatoes on top, taking care to reach all 4 corners. Use the back of a spoon to smooth the potatoes into a uniform layer.

8. Bake for 20 minutes or until the potatoes are browned and the meat mixture is bubbly.

PER SERVING Calories: 408 | Fat: 24 g | Protein: 20 g | Sodium: 478 mg | Fiber: 5 g | Carbohydrates: 28 g | Sugar: 6 g

Papaya Pulled Pork

Papaya provides moisture, body, and flavor to this tropical pulled pork.

INGREDIENTS | SERVES 8

3-pounds boneless pork shoulder roast, trimmed of fat

3 cups cubed papaya, peeled

2 tablespoons ginger juice

¼ cup pineapple juice

¼ cup tomato paste

3 serrano peppers, diced

1 onion, diced

5 cloves garlic, sliced

1 tablespoon yellow hot sauce

1 teaspoon sea salt

1 teaspoon chili powder

1 teaspoon paprika

1. Place all ingredients in a 4-quart slow cooker. Cook on low for 8–10 hours.

2. Remove the meat and pull apart with forks. Mash any solids in the slow cooker with a potato masher.

3. Return the meat to the slow cooker and stir to combine.

PER SERVING Calories: 297 | Fat: 12 g | Protein: 34 g | Sodium: 243 mg | Fiber: 2 g | Carbohydrates: 11 g | Sugar: 5 g

Papaya Tips

One large papaya contains more than 300 percent of the recommended RDA of vitamin C. Papayas also have 30 percent of the RDA of fiber and potassium. Papaya contains an enzyme that helps lower inflammation and improves healing from burns.

Leek-Smothered Pork Chops

Mild leeks melt and form a savory-sweet sauce for pork chops.

INGREDIENTS | SERVES 6

1 teaspoon kosher salt
1 teaspoon freshly ground pepper
1¼ pounds thin-cut boneless pork chops
¼ cup flour
2 tablespoons canola oil
1 onion, chopped
2 leeks, chopped
1 cup pork or chicken stock
¼ cup lemon juice
2 tablespoons balsamic vinegar
1 teaspoon thyme leaves

1. Sprinkle salt and pepper on both sides of each chop. Place flour in a shallow bowl; dredge the chops in flour.

2. Heat the oil in a skillet, brown the chops on both sides, about 3–5 minutes. Remove to a covered dish.

3. Add the onion and leeks to the pan and sauté until they start to brown.

4. Return the pork chops to the pan. Add the remaining ingredients. Cover and cook for 15 minutes or until everything is fully cooked and the sauce thickens.

PER SERVING Calories: 223 | Fat: 8 g | Protein: 23 g | Sodium: 504 mg | Fiber: 1 g | Carbohydrates: 12 g | Sugar: 3 g

Pineapple-Mango Meatballs

Fresh tropical fruit sweetens these meatballs naturally.

INGREDIENTS | SERVES 6

1 pound fresh pineapple, diced
1 mango, peeled and diced
1-inch knob ginger, minced
2 cloves garlic, minced
½ cup pineapple juice
¼ cup soy sauce
1 habanero pepper, minced, seeds removed
1 pound ground pork
¼ cup panko
1 tablespoon dark soy sauce
1 tablespoon sesame oil
1 teaspoon freshly ground black pepper

1. Bring the pineapple, mango, ginger, garlic, pineapple juice, soy sauce, and habanero pepper to a boil in a medium pan. Remove from heat.

2. Meanwhile, in a large bowl, combine the pork, panko, dark soy sauce, sesame oil, and pepper. Form into 1-inch meatballs. Place on a broiling pan and broil for 8 minutes.

3. Bring the sauce back up to a simmer. Add the meatballs and cook, stirring occasionally, until they are coated in sauce and fully cooked, about 10–20 minutes.

PER SERVING Calories: 320 | Fat: 19 g | Protein: 15 g | Sodium: 827 mg | Fiber: 2 g | Carbohydrates: 24 g | Sugar: 16 g

Tamarind Pot Roast

Fresh tamarind pods have a fresh, bright taste that perks up any pot roast.

INGREDIENTS | SERVES 6–8

2½ pounds top round roast

1 teaspoon salt

1 teaspoon freshly ground black pepper

1 teaspoon paprika

1 cup flour

2 tablespoons canola oil

2 onions, chopped

4 cloves garlic, minced

1-inch knob ginger, minced

2 carrots, sliced into coins

2 cups beef stock

4 tamarind pods, skin removed

¼ cup lemon juice

2 tablespoons dark soy sauce

Terrific Tamarind

Tamarind comes in brown, papery-looking pods with soft, edible brown pulp. It has a sour-sweet taste. It is used in a variety of candies, sauces, juices, and jams. In Ayurvedic medicine, tamarind is used to treat digestive issues.

1. Preheat oven to 350°F.

2. Season the pot roast with salt, pepper, and paprika.

3. Sprinkle the flour on a plate. Dredge the roast in the flour.

4. Heat the oil in a Dutch oven. Brown the beef on all sides. Remove to a covered dish. Add the onion, garlic, ginger, and carrots to the Dutch oven. Sauté 5 minutes.

5. Meanwhile, bring the stock and tamarind to a boil in a small saucepan, stirring frequently.

6. Add the beef back to the Dutch oven. Whisk the tamarind mixture through a strainer over the beef. Add the lemon juice and soy sauce. Bring to a boil.

7. Place Dutch oven into the oven. Cover and bake for 2½ hours.

PER SERVING Calories: 310 | Fat: 9 g | Protein: 36 g | Sodium: 738 mg | Fiber: 2 g | Carbohydrates: 19 g | Sugar: 3 g

Garlic-Studded Pork Roast

Inserting garlic into the roast not only infuses it with flavor; it seems to keep it moist as well.

INGREDIENTS | SERVES 8

1 (2-pound) pork loin

1 head garlic, peeled

1 cup basil

1 cup Italian parsley

2 tablespoons olive oil

¼ cup lemon juice

2 tablespoons lemon zest

1 teaspoon sea salt

1 teaspoon freshly ground pepper

Go, Garlic!

Garlic is fundamental ingredient in thousands of dishes around the world. Garlic has been traditionally used to treat the common cold. It also has antibacterial activity and has been used as an antiseptic.

1. Preheat oven to 350°F.

2. Cut slits on all sides of the loin and insert a garlic clove in each one.

3. Place the basil, parsley, olive oil, lemon juice, zest, salt, and pepper in a food processor. Pulse until a paste forms.

4. Rub the paste over the pork. Place in a Dutch oven and roast for 40 minutes or until the pork is fully cooked.

PER SERVING Calories: 115 | Fat: 10 g | Protein: 5 g | Sodium: 318 mg | Fiber: 0 g | Carbohydrates: 1 g | Sugar: 0 g

Grilled Steak Fajitas

Grilling is a great way to infuse lean cuts of steak with flavor instead fat.

INGREDIENTS | SERVES 6

2 pounds skirt steak

5 cloves garlic, minced

2 serrano peppers, minced

1 jalapeño pepper, minced

⅔ cup lime juice

3 tablespoons minced fresh oregano

2 tablespoons Worcestershire sauce

1 teaspoon cracked black pepper

1 teaspoon ground chipotle

¼ teaspoon ground cumin

1 onion, thinly sliced

3 poblano peppers, sliced

¾ cup pico de gallo

6–10 regular or whole-wheat tortillas

Pico de Gallo

This fresh Mexican condiment peps up any fajita or taco. In a small bowl, stir together 1 white onion, chopped; 2 jalapeños, minced; 1 large tomato, diced; 1 clove garlic, minced; salt and pepper to taste. Stir in 1 tablespoon minced cilantro and ¼ cup lime juice. Cover and refrigerate 1 hour.

1. Place the steak in a marinating container or resealable bag. Add the garlic, serrano peppers, jalapeño peppers, lime juice, oregano, Worcestershire sauce, black pepper, chipotle, and cumin. Refrigerate overnight.

2. Prepare your grill according to manufacturer's instructions. Meanwhile, in a nonstick skillet, sauté the onion and poblano peppers until soft, about 5–10 minutes. Cover to keep warm.

3. Place the steak on the grill and cook about 3 minutes on each side or until medium-rare. Allow to rest 5 minutes before slicing thinly.

4. Serve with pico de gallo, tortillas, and the pepper and onion mixture.

PER SERVING Calories: 473 | Fat: 23 g | Protein: 35 g | Sodium: 560 mg | Fiber: 3 g | Carbohydrates: 30 g | Sugar: 5 g

Spiced Baked Ham

Using whole spices instead of ground helps the mixture really permeate the ham.

INGREDIENTS | SERVES 8–10

1 (8-pound) fresh ham
1 teaspoon salt
1 tablespoon cracked pepper
1 teaspoon ground cayenne
3 tablespoons whole cloves
2 tablespoons whole mace
1 teaspoon allspice berries
1 teaspoon crushed star anise
¼ cup dark brown sugar
2 cinnamon sticks
2 cups water

1. Preheat oven to 325°F.

2. Score the outside of the ham with a sharp knife. Place it on a rack in a roasting pan.

3. In a small bowl, stir together the salt, pepper, cayenne, cloves, mace, allspice, star anise, and brown sugar. Rub into the skin of the ham.

4. Place the cinnamon sticks and water in the bottom of the pan. Bake 2½ hours. Wait 10 minutes prior to carving.

PER SERVING Calories: 593 | Fat: 31 g | Protein: 66 g | Sodium: 4,822 mg | Fiber: 1 g | Carbohydrates: 10 g | Sugar: 0 g

Ham Salad

Have leftovers? Grind together 2 cups cubed ham, ¼ cup fresh mayonnaise, 3 gherkins and 1 shallot. Serve on crackers or as a sandwich spread.

Beef and Zucchini Stuffed Eggplant

An easy variation is to swap out the dill for basil and sprinkle the finished product with Parmesan.

INGREDIENTS | SERVES 4

2 large eggplants, halved
½ pound 94% lean ground beef
1 onion, minced
1 zucchini, diced
1½ cups prepared quinoa
1 tablespoon minced fresh dill
½ teaspoon salt
½ teaspoon freshly ground black pepper

1. Preheat the oven to 350°F.

2. Scoop out the center of each eggplant half to form a "boat." Discard the innards. Bake for 5 minutes on a baking sheet. Set aside.

3. Brown the beef in a nonstick skillet. Drain off excess fat and add the onion and zucchini. Sauté until the zucchini is fork-tender, about 5–10 minutes.

4. Remove from heat and stir in the quinoa, dill, salt, and pepper.

5. Scoop the filling into each half of the eggplant. Return the eggplant to oven and bake for 10 minutes or until warmed through.

PER SERVING Calories: 397 | Fat: 7 g | Protein: 25 g | Sodium: 345 mg | Fiber: 15 g | Carbohydrates: 61 g | Sugar: 9 g

Rosemary-Rubbed Pan-Fried Flank Steak

Flank steak is a long, lean cut of beef. If unavailable, use skirt steak.

INGREDIENTS | SERVES 6

1¾ pounds flank steak

2½ tablespoons crushed rosemary

1 teaspoon coarse smoked sea salt

1 tablespoon cracked pepper

2 tablespoons olive oil

Grass-Fed Beef

When possible, buy grass-fed beef. Grass-fed beef is leaner than grain-fed and has a more favorable ratio of omega fatty acids. It is also a more sustainable way to farm and is community friendly. Most grass-fed cows are raised on independently owned ranches.

1. Heat a cast-iron skillet until it is very hot.

2. Meanwhile, thoroughly rub the steak on all sides with rosemary, salt, and pepper.

3. Add oil to the skillet. Add the steak and cook for 4–6 minutes on each side.

4. Remove to a platter. Tent with foil and allow to rest for 10 minutes before slicing.

PER SERVING Calories: 250 | Fat: 14 g | Protein: 28 g | Sodium: 465 mg | Fiber: 1 g | Carbohydrates: 2 g | Sugar: 0 g

Sausage with Rapini and White Beans

Try this with freshly made sausage from a butcher shop; it is head and shoulders above national brand sausage.

INGREDIENTS | SERVES 4

2 tablespoons olive oil

1 pound fresh hot Italian sausage links (4 links)

1 bunch rapini, chopped

4 cloves garlic, minced

2 shallots, minced

1 teaspoon crushed red pepper flakes

30 ounces cooked cannellini beans

1. Heat the oil in a large skillet. Add the sausage and cook for 1 minute.

2. Add the rapini, garlic, shallots, and red pepper flakes and sauté until the greens have wilted and the sausage is cooked through and browned on both sides, about 5–10 minutes. If the sausages are really thick, cover the mixture briefly to help them cook more rapidly.

3. Stir in the cannellini beans and cook 5 additional minutes or until warmed through. Serve immediately.

PER SERVING Calories: 622 | Fat: 38 g | Protein: 30 g | Sodium: 1,341 mg | Fiber: 11 g | Carbohydrates: 41 g | Sugar: 4 g

Grilled Chipotle Lamb Roast

Boneless lamb roast can be slightly tricky to find but the lean, flavorful meat is worth it.

INGREDIENTS | SERVES 6–8

1 onion, quartered

4 cloves garlic

4 chipotle chiles in adobo sauce

½ cup apple cider vinegar

2 tablespoons minced oregano

2 tablespoons olive oil

1 teaspoon dried epazote

2 tablespoons minced flat leaf parsley

½ teaspoon cayenne pepper

1 jalapeño

1 (3-pound) lamb roast

1. Place the onion, garlic, chipotles in adobo, vinegar, oregano, olive oil, epazote, parsley, cayenne, and jalapeño in a blender. Pulse until a paste forms.

2. Rub the lamb thoroughly with the paste and place in a marinating container or resealable bag. Refrigerate for 24 hours.

3. Prepare your grill according to manufacturer's instructions. Place the lamb on the grill. Cook for 15 minutes on each side, or until the internal temperature reaches 145°F.

PER SERVING Calories: 576 | Fat: 47 g | Protein: 34 g | Sodium: 77 mg | Fiber: 0 g | Carbohydrates: 3 g | Sugar: 1 g

Braised Short Ribs

Short ribs are an inexpensive cut of meat but they can be tough.
A long cooking time helps tenderize the meat.

INGREDIENTS | SERVES 4–6

5 pounds short ribs
3 cups flour
1 tablespoon sea salt
1 tablespoon cracked pepper
2 tablespoons olive oil
4 cloves garlic, sliced
1 pound pearl onions
3 carrots, sliced into coins
3 parsnips, peeled and sliced into coins
1 tablespoon minced bush sage
2 cups beef stock

1. Preheat oven to 350°F.

2. Dredge ribs in flour. Sprinkle with salt and pepper.

3. Heat oil in a large Dutch oven. Add the ribs and brown on all sides. Add the garlic, onions, carrots, parsnips, sage, and stock.

4. Cover and braise in the oven 2–2 ½ hours or until the meat is falling off the bone and tender.

PER SERVING Calories: 980 | Fat: 44 g | Protein: 80 g | Sodium: 1,565 mg | Fiber: 4 g | Carbohydrates: 60 g | Sugar: 5 g

Sea Salt FYI

Sea salt is made by evaporating seawater. Unlike table salt, it is unrefined and does not contain added iodine. Once a "gourmet" ingredient, sea salt now can be found at most grocery stores.

CHAPTER 9

Salads and Sandwiches

Asparagus Salad with Hard-Boiled Egg

This is a lovely salad to serve during the all-too-brief asparagus season. For an easy variation, toss in some leftover cooked or smoked salmon.

INGREDIENTS | SERVES 4

1½ pounds steamed asparagus

2 hard-boiled eggs, coarsely grated

3 tablespoons white wine vinegar

3 tablespoons olive oil

½ teaspoon Dijon mustard

2 tablespoons lemon juice

½ tablespoon lemon zest

2 tablespoons minced fresh dill

1 tablespoon minced Italian parsley

¼ teaspoon sea salt

1. In a large bowl, toss together the asparagus and eggs. Set aside.

2. In a small bowl, whisk together the vinegar, oil, mustard, lemon juice, lemon zest, dill, parsley, and salt. Drizzle over the asparagus and egg. Toss lightly. Serve immediately.

PER SERVING Calories: 167 | Fat: 13 g | Protein: 7 g | Sodium: 194 mg | Fiber: 4 g | Carbohydrates: 8 g | Sugar: 3 g

The Perfect Hard-Boiled Egg

Place eggs in a pan with a lid. Fill the pan with cold water until it is ¾–1 inch above the eggs. Bring to a full boil. Remove from heat and cover. Allow the eggs to sit 15 minutes. Drain and run under cool water. Use immediately or refrigerate.

Green Bean Salad with Orange Vinaigrette

Try this instead of green bean casserole at your next holiday meal.

INGREDIENTS | SERVES 8

2 pounds French green beans (haricot verts), steamed

⅓ cup toasted hazelnuts

¼ cup dried, tart cherries

1 small onion, minced

2 tablespoons extra virgin olive oil

3 tablespoons white wine vinegar

3 tablespoons fresh orange juice

1 tablespoon orange zest

½ teaspoon Dijon mustard

1. Toss together the green beans, hazelnuts, and cherries in a large bowl. Set aside.

2. Whisk together the onion, oil, vinegar, juice, zest, and mustard until well combined. Drizzle over the green bean mixture and toss again. Serve warm or cold.

PER SERVING Calories: 107 | Fat: 7 g | Protein: 3 g | Sodium: 12 mg | Fiber: 4 g | Carbohydrates: 11 g | Sugar: 6 g

Peppery Corn and Tomato Salad

Peppers in the salad and hot sauce in the dressing equal one zippy corn salad.

INGREDIENTS | SERVES 6

2 cups fresh corn kernels

1¼ cups halved cherry tomatoes

1 cup chopped red onion

1 bulb fennel, diced

1 cubanelle pepper, diced

1 bunch scallions, diced

¼ cup red wine vinegar

¼ cup olive oil

¼ cup lime juice

½ teaspoon Scotch bonnet hot sauce

1. In a medium bowl, toss together the corn, tomatoes, onion, fennel, cubanelle, and scallions. Take care to break the corn into individual kernels, as needed.

2. In a small bowl, whisk together the vinegar, oil, lime juice, and hot sauce. Pour over the salad and toss to combine. Serve immediately.

PER SERVING Calories: 151 | Fat: 10 g | Protein: 2 g | Sodium: 17 mg | Fiber: 2 g | Carbohydrates: 17 g | Sugar: 4 g

Dill-Yogurt Potato Salad

This Greek-inspired potato salad has more vegetables and crunch than your typical potato salad.

INGREDIENTS | SERVES 8

2 pounds whole baby red-skin potatoes

1 onion, diced

1 shallot, minced

4 large red radishes, diced

⅓ cup diced cucumber

2 stalks celery, diced

¾ cup chopped fresh dill

1¼ cups plain Greek yogurt

¼ cup lemon juice

2 tablespoons lemon zest

½ teaspoon sea salt

½ teaspoon white pepper

1. Combine the potatoes, onion, shallot, radishes, cucumbers, and celery in a medium bowl. Set aside.

2. In a small bowl, stir together the dill, yogurt, lemon juice, lemon zest, salt, and pepper. Pour over the potato mixture and stir to evenly coat.

3. Refrigerate for 2 hours prior to serving.

PER SERVING Calories: 117 | Fat: 0 g | Protein: 6 g | Sodium: 180 mg | Fiber: 3 g | Carbohydrates: 23 g | Sugar: 4 g

What's the Dillio?

Dill is a popular herb that is used in many ways. However, the terms that refer to the various forms of dill can be confusing. Fresh dill is always referred to as *dill*, while *dillweed* refers to dried dill. Dill seeds are, of course the seeds of the dill plant. Dill flowers (flowering dill) can also be used in pickling.

Ginger-Sesame Coleslaw

This vegan, crunchy slaw goes great with grilled foods and on sandwiches.

INGREDIENTS | SERVES 10

4 cups shredded green cabbage

1 cup shredded red cabbage

4 carrots, shredded

½ cup shredded jicama

1 bunch scallions, minced

2-inch knob ginger, grated

2 tablespoons toasted sesame seeds

1½ tablespoons toasted sesame oil

¾ cup rice vinegar

¼ teaspoon kosher salt

¼ teaspoon celery seed

1. In a large bowl, toss together the cabbage, carrots, jicama, and scallions. Set aside.

2. In a small bowl, whisk together the ginger, sesame seeds, oil, vinegar, salt, and celery seed. Drizzle over the cabbage mixture and toss.

PER SERVING Calories: 57 | Fat: 3 g | Protein: 1 g | Sodium: 87 mg | Fiber: 2 g | Carbohydrates: 7 g | Sugar: 3 g

Awesome Cabbage

Cabbage is a very low-calorie food, making it perfect for dieters and the health conscious. Cabbage is also an excellent source of vitamin C. It contains glutamine, which is an anti-inflammatory.

Green Papaya and Green Mango Salad

The "green" in this recipe does not refer to the color of the fruit but to the state of ripeness. Use unripe papaya and mango in this dish.

INGREDIENTS | SERVES 4

1 green papaya, peeled and cut into matchsticks

1 green mango, peeled and cut into matchsticks

1 carrot, cut into matchsticks

1 seedless cucumber, peeled and cut into matchsticks

¼ cup chopped fresh mint

¼ cup chopped cilantro

1 Thai Bird's Eye pepper, sliced

1 teaspoon Thai garlic-chili paste

1 tablespoon palm sugar

⅓ cup lime juice

⅓ cup Thai fish sauce

1. In a large bowl, toss together the papaya, mango, carrot, cucumber, mint, cilantro, and chile pepper. Set aside.

2. In a small bowl, whisk together the garlic-chili paste, palm sugar, lime juice, and fish sauce. Pour over the salad and toss.

3. Garnish with peanuts and lime wedges if desired.

PER SERVING Calories: 98 | Fat: 0 g | Protein: 2 g | Sodium: 18 mg | Fiber: 3 g | Carbohydrates: 25 g | Sugar: 18 g

Exotic Ingredient Demystified: Palm Sugar

Palm sugar is made from the sago or coconut palm. It looks a bit like brown sugar but tastes like caramel. It is often sold as a solid brick. To use, simply break off a piece and either crush it and measure it or estimate the amount and allow it to dissolve in the dish whole.

Beet-Grapefruit Salad

Just the salad to get one through a long, cold winter.

INGREDIENTS | SERVES 4

3 large beets with greens
1 shallot, grated
¼ cup sherry vinegar
3 tablespoons extra virgin olive oil
2 tablespoons fresh grapefruit juice
1½ teaspoons Dijon mustard
½ teaspoon grapefruit zest
2 grapefruits, supremed

Zest Tips

When zesting, you only want to take the outermost part of the skin. No pith (the white part) should be removed. Use a box grater or Microplane for very fine zest and zester for more coarse zest. Use the freshest citrus possible for best flavor.

1. Preheat oven to 350°F.

2. Chop off the beet greens and tear into bite-sized pieces. Set aside.

3. Peel and quarter the beets. Arrange the beets in a single layer on a baking pan and roast for 60 minutes or until tender.

4. Meanwhile, in a small bowl, whisk together the shallot, vinegar, oil, grapefruit juice, mustard, and zest. Set aside.

5. Arrange the beet greens in a serving bowl or plate. Top with cooked (hot or cold) beets and grapefruit. Drizzle with the dressing and serve.

PER SERVING Calories: 186 | Fat: 11 g | Protein: 3 g | Sodium: 119 mg | Fiber: 3 g | Carbohydrates: 22 g | Sugar: 14 g

Summer Salad with Poached Egg

This salad is pretty and festive enough to serve at a summer dinner party.

INGREDIENTS | SERVES 4

10 ounces fresh baby spinach or baby lettuces

1½ cups diced heirloom tomatoes

3 banana peppers, thinly sliced into rounds

1 bulb fennel, shaved

1 avocado, thinly sliced

5 French Breakfast radishes, thinly sliced

¾ cup fresh corn kernels

1 zucchini, thinly sliced

¼ cup tarragon vinegar

3 tablespoons avocado oil

1 teaspoon Dijon mustard

3 tablespoons minced chives

4 eggs, poached

1. Divide the spinach or lettuce among 4 dinner plates. Top each with tomato, peppers, fennel, avocado, radishes, corn, and zucchini.

2. In a small bowl, whisk together the vinegar, oil, and mustard. Drizzle over each salad.

3. Sprinkle each with chives. Top with a poached egg.

PER SERVING Calories: 336 | Fat: 24 g | Protein: 13 g | Sodium: 461 mg | Fiber: 9 g | Carbohydrates: 24 g | Sugar: 6 g

How to Poach an Egg

While slightly daunting at first, poached eggs are so delicious that it is worth mastering the technique. The easiest way is to use special silicon pods that float in water, but eggs can be poached in a simple pot. Heat a few inches of water in a saucepan until it is almost simmering. Add a splash of vinegar. Stir to create a "whirlpool," crack open the egg, and drop it gently in. Cook for 3–4 minutes. Voilà!

Celeriac-Pear Salad with Fig Vinaigrette

Celeriac, also known as celery root, is a crisp counterpoint to the lush, soft pear.

INGREDIENTS | SERVES 6

1 bulb celeriac, cut into matchsticks

2 Bosc pears, peeled, halved and thinly sliced

1 red onion, cut into half-moons

1 tablespoon Dijon mustard

3 tablespoons sherry vinegar

1 tablespoon lemon juice

¼ cup grapeseed oil

2 tablespoons minced fresh fig

¼ teaspoon salt

¼ teaspoon celery seed

¼ teaspoon white pepper

1. In a large bowl, toss together celeriac, pears, and onion.

2. In a small bowl, whisk together the mustard, vinegar, lemon juice, oil, fig, salt, celery seed, and pepper. Drizzle over salad and serve.

PER SERVING Calories: 129 | Fat: 9 g | Protein: 1 g | Sodium: 135 mg | Fiber: 2 g | Carbohydrates: 12 g | Sugar: 7 g

Straight Talk about Celeriac

Celeriac is a bulbous root vegetable. Unlike many root vegetables, it is very low in starch. While it can be eaten cooked or raw, the rough, bumpy skin needs to be removed. It has a light, celery-like flavor.

Cucumber-Carrot Salad

This salad makes a great side dish, but an even better topper for grilled fish or a sandwich.

INGREDIENTS | SERVES 6

2 seedless cucumbers, thinly sliced

2 carrots, cut into matchsticks

1 stalk celery, thinly sliced

1 red onion, shaved

1 bunch scallions, diced

1 tablespoon sesame seeds

3 tablespoons rice vinegar

½ teaspoon sesame oil

1 teaspoon mirin

¼ teaspoon sea salt

In a medium bowl with a lid, add all of the ingredients. Cover and shake. Refrigerate for 1 hour prior to serving.

PER SERVING Calories: 46 | Fat: 1 g | Protein: 1 g | Sodium: 124 mg | Fiber: 2 g | Carbohydrates: 8 g | Sugar: 4 g

Peach and Chèvre Panino

Sweet peaches make this grilled sandwich an unusual delight.

INGREDIENTS | SERVES 1

2 ounces chèvre, at room temperature

¼ teaspoon ground ginger

¼ baguette, sliced in half

1 peach, peeled and sliced

1. In a small bowl, mix the chèvre and ginger together.

2. Spread mixture on ½ of the baguette.

3. Layer the peach slices on top of the cheese. Top with the other half of the baguette.

4. Heat a panini press to medium and press until the cheese is soft and the sandwich is hot.

PER SERVING Calories: 139 | Fat: 1 g | Protein: 5 g | Sodium: 182 mg | Fiber: 3 g | Carbohydrates: 30 g | Sugar: 13 g

Berry-Kiwi Fruit Salad

Berries are packed with antioxidants!

INGREDIENTS | SERVES 8

1 cup raspberries
1 cup blackberries
1 cup blueberries
2 cups peeled, diced kiwi
1 cup water
1 cup sugar
¼ cup fresh mint

Kiwi Facts

Known as "kiwifruit" in much of the world, so as to differentiate it from the flightless kiwi bird, the kiwi is an edible berry. Bright green or yellow inside and studded with black seeds, the kiwi contains over 100 percent of the RDA of vitamin C. It is also rich in a protein-tenderizing enzyme that makes it a popular ingredient in recipes that use tough cuts of meat such as beef ribs.

1. In a large bowl, toss together the berries and kiwi.

2. In a medium saucepan, heat the water, sugar, and mint to a boil. Stir until the sugar is dissolved then boil, uncovered, for about 20 minutes. (It should reduce slightly and look thick.) Strain out any large pieces of mint. Allow to cool.

3. Drizzle the syrup over the fruit and then toss. Serve immediately.

PER SERVING Calories: 113 | Fat: 0 g | Protein: 0 g | Sodium: 1 mg | Fiber: 2 g | Carbohydrates: 29 g | Sugar: 27 g

Meatball-Eggplant Sub

This is an unexpected, lighter twist on the traditional eggplant or meatball sub.
No heavy sauce, no extra cheese, just natural flavor.

INGREDIENTS | SERVES 4

1 pound ground pork
1 shallot, minced
1 clove garlic, minced
⅓ cup fresh bread crumbs
¼ cup shredded Parmesan cheese
1 tablespoon minced fresh basil
1 tablespoon minced fresh Italian parsley
1 tablespoon balsamic vinegar
¼ teaspoon kosher salt
¼ teaspoon freshly ground black pepper
1 egg
2 Italian eggplants, sliced into ¼-inch thick slices
2 tablespoons Dijon mustard
1½ tablespoons nonpareil capers
1 teaspoon mayonnaise
4 Italian sandwich rolls, sliced lengthwise

1. Preheat oven to 350°F.

2. In a medium bowl and with a gentle hand, mix together the pork, shallot, garlic, bread crumbs, Parmesan, basil, parsley, vinegar, salt, pepper, and egg. Form into 1–2-inch balls. Arrange on a broiling pan. Set aside.

3. Arrange the eggplant slices on 2 baking sheets. Place the meatballs and the eggplant in the oven. Bake the meatballs 20 minutes, turning once, or until cooked through. Bake the eggplant 10 minutes or until soft.

4. Meanwhile, whisk together the mustard, capers, and mayonnaise. Spread on 1 side of each roll.

5. When the meatballs are ready, alternate the meatballs and a slice of eggplant on each roll. Serve immediately.

PER SERVING Calories: 539 | Fat: 29 g | Protein: 29 g | Sodium: 639 mg | Fiber: 10 g | Carbohydrates: 41 g | Sugar: 9 g

Capers Caper

Capers are the pickled bud of the caper bush. They come in several sizes but two are the most popular. The smallest is the nonpareil and is used frequently in salads and other dishes. The slightly larger caper is the capote, which is great when more caper flavor is needed. The caperberry, which is the size of a lima bean, is the berry that results when the bud is not picked.

Tuna Cannellini Sandwiches

This protein-packed, mayo-less tuna sandwich is an elegant addition at a picnic.

INGREDIENTS | SERVES 4

10 ounces cooked tuna, chopped

2 tablespoons minced Italian parsley

3 tablespoons capote capers

1 stalk celery, chopped

2 tablespoons avocado oil

2 tablespoons lemon juice

1 shallot, minced

1 teaspoon lemon zest

½ teaspoon smoked paprika

¼ teaspoon salt

¼ teaspoon freshly ground black pepper

14 ounces cooked cannellini beans

2 cloves garlic, minced

1 tablespoon white wine vinegar

2 tablespoons olive oil

1½ tablespoons fresh thyme leaves

8 thick slices of white or whole-wheat Italian bread

1. In a large bowl, stir together the tuna, parsley, capers, celery, avocado oil, lemon juice, shallot, lemon zest, smoked paprika, salt, and pepper until well combined.

2. In a medium bowl, place the beans, garlic, vinegar, olive oil, and thyme. Mash lightly with a fork.

3. Evenly split the bean mixture between 4 slices of bread. Top each with the tuna. Add remaining slice of bread. Serve immediately.

PER SERVING Calories: 330 | Fat: 18 g | Protein: 23 g | Sodium: 669 mg | Fiber: 6 g | Carbohydrates: 20 g | Sugar: 2 g

Chicken-Sage Burgers

An lighter, more adult take on the typical burger.

INGREDIENTS | SERVES 4

1 pound ground chicken breast

1 shallot, minced

½ cup fresh whole-wheat or white bread crumbs

1 tablespoon creamy mustard

1 tablespoon champagne vinegar

2 tablespoons minced sage

1 clove garlic, minced

4 slices fontina cheese

4 whole-wheat or white hamburger buns

1. In a medium bowl, with a gentle hand, mix together the chicken, shallot, bread crumbs, mustard, vinegar, sage, and garlic. Form into 4 equal, flattish patties.

2. Spray a skillet with cooking spray. Cook the burgers, turning once, until fully cooked, about 10–15 minutes.

3. Add a slice of cheese to each, cook 30 seconds or until the cheese is starting to melt. Serve on buns.

PER SERVING Calories: 354 | Fat: 14 g | Protein: 34 g | Sodium: 515 mg | Fiber: 1 g | Carbohydrates: 21 g | Sugar: 2 g

Chicken Cherry Salad Sandwiches

A pop of cherry is in every bite of this unique sandwich.

INGREDIENTS | SERVES 4

1½ pounds poached chicken breast, cubed

½ Vidalia onion, diced

⅔ cup halved fresh sweet cherries

¼ cup mayonnaise

2 tablespoons tarragon vinegar

¼ teaspoon celery seed

¼ teaspoon sea salt

¼ teaspoon white pepper

¼ teaspoon summer savory

4 Boston lettuce leaves

4 whole-wheat or white kaiser rolls

1 avocado, sliced

1. In a medium bowl, combine the chicken, onion, cherries, mayonnaise, vinegar, celery seed, sea salt, pepper, and summer savory until all ingredients are evenly distributed.

2. Place a lettuce leaf on the bottom half of each roll. Evenly distribute the chicken salad among the rolls. Top each with avocado slices. Close the sandwiches and serve.

PER SERVING Calories: 475 | Fat: 24 g | Protein: 40 g | Sodium: 566 mg | Fiber: 5 g | Carbohydrates: 24 g | Sugar: 6 g

Falafel Pita

Though fried, falafel is made with chickpeas, which are high in protein, fiber, and complex carbohydrates, making it a healthier "fast food" alternative.

INGREDIENTS | SERVES 6

2 cups cooked chickpeas

1 tablespoon baking powder

1 onion, sliced

4 cloves garlic

¼ cup chopped Italian parsley

1 teaspoon cumin

1 teaspoon ground coriander

½ teaspoon salt

½ teaspoon freshly ground black pepper

¼ cup flour

Canola oil, for frying

1 cup Classic Hummus (see Chapter 14)

6 whole-wheat or regular pita pockets

1 cucumber, sliced

1 large tomato, sliced

1. Place the chickpeas, baking powder, onion, garlic, parsley, cumin, coriander, salt, and pepper into a food processor. Pulse on high until a paste forms.

2. Scrape the paste into a large bowl. Stir in the flour. Cover and refrigerate for 1 hour.

3. Heat 1 inch of canola oil in a large skillet. Roll the chickpea mixture into 1–2-inch balls and fry until golden on all sides, about 5 minutes. Drain on paper towel–lined plates.

4. Spread some hummus into each of the pita pockets. Add cucumber and tomato slices to the pockets. Stuff with falafel.

PER SERVING Calories: 519 | Fat: 9 g | Protein: 23 g | Sodium: 940 mg | Fiber: 16 g | Carbohydrates: 90 g | Sugar: 10 g

Chickpea Facts

Chickpeas, also known as garbanzo beans or chana, are edible legumes. They are very high in protein and fiber, making them a particularly excellent choice for vegan or vegetarian meals.

Hummus and Tofu Sandwiches

This easy, vegan sandwich is the perfect protein-packed pick-me-up for a long day at school or work.

INGREDIENTS | SERVES 2

4 slices whole-grain bread
½ cup Classic Hummus (see Chapter 14)
1 seedless cucumber, sliced
1 small red onion, sliced
2 tablespoons minced oregano
4 ounces firm tofu, cut into slices
1 tablespoon dill mustard

1. Divide the hummus between 2 slices of bread. Top with cucumber, onion, oregano, and tofu.

2. Spread the remaining 2 slices of bread with mustard. Top the sandwiches. Serve.

PER SERVING Calories: 272 | Fat: 8 g | Protein: 14 g | Sodium: 445 mg | Fiber: 7 g | Carbohydrates: 39 g | Sugar: 6 g

Healthful Hummus

Providing that one does not overdo it with the olive oil, hummus is a healthy treat. Due to its individual ingredients, it is high in iron and vitamin C, and is also a good source of protein and fiber. Hummus serves as a complete protein when served with bread.

Turkey-Pear Melt

A cross between a grilled cheese and a patty melt, this is a sandwich the whole family can enjoy.

INGREDIENTS | SERVES 4

8 thick slices white or whole-grain bread
1 Bosc pear, thinly sliced vertically
4 thick-cut slices fresh turkey
4 slices lean capicola
2 tablespoons grainy mustard
4 slices smoked Gouda cheese
3 tablespoons unsalted butter

1. On 4 slices of bread, layer the pear, then turkey, then the capicola. Spread the capicola with mustard. Top with a slice of Gouda.

2. Melt the butter in a large skillet (or work in 2 batches with 1½ tablespoons of butter at a time). Add the sandwiches bread side down until the cheese starts to melt. Top with remaining slices of bread and flip. Press down with the spatula to compress the sandwich. Flip again if needed for both sides to be deep, golden brown.

PER SERVING Calories: 215 | Fat: 11 g | Protein: 14 g | Sodium: 217 mg | Fiber: 2 g | Carbohydrates: 15 g | Sugar: 4 g

Dilled Shrimp on Rye Crisp Bread

This recipe is inspired by the open-faced "sandwiches" that are so popular in Sweden.

INGREDIENTS | SERVES 4

8 rye crisp flatbreads

4 hard-boiled eggs, sliced

3 tablespoons mayonnaise

1 tablespoon Dijon mustard

3 tablespoons minced fresh dill

2 tablespoons lemon juice

8 ounces small salad shrimp

Keep Your Herbs Fresh Longer

It is often difficult to make it through an entire bunch of herbs in one sitting. Keep them fresh by storing them in a glass of water in the refrigerator. Clip off the ends as needed.

1. Create a single layer of egg on each of the rye crisp breads. Set aside.

2. In a small bowl, whisk together the mayonnaise, mustard, dill, and lemon juice. Stir in the shrimp.

3. Top each crisp bread with an equal portion of the shrimp mixture. Serve open-faced, with a dill or caper garnish if desired.

PER SERVING Calories: 388 | Fat: 12 g | Protein: 22 g | Sodium: 384 mg | Fiber: 9 g | Carbohydrates: 47 g | Sugar: 2 g

CHAPTER 10

Dressings and Sauces

Fresh Blackberry Vinaigrette

Try this over a summer salad of mixed greens and tomatoes.

INGREDIENTS | SERVES 4

¼ cup fresh blackberries
2 ounces balsamic vinegar
2 ounces olive oil
1 teaspoon Dijon mustard
¼ teaspoon sea salt
¼ teaspoon freshly ground black pepper

Muddle the blackberries in the bottom of a resealable jar or dressing container. Add the remaining ingredients. Cover and shake to thoroughly mix.

PER SERVING Calories: 140 | Fat: 14 g | Protein: 0 g | Sodium: 166 mg | Fiber: 1 g | Carbohydrates: 3 g | Sugar: 3 g

Fresh Dill Vinaigrette

Pepper sherry, a popular condiment in the Caribbean, adds a spicy kick to this otherwise classic dressing.

INGREDIENTS | SERVES 4

¼ cup minced fresh dill
¼ cup white wine vinegar
¼ cup olive oil
2 tablespoons lemon juice
2 tablespoons pepper sherry
1 tablespoon Dijon mustard

Add all ingredients to a resealable jar or dressing container. Cover and shake to thoroughly mix.

PER SERVING Calories: 136 | Fat: 14 g | Protein: 0 g | Sodium: 47 mg | Fiber: 0 g | Carbohydrates: 1 g | Sugar: 1 g

Jalapeño-Lime Vinaigrette

This light, spicy vinaigrette is especially good over crunchy greens like cabbage.

INGREDIENTS | SERVES 6

¼ cup avocado oil

¼ cup lime juice

¼ cup white vinegar

1 tablespoon lime zest

2 jalapeño peppers, halved

¼ teaspoon salt

¼ teaspoon freshly ground black pepper

1. Add all ingredients to a resealable jar or dressing container. Cover and shake to thoroughly mix.

2. Strain the mixture prior to serving.

PER SERVING Calories: 83 | Fat: 9 g | Protein: 0 g | Sodium: 98 mg | Fiber: 0 g | Carbohydrates: 0 g | Sugar: 0 g

Too Many Jalapeños?

Jalapeños are wonderful fresh but sometimes one ends up with more than they can use. Luckily, jalapeños can be pickled and canned for use on tacos or nachos. Peppers can also be frozen. Either chop or freeze whole in a freezer-safe container.

Apricot-Basil Salad Dressing

This light dressing is perfect over fruit or vegetable salads. Keep any leftovers refrigerated.

INGREDIENTS | SERVES 4

¼ cup fresh apricot purée

¼ cup sherry vinegar

3 tablespoons olive oil

2 tablespoons minced fresh basil

½ teaspoon salt

½ teaspoon white pepper

½ teaspoon Dijon mustard

In a small bowl, whisk together all ingredients. Cover and refrigerate 20 minutes prior to serving.

PER SERVING Calories: 98 | Fat: 10 g | Protein: 0 g | Sodium: 205 mg | Fiber: 0 g | Carbohydrates: 1 g | Sugar: 1 g

Dressing Tips

Vinaigrettes are made by whisking vinegar and oil together. To keep them lighter, use more vinegar than oil. Adding a bit of mustard or even egg yolk to the mix will keep the ingredients from separating. Most dressings with fresh herbs will keep in the refrigerator up to 3 days.

Fresh Tomato Marinara

Use this in any recipe that calls for a basic tomato sauce or as is, over fresh pasta. For best results use Roma or San Marzano tomatoes.

INGREDIENTS | SERVES 6

2 pounds fresh tomatoes
2 tablespoons olive oil
4 cloves garlic, minced
1 shallot, minced
1 tablespoon minced fresh basil
½ tablespoon minced fresh oregano
¼ cup chopped fresh Italian parsley

Tomato Typecasting

There are several general varieties of tomatoes. It is easy to tell how some varieties got their names; cherry tomatoes are small and round, grape tomatoes are small and oblong, and pear tomatoes are dense and pear-shaped. Others are not so obvious. Campari tomatoes look like big cherry tomatoes and are similarly sweet, while beefsteaks are very large tomatoes suitable for slicing.

1. Blanch and peel the tomatoes. Dice the tomatoes. Set aside.

2. In a Dutch oven heat the oil. Add the garlic and shallot and sauté until soft and fragrant, about 5–8 minutes.

3. Add the tomato, basil, and oregano. Simmer until the tomato is cooked through, about 10–20 minutes.

4. Remove from heat and stir in the parsley.

PER SERVING Calories: 83 | Fat: 5 g | Protein: 2 g | Sodium: 10 mg | Fiber: 2 g | Carbohydrates: 10 g | Sugar: 4 g

Roasted Eggplant Tomato Sauce

Eggplants become meltingly smooth in this easy sauce.

INGREDIENTS | SERVES 8

2 (1-pound) eggplants, cubed
2 pounds fresh tomatoes, sliced thickly
3 cloves garlic, minced
3 tablespoons olive oil
½ teaspoon sea salt
½ teaspoon freshly ground black pepper
1 tablespoon minced fresh basil
1 tablespoon minced oregano

Eggplant Edification

Eggplants can be slightly bitter or watery. To combat this, salt the eggplant slices and allow it to drain for 20 minutes, then rinse.

1. Preheat oven to 350°F.

2. Arrange the eggplant and tomato on a 9" × 13" baking dish. Sprinkle with garlic. Drizzle with oil. Toss to coat. Sprinkle with salt and pepper.

3. Bake for 30 minutes or until the tomatoes are soft and juicy and the eggplant is tender. Stir in the herbs. Serve over hot pasta.

PER SERVING Calories: 79 | Fat: 4 g | Protein: 2 g | Sodium: 155 mg | Fiber: 5 g | Carbohydrates: 11 g | Sugar: 6 g

Meyer Lemon Curd

Meyer lemons are just a bit sweeter than regular lemons, making this curd a decadent treat.

INGREDIENTS | YIELDS 8 OUNCES

6 tablespoons unsalted butter
3 eggs
½ cup sugar
⅔ cup Meyer lemon juice
1½ tablespoons Meyer lemon zest

Salted or Unsalted Butter

When cooking it is important to always use unsalted butter unless otherwise instructed. One can always add salt but if your salted butter makes the dish too salty, you cannot reduce the salt.

1. Over low heat, melt the butter in a small, heavy saucepan. Add the remaining ingredients and whisk continuously for about 8–10 minutes or until it forms a custard.

2. Allow to cool. Pour into a jar and refrigerate. The curd will thicken considerably as it cools.

PER SERVING Calories: 129 | Fat: 9 g | Protein: 0 g | Sodium: 6 mg | Fiber: 0 g | Carbohydrates: 14 g | Sugar: 13 g

Homemade Peach Barbecue Sauce

Use this fresh tasting, preservative-free barbecue sauce as a glaze or dip for pork or poultry.

INGREDIENTS | YIELDS ABOUT 2 CUPS

1 shallot, chopped

1¾ pounds peeled, halved peaches

2 tablespoons water

¼ cup Worcestershire sauce

½ cup apple cider vinegar

2 tablespoons mustard powder

½ teaspoon cayenne pepper

1 tablespoon unsalted butter

½ teaspoon hickory liquid smoke (optional)

1. Pulse all ingredients in a blender until smooth.

2. Pour into a small saucepan and simmer on the lowest setting for 15 minutes or until heated through and slightly thickened.

3. Allow to cool completely. Pour into an airtight container and refrigerate until ready to use.

PER SERVING Calories: 73 | Fat: 2 g | Protein: 1 g | Sodium: 131 mg | Fiber: 2 g | Carbohydrates: 14 g | Sugar: 9 g

Chile-Garlic-Peanut Sauce

This is lovely on steamed or roasted eggplant or over thin, Vietnamese noodles.

INGREDIENTS | SERVES 4

¾ cup water

⅓ cup lightly salted, roasted peanuts

1½ tablespoons nuoc mam

2 tablespoons tuong ot toi (Vietnamese chili garlic sauce)

2 cloves garlic

1 tablespoon canola oil

In a high-powered blender, pulse all ingredients until very smooth.

PER SERVING Calories: 110 | Fat: 9 g | Protein: 3 g | Sodium: 116 mg | Fiber: 2 g | Carbohydrates: 4 g | Sugar: 1 g

Exotic Ingredient Demystified: Nước Mắm

Nước mắm is Vietnamese fish sauce. It is made by fermenting anchovies, salt, and water. It has a pungent, tangy flavor.

Orange Cranberry Sauce

Cranberries are packed with antioxidants and are advertised as being a superfruit.

INGREDIENTS | SERVES 8

2 cups fresh cranberries
½ cup sugar
¾ cup water
¼ cup fresh-squeezed orange juice
2 tablespoons orange zest

Place the cranberries, sugar, water, juice, and zest in a medium saucepan over medium-high heat, and cook for 20 minutes, stirring occasionally, to reduce and thicken. Remove from heat. Serve hot or cold.

PER SERVING Calories: 64 | Fat: 0 g | Protein: 0 g | Sodium: 1 mg | Fiber: 1 g | Carbohydrates: 17 g | Sugar: 14 g

Ways to Use Up Leftover Cranberry Sauce

Cranberry sauce has a tendency to stick around the fridge long after the meal is over. Try some on your yogurt or on a sandwich instead of jelly. Swirl it in muffin or cake batter. Use it as a glaze on meat.

Tzatziki

Try this not only as a dip or sauce but as a topping for lamb burgers, souvlaki, and gyros.

INGREDIENTS | SERVES 4

1 cup low-fat plain Greek yogurt
½ cup finely diced, seedless cucumber
1½ tablespoons finely minced fresh dill
1½ tablespoons lemon juice
¼ teaspoon sea salt
¼ teaspoon freshly ground black pepper

Place all ingredients in a small bowl. Stir until all ingredients are evenly distributed. Refrigerate at least 1 hour prior to serving.

PER SERVING Calories: 35 | Fat: 0 g | Protein: 6 g | Sodium: 171 mg | Fiber: 0 g | Carbohydrates: 3 g | Sugar: 3 g

Mango Sauce

Use this sauce as a salad dressing, topping for ice cream, or as a marinade and sauce for fish.

INGREDIENTS | YIELDS ABOUT 2 CUPS

3 mangoes, peeled and pitted
¼ cup lime juice
½ teaspoon cayenne
2 tablespoons ginger juice

1. Place all ingredients in a blender. Pulse until smooth.

2. Refrigerate until ready to use.

PER SERVING Calories: 52 | Fat: 0 g | Protein: 0 g | Sodium: 2 mg | Fiber: 1 g | Carbohydrates: 14 g | Sugar: 12 g

Mango Mania
Mango is the most cultivated fruit in the tropics. It is used both raw (green) and ripe, cooked and raw. There are over 1,000 varieties of mangoes around the world. Mango skin has a chemical which may cause mild skin irritation when touched or consumed.

Chimichurri

This Argentinian sauce is traditionally served over steak.

INGREDIENTS | YIELDS ABOUT 1 CUP

1½ cups fresh Italian parsley
3 tablespoons chopped fresh oregano
¾ cup olive oil
½ cup red wine vinegar
3 cloves garlic
1 dried red pepper
¼ teaspoon cumin
¼ teaspoon salt

Place all ingredients in a food processor. Pulse until mostly liquid. Pour into a bowl. Serve at room temperature.

PER SERVING Calories: 187 | Fat: 20 g | Protein: 0 g | Sodium: 82 mg | Fiber: 0 g | Carbohydrates: 1 g | Sugar: 0 g

Chunky Salsa Verde

This chunky sauce is great on tacos or over fish. If you would like a smoother sauce, combine the ingredients in a food processor rather than by hand.

INGREDIENTS | YIELDS ABOUT 3 CUPS

1¾ pounds tomatillos

¾ cup finely chopped white onion

½ cup finely chopped cilantro or flat leaf parsley

1 tablespoon minced oregano

3 tablespoons lime juice

2 serrano peppers, chopped

2 cloves garlic, minced

½ teaspoon salt

½ teaspoon freshly ground black pepper

1. Bring a pot of water to boil. Add the tomatillos and cook for 5 minutes. Remove from the water and allow to cool slightly.

2. Dice the tomatillos. Place in a large bowl. Add the remaining ingredients and stir to evenly distribute. Refrigerate leftovers.

PER SERVING Calories: 28 | Fat: 1 g | Protein: 1 g | Sodium: 100 mg | Fiber: 2 g | Carbohydrates: 6 g | Sugar: 3 g

Tomatillo Tips

Tomatillos look like small green, yellow, or purple tomatoes in a papery husk. Look for unblemished fruits that are firm to the touch. The husk needs to be removed prior to eating.

Harissa

This Tunisian paste-like sauce is extremely flexible. Try it rubbed into meat and fish or as a condiment on eggs, potatoes, anything you can think of!

INGREDIENTS | YIELDS ABOUT 1 CUP

3 ounces dried guajillo chiles, seeded

2 ounces dried New Mexico chiles, seeded

1 teaspoon ground coriander

1 teaspoon ground caraway seeds

¼ teaspoon cumin

¼ tablespoon olive oil

¼ cup lemon juice

6 cloves garlic

½ teaspoon salt

1. Place all of the dried chiles in a heat-safe bowl. Pour boiling water over the chiles. Allow them to soak for 20 minutes.

2. Drain the chiles and add them to a food processor. Add the remaining ingredients and pulse until very smooth.

3. Scrape into an airtight jar or bowl. Refrigerate.

PER SERVING Calories: 14 | Fat: 1 g | Protein: 0.5 g | Sodium: 149 mg | Fiber: 0.4 g | Carbohydrates: 2 g | Sugar: 1 g

Grinding Spices

Buying whole spices is both economical and flavorful. Whole spices stay fresh longer. Before grinding, lightly toast the spices in a dry, nonstick pan to bring out their flavor even more. Turn them into powder in a clean coffee grinder, a spice mill, or by using a mortar and pestle or molcajete.

Rémoulade

Similar to tartar sauce, rémoulade is most popularly served with seafood.

INGREDIENTS | YIELDS 1½ CUPS

¾ cup mayonnaise

½ cup diced scallions

¼ cup Dijon mustard

3 tablespoons nonpareil capers

2 tablespoons minced fresh dill

2 tablespoons minced Italian parsley

2 tablespoons lemon juice

1 tablespoon white wine vinegar

½ teaspoon hot sauce

½ teaspoon white pepper

¼ teaspoon salt

¼ teaspoon celery seed

Stir all ingredients together in a bowl. Cover and refrigerate at least 1 hour prior to serving.

PER SERVING Calories: 209 | Fat: 22 g | Protein: 1 g | Sodium: 414 mg | Fiber: 1 g | Carbohydrates: 2 g | Sugar: 1 g

Blueberry Sauce

Try this sauce over ice cream, frozen yogurt, or panna cotta.

INGREDIENTS | YIELDS ABOUT 1½ CUPS

2 pints blueberries

¼ cup lemon juice

3 tablespoons lemon zest

½ cup sugar

1. Place all ingredients in a small saucepan. Cook, stirring occasionally, until the blueberries release their juices and the mixture starts to boil.

2. Reduce heat and simmer until slightly thickened, about 5 minutes.

3. Refrigerate. Serve cold.

PER SERVING Calories: 60 | Fat: 0 g | Protein: 1 g | Sodium: 4 mg | Fiber: 2 g | Carbohydrates: 17 g | Sugar: 13 g

Piri-Piri Sauce

Piri-Piri peppers are found in well-stocked supermarkets and spice shops.
Dried cayenne or piquins are acceptable substitutes.

INGREDIENTS | YIELDS ABOUT 1½ CUPS

¼ cup crushed dried piri-piri peppers
3 cloves garlic, minced
¼ cup white vinegar
2 tablespoons dark brown sugar
2 tablespoons lime juice
1 tablespoon olive oil
1-inch knob ginger, grated
½ teaspoon salt

1. Place the ingredients in a blender and purée until very smooth.

2. Use immediately or pour into a lidded container and refrigerate up to 2 weeks.

PER SERVING Calories: 46 | Fat: 2 g | Protein: 0 g | Sodium: 200 mg | Fiber: 0 g | Carbohydrates: 6 g | Sugar: 5 g

Strawberry-Star Anise Compote

The unexpected addition of star anise makes this strawberry compote stand out.

INGREDIENTS | YIELDS 1 CUP

1½ cups diced strawberries
¼ cup water
¼ cup sugar
2 tablespoons lemon juice
2 whole star anise
1 teaspoon arrowroot powder

1. Place the strawberries, water, sugar, lemon juice, and star anise in a small, heavy-bottomed saucepan. Cook until the mixture starts to thicken, stirring occasionally, about 10 minutes.

2. Remove and discard the star anise. Stir in the arrowroot powder.

3. Serve hot or cold. Allow to cool completely before refrigerating any leftovers.

PER SERVING Calories: 70 | Fat: 0 g | Protein: 0 g | Sodium: 2 mg | Fiber: 1 g | Carbohydrates: 18 g | Sugar: 15 g

Carolina Gold Sauce

This mustard-based sauce is how South Carolina does barbecue.

INGREDIENTS | YIELDS ABOUT 1½ CUPS

1½ cups yellow mustard
¾ cup apple cider vinegar
¼ cup dark brown sugar
1 teaspoon freshly ground black pepper
1 teaspoon chili powder
1 teaspoon Worcestershire sauce
1 teaspoon red hot sauce
½ teaspoon garlic powder

1. Place all of the ingredients in a small pan. Heat over the lowest heat setting possible, whisking continuously, until the sugar is fully dissolved.

2. Remove from heat. Scrape into a lidded bowl or jar and allow to cool. Use immediately or refrigerate up to 2 weeks.

PER SERVING Calories: 85 | Fat: 3 g | Protein: 3 g | Sodium: 743 mg | Fiber: 2 g | Carbohydrates: 13 g | Sugar: 10 g

Why Make Your Own Sauces and Condiments?

Commercially made sauces are full of preservatives and often high fructose corn syrup as well. Making your own sauces and condiments at home means you know exactly what goes into the finished product. Homemade sauces taste fresher and better than commercially made as well.

CHAPTER 11

Soups, Stews, and Chili

Escarole, Spring Onion, and Rice Soup

Spring onions look like scallions but have a larger bulb at the bottom and a leek-like flavor. Chop off the roots and use the whole rest of the plant.

INGREDIENTS | SERVES 6

1 tablespoon olive oil

1 tablespoon unsalted butter

2 cloves garlic, minced

1 bunch curly escarole, chopped

1 bunch spring onions, sliced

¾ cup uncooked jasmine rice

6 cups chicken stock

¼ cup lemon juice

1 bay leaf

½ teaspoon sea salt

½ teaspoon freshly ground black pepper

1. In a Dutch oven, heat the olive oil and butter over medium heat. Add the garlic, escarole, and spring onions. Sauté until the onions start to soften and the escarole starts to wilt, about 2–3 minutes.

2. Add the remaining ingredients. Cover and cook until the rice is fully cooked, about 15 minutes.

3. Remove the bay leaf and serve.

PER SERVING Calories: 215 | Fat: 7 g | Protein: 8 g | Sodium: 542 mg | Fiber: 1 g | Carbohydrates: 29 g | Sugar: 4 g

Confusing Escarole

Escarole, also known as broad-leaved endive, is a member of the same family as Belgian endive and radicchio but features loose, curly leaves instead of a tightly wrapped head. It is less bitter than other members of the chicory family despite also being rich in vitamins and folate.

Salmon Chowder

This is a wonderful way to use up any leftover salmon.

INGREDIENTS | SERVES 8

1 onion, chopped

1 large shallot, minced

2 cloves garlic, minced

2 cups peeled, diced red-skin potatoes

2 stalks celery, diced

2 carrots, diced

2 tablespoons olive oil

6 cups fish stock

1 pound diced tomatoes

¼ teaspoon ground cayenne

1 teaspoon Worcestershire sauce

1 teaspoon sherry vinegar

1 bay leaf

3 tablespoons fresh thyme leaves

3 tablespoons chopped Italian parsley

3 green onions, diced

1 pound cooked salmon, cut into chunks

1. In a large pot, sauté the onion, shallot, garlic, potatoes, celery, and carrots in the olive oil until the onions are softened and translucent, about 8–12 minutes.

2. Add the stock, tomatoes, cayenne, Worcestershire sauce, and vinegar. Bring to a boil then reduce the heat. Simmer until the potatoes are nearly fork-tender, about 10–20 minutes.

3. Stir in the herbs, green onion, and salmon. Cook until the salmon is heated through, about 5–15 minutes depending on thickness. Discard the bay leaf prior to serving.

PER SERVING Calories: 195 | Fat: 6 g | Protein: 20 g | Sodium: 340 mg | Fiber: 3 g | Carbohydrates: 14 g | Sugar: 4 g

Sock It to Me, Salmon!

Salmon is an oily fish that has high levels of omega-3 fatty acids. Wild-caught salmon has a higher percentage of these brain-nourishing acids than farm-raised. It is also an excellent source of protein and is available in several forms, such as fresh, canned, cold smoked lox, and gravlax.

Summer Borscht

There are two versions of borscht. Both use beets but the summer version is served chilled.

INGREDIENTS | SERVES 4

8 small beets, peeled
1 small onion, chopped
1 teaspoon salt
½ teaspoon freshly ground pepper
4 cups water
2 teaspoons sugar
¼ cup lemon juice
1 egg
1 cup sour cream, for garnish
4 red radishes, diced, for garnish
1 cucumber, diced, for garnish

1. In a large pot, bring the beets, onion, salt, pepper, and water to a boil. Boil for 1 hour.

2. Add the sugar and lemon juice and simmer for ½ hour.

3. Remove the beets and grate half. Set aside. Reserve the other half for another recipe. Pour the liquid into a large measuring cup or bowl.

4. In a separate large bowl, beat the egg until very fluffy. Add about ¼ cup of the liquid to the egg and whisk. Continue adding the soup in a slow stream to the egg, whisking continuously.

5. Stir in the grated beets.

6. Chill at least 4 hours or overnight. Ladle into bowls and top with a dollop of sour cream, diced radish, and diced cucumber.

PER SERVING Calories: 230 | Fat: 13 g | Protein: 6 g | Sodium: 785 mg | Fiber: 6 g | Carbohydrates: 25 g | Sugar: 18 g

Chesapeake Oyster Stew

Use fresh, Chesapeake Bay oysters for the authentic touch.

INGREDIENTS | SERVES 4

2 tablespoons unsalted butter

1 large onion, chopped

1 jalapeño pepper, chopped

1 large russet potato, chopped

2 stalks celery, chopped

2 cloves garlic, minced

¼ cup diced country ham

4 cups milk

1 pound shucked fresh oysters in their liquor

1. Heat the butter in a Dutch oven over medium heat. Sauté the onion, pepper, potato, celery, garlic, and ham until the vegetables are softened, about 8–15 minutes.

2. Add the remaining ingredients and simmer until the oysters are cooked through, about 5–10 minutes.

PER SERVING Calories: 344 | Fat: 17 g | Protein: 19 g | Sodium: 474 mg | Fiber: 2 g | Carbohydrates: 29 g | Sugar: 15 g

Seafood Watch List

The Monterey Bay Aquarium has compiled a seafood watch list that includes a ranking system for how safe and sustainable many popular seafood choices are, along with alternatives. Topping the list are farmed oysters, farmed salmon, Pacific halibut, sablefish, and Arctic char. It is available for download and as an app at *www.monterey bayaquarium.org/cr/seafoodwatch.aspx*.

Summer Vegetable Stew

Make this light stew in July or August when all of these vegetables will be at their peak.

INGREDIENTS | SERVES 6

1½ tablespoons canola oil

1 medium yellow squash, diced

1 carrot, diced

1 stalk celery, diced

1 Vidalia onion, diced

5 cloves of garlic, minced

4 cubanelle peppers, diced

2 ears' worth of corn kernels

2 cups diced okra

6½ cups chicken stock

3 medium tomatoes, diced

2 tablespoons minced fresh basil

2 tablespoons minced fresh Italian parsley

¼ teaspoon salt

¼ teaspoon freshly ground black pepper

1. Heat the oil in a large, heavy-bottomed pan. Add the squash, carrot, celery, onion, garlic, and cubanelle peppers. Cook, stirring occasionally, until the onion is soft and translucent but not browned, about 8–12 minutes.

2. Add the remaining ingredients and simmer until the vegetables are tender, about 20 minutes.

PER SERVING Calories: 219 | Fat: 7 g | Protein: 10 g | Sodium: 495 mg | Fiber: 5 g | Carbohydrates: 31 g | Sugar: 11 g

Split Pea Soup

Split pea soup might be a classic but that does not mean it has to be boring!
This version has extra vegetables for texture and flavor.

INGREDIENTS | SERVES 8

2 cups split peas

5 cups water or ham stock

2 carrots, diced

3 cloves garlic, minced

1 onion, diced

1 shallot, minced

1 parsnip, peeled and diced

1 tablespoon ground mustard

1 tablespoon tarragon vinegar

½ tablespoon minced sage

¼ teaspoon sea salt

¼ teaspoon freshly ground black pepper

Place all ingredients in a 4-quart slow cooker. Stir. Cook on low for 10 hours. Stir prior to serving.

PER SERVING Calories: 61 | Fat: 0 g | Protein: 3 g | Sodium: 113 mg | Fiber: 3 g | Carbohydrates: 12 g | Sugar: 4 g

Picking a Slow Cooker

Look for a slow cooker with a removable inside crock for easy cleanup. Oval slow cookers can accommodate longer cuts of meat than round models. Four-quart slow cookers are perfect for families of 2–4 while 6–8-quart slow cookers can feed a crowd.

Caramelized Onion Soup

This lighter version of French onion soup is just as flavorful and easy to make.

INGREDIENTS | SERVES 6

2 tablespoons olive oil

2 tablespoons unsalted butter

4 pounds onions, sliced

2 tablespoons balsamic vinegar

2 quarts beef stock or water

2 bay leaves

4 sprigs thyme

Crispy Baked Croutons

Preheat oven to 350°F. Place day-old bread cubes in a lidded container or resealable bag. Drizzle with 2 tablespoons olive oil. Sprinkle with 1 teaspoon each garlic powder, onion powder, dried parsley, dried basil, and dried oregano. Seal and shake to coat. Bake in a single layer 10 minutes or until crispy and golden.

1. Heat the olive oil and butter in large skillet or saucepan. Add the onions. (It is okay if they are mounded high in the pan, they will cook down quickly.) Cover and cook the onions until just beginning to soften, stirring occasionally so they cook evenly, about 5–10 minutes.

2. Stir in the balsamic vinegar. Cook until the onions are caramelized, stirring occasionally, about 40 minutes.

3. Deglaze the pan with ¼ cup of stock. Add the remaining stock, bay leaves, and thyme.

4. Bring to a boil then reduce the heat and simmer for 30 minutes. Remove bay leaves and thyme before serving.

PER SERVING Calories: 194 | Fat: 9 g | Protein: 3 g | Sodium: 13 mg | Fiber: 5 g | Carbohydrates: 28 g | Sugar: 13 g

Hot and Spicy Chicken Tomato Soup

Try serving this zesty soup with sliced avocado and a garnish of diced green onion.

INGREDIENTS | SERVES 8

1½ tablespoons canola oil

1 onion, chopped

2 cubanelle peppers, chopped

2 cloves garlic, minced

2 jalapeño peppers, minced

24 ounces crushed tomatoes

14 ounces diced fire-roasted tomatoes

3 cups chicken stock

2 cups shredded cooked chicken

1 cup fresh corn kernels

1 teaspoon hot Mexican chili powder

1 teaspoon hot paprika

¼ teaspoon salt

½ teaspoon freshly ground black pepper

1. Heat the oil in a large stock pot. Sauté the onion, cubanelle peppers, garlic, and jalapeños until the onions are soft, about 5–10 minutes.

2. Add the remaining ingredients and bring to a rolling boil. Reduce heat and cook, stirring occasionally, until the chicken is heated through, about 5–20 minutes depending on the size of the chicken pieces.

PER SERVING Calories: 148 | Fat: 6 g | Protein: 12 g | Sodium: 116 mg | Fiber: 3 g | Carbohydrates: 13 g | Sugar: 6 g

Stock Versus Water

Using stock in recipes instead of water makes for a more flavorful finished product. Chicken stock makes poultry dishes taste richer and is mild enough to use with other meats or vegetables. Water can dilute the taste of soups and stews.

Mushroom Barley Soup

It takes a bit of time but this hearty, New York deli–inspired soup is sure to be a new favorite.

INGREDIENTS | SERVES 6–8

½ pound pearl barley

10 cups chicken or beef stock

2 tablespoons olive oil

2 onions, chopped

3 stalks celery, chopped

3 carrots, diced

2 parsnips, peeled and diced

4 cloves garlic, minced

1 pound fresh porcini mushrooms, sliced

½ pound sliced fresh shiitake mushrooms

3 ounces dried porcini mushrooms

½ teaspoon salt

½ teaspoon freshly ground black pepper

1. In a large pot, bring the barley and stock to a boil. Reduce the heat and simmer 1 hour.

2. Heat the oil in a skillet and sauté the onions until just starting to soften. Add the celery, carrots, parsnips, garlic, fresh porcini and shiitake mushrooms. Sauté until the celery and carrots are tender, about 8–12 minutes.

3. Meanwhile, place the dried mushrooms in a heat-proof container. Pour 1 cup of boiling water over the mushrooms and soak until softened, about 10 minutes. Drain and discard the water.

4. Add the onion mixture, salt, pepper, and the rehydrated mushrooms to barley and stock.

5. Simmer 1 hour, stirring occasionally.

PER SERVING Calories: 186 | Fat: 4 g | Protein: 7 g | Sodium: 188 mg | Fiber: 7 g | Carbohydrates: 33 g | Sugar: 6 g

Vegetable Miso Soup

Making your own dashi with kombu and bonito flakes is the secret to authentic miso soup.

INGREDIENTS | SERVES 4

5 cups water, divided use

1 (2-inch) square kombu

½ ounce bonito flakes

¼ cup red miso

6 ounces extra-firm tofu, cubed

¾ cup snow peas

2 baby bok choy, chopped

½ cup fresh baby corn

4 ounces enoki mushrooms

1 bunch scallions, chopped

Switch It Up!

Instead of tofu, try baby shrimp or sea scallops. Instead of bok choy, try some chopped chives. Swap out the enoki mushrooms for fresh shiitake.

1. Add 4½ cups water and the kombu to a 4-quart pot. Bring to an almost boil. Remove the kombu and add the bonito flakes. Return it to a high simmer for 5 minutes then skim out the bonito flakes.

2. Dissolve the miso in ½ cup of water. Set aside.

3. Add the tofu, snow peas, bok choy, baby corn, and enoki mushrooms to the kombu water. Simmer until the vegetables are just softened, about 5 minutes.

4. Add the dissolved miso to the pot. Simmer for 1 minute. Garnish with scallions.

PER SERVING Calories: 152 | Fat: 3 g | Protein: 14 g | Sodium: 934 mg | Fiber: 6 g | Carbohydrates: 22 g | Sugar: 9 g

Bison Chili with Beans

Bison is a naturally lean meat so you can eat this chili without worry!

INGREDIENTS | SERVES 8

1½ tablespoons canola oil
1½ pounds ground bison
1 onion, chopped
3 cloves garlic, minced
1 habanero chile, minced
2 poblano peppers, diced
2 pounds tomatoes, diced
1 pound cooked kidney beans
1 teaspoon chipotle pepper flakes
1 teaspoon ground cayenne
½ teaspoon hot paprika
½ teaspoon cumin
½ teaspoon cocoa

1. Heat the oil in a large pot over medium heat. Add the bison, onion, garlic, habanero, and poblano peppers. Cook, stirring occasionally, until the onions are softened and bison is nearly fully cooked, about 10–20 minutes.

2. Add the tomatoes and cook until they release their juices, about 5 minutes.

3. Add all of the remaining ingredients. Stir and continue to cook until all ingredients are piping hot, about 10–30 minutes.

PER SERVING Calories: 239 | Fat: 3 g | Protein: 15 g | Sodium: 20 mg | Fiber: 16 g | Carbohydrates: 40 g | Sugar: 5 g

The Great Chili Debate

There is a lot of argument over what a true chili should contain. Texas-style chili traditionally is meat only, but in the rest of the country, beans are common. Some chili purists do not agree that tomatoes have a place in chili at all. All that is agreed upon is that chili needs chiles!

Acorn Squash Chili

Slow cooking results in the perfect toothsome bite to the squash.

INGREDIENTS | SERVES 8

3 cups peeled, cubed acorn squash

2 pounds diced fresh tomatoes

1 pound cooked pinto beans

2 poblano chiles, diced

1 Scotch bonnet chile, minced

4 cloves garlic, minced

1 tablespoon Worcestershire sauce

1 teaspoon yellow hot sauce

1 teaspoon ground jalapeño

½ teaspoon cumin

½ teaspoon smoked paprika

½ teaspoon ground cayenne

Place all ingredients in a 4-quart slow cooker. Stir. Cook on low for 6–8 hours. Stir prior to serving.

PER SERVING Calories: 98 | Fat: 1 g | Protein: 4 g | Sodium: 210 mg | Fiber: 5 g | Carbohydrates: 20 g | Sugar: 4 g

Toast the Seeds!

Acorn squash seeds are perfectly edible. Simply rinse them off, toss them with salt and your favorite spices, and roast them for 20 minutes, stirring occasionally, in a pre-heated 325°F oven. Store leftovers in an airtight container.

Maryland Crab Soup

Possibly the quintessential soup of the Mid-Atlantic, Maryland Crab soup boasts a spicy tomato broth and lots of crab.

INGREDIENTS | SERVES 8

6 cups crab stock or water

1 onion, chopped

1 shallot, minced

1 jalapeño chile, diced

3 stalks celery, diced

2 carrots, diced

1¾ cups diced green beans

1½ cups fresh corn kernels

1½ cups fresh peas

1½ cups fresh lima beans

2 large russet potatoes, diced

3 tablespoons Chesapeake Bay Seasoning

2 tablespoons Worcestershire sauce

28 ounces canned whole tomatoes

1 pound blue crab jumbo lump or claw meat

1. In a large stockpot, stir together the stock, all of the vegetables, seasoning, Worcestershire sauce, and tomatoes. Bring to a boil then reduce the heat and simmer for 30 minutes, stirring occasionally.

2. Add the crabmeat and continue to cook for 30–40 minutes, stirring occasionally.

PER SERVING Calories: 305 | Fat: 2 g | Protein: 23 g | Sodium: 251 mg | Fiber: 13 g | Carbohydrates: 53 g | Sugar: 12 g

Turkey-Apple Chili

Try this unusual chili with leftover roasted turkey.

INGREDIENTS | SERVES 6

2 tablespoons canola oil

3 shallots, minced

3 Granny Smith apples, cubed

1 carrot, diced

3 cloves garlic, minced

2 jalapeños, diced

3½ cups cubed cooked turkey breast

15 ounces canned diced tomato

1 tablespoon cocoa

1 tablespoon chili powder

½ teaspoon ground cinnamon

¼ teaspoon ground allspice

¼ teaspoon ground cloves

1. Heat the oil in a Dutch oven. Add the shallots, apples, carrot, garlic, and jalapeños. Sauté until the onions are just turning golden, about 15–20 minutes.

2. Add the turkey, tomatoes, cocoa, and spices. Cover and cook, stirring occasionally, for 20 minutes.

PER SERVING Calories: 147 | Fat: 5 g | Protein: 3 g | Sodium: 32 mg | Fiber: 3 g | Carbohydrates: 26 g | Sugar: 11 g

Easy Roasted Turkey

For an easy roasted turkey try this: Rub a 16-pound turkey with lemon juice, coarse salt, pepper, and rubbed sage. Roast for 3–4 hours at 350°F. Allow to sit for 10 minutes before carving.

Black Bean and King Oyster Mushroom Soup

Look for large, meaty King Oyster mushrooms at an Asian grocery for the best selection and prices.

INGREDIENTS | SERVES 4

2 tablespoons olive oil

1 onion, minced

1 shallot, minced

2 carrots, minced

2 stalks celery, diced

1 bulb fennel, diced

6 King Oyster mushrooms, diced

30 ounces cooked black beans

4 cups chicken or vegetable stock

1 tablespoon thyme leaves

½ tablespoon minced rosemary

1. Heat the oil in a Dutch oven. Sauté the onion, shallot, carrots, celery, fennel, and mushrooms until soft and fragrant, about 10–15 minutes.

2. Add the beans, stock, thyme, and rosemary. Stir. Cover and simmer 30 minutes.

PER SERVING Calories: 377 | Fat: 9 g | Protein: 21 g | Sodium: 736 mg | Fiber: 20 g | Carbohydrates: 60 g | Sugar: 10 g

Zucchini-Garlic Chili

Perfect for summer, this vegan chili will satisfy anyone!

INGREDIENTS | SERVES 6

5 medium zucchini, cubed

1 red onion, diced

7 cloves garlic, minced

8 ounces sliced crimini mushrooms

28 ounces canned diced fire-roasted tomatoes

1 teaspoon hot paprika

1 teaspoon garlic powder

½ teaspoon cayenne

½ teaspoon sea salt

½ teaspoon freshly ground black pepper

1. Sauté the zucchini, onion, garlic, and mushrooms in oil or butter in a Dutch oven until the onion is just browned, about 15–20 minutes.

2. Add the remaining ingredients. Simmer until warmed through, about 10–20 minutes, stirring occasionally.

PER SERVING Calories: 73 | Fat: 1 g | Protein: 5 g | Sodium: 400 mg | Fiber: 4 g | Carbohydrates: 15 g | Sugar: 9 g

Gazpacho

Perfect for a hot summer day, this gazpacho uses the best of in-season ingredients.

INGREDIENTS | SERVES 8

4 pounds tomatoes, finely diced

1 red onion, diced

1 seedless cucumber, diced

2 jalapeños, diced

2 stalks celery, diced

2 cloves garlic, minced

2 tablespoons minced Italian parsley

¼ cup lemon juice

½ tablespoon Worcestershire sauce

⅓ cup red wine vinegar

¼ cup olive oil

3½ cups unsalted tomato juice

Combine all ingredients in a food processor; pulse until mostly smooth. Pour into a nonreactive container. Refrigerate overnight. Stir prior to serving.

PER SERVING Calories: 136 | Fat: 7 g | Protein: 3 g | Sodium: 43 mg | Fiber: 4 g | Carbohydrates: 17 g | Sugar: 11 g

Suggested Garnishes

While gazpacho is wonderful on its own, it is also fun to garnish. Try some chopped parsley, cucumber, or avocado. Or for a seafood-eaters version, steamed shrimp or crawfish.

Seafood Gumbo

This gumbo uses a quick roux to provide a depth of flavor that cannot be beat!

1. In a Dutch oven, melt the butter. Add the flour, Cajun seasoning, and ground cayenne. Whisk continuously until it turns a nutty, golden brown, about 3–8 minutes.

2. Add the thyme, garlic, peppers, and onion, and sauté until all ingredients begin to soften, about 5–10 minutes.

3. Add the stock and bring to a simmer. Stir in the sausages and okra. Cook for 30 minutes.

4. Add the shrimp, catfish, crawfish, and parsley. Simmer until the seafood is fully cooked, about 10–20 minutes. Serve over rice and top with a sprinkle of filé powder.

PER SERVING Calories: 712 | Fat: 14 g | Protein: 51 g | Sodium: 563 mg | Fiber: 5 g | Carbohydrates: 91 g | Sugar: 3 g

Chicken-Tomatillo Chili

A change from the typical chili, this chicken chili tastes light and fresh.

INGREDIENTS | SERVES 6

2 pounds boneless, skinless chicken breast

¼ cup lime juice

1 teaspoon ground cayenne

2 teaspoons ground chipotle

1 tablespoon red pepper flakes

2 onions, chopped

3 cloves garlic, minced

3 poblano peppers

3 Anaheim peppers

2 tablespoons canola oil

2 pounds chopped tomatillos

1½ cups chicken stock

2 cups cooked white beans

Checking Out Chicken

Boneless skinless chicken breasts are incredibly popular. They are easy to pre-pare; no deboning or skin removal needed. They are also good sources of protein and only contain 1.5 grams of fat per 4 ounce serving.

1. Place the chicken, lime juice, spices, onions, and garlic in a marinating container or resealable bag. Refrigerate for 30 minutes.

2. Meanwhile, place the peppers in a heat-safe dish or broiling pan and broil for 5 minutes on each side. Allow to cool enough to be safely handled, about 5 minutes. Use a towel to rub the skins off of the peppers. Cut a slit into one side of the chile and remove the seeds. Discard the seeds. Dice the peppers.

3. Heat the oil in a Dutch oven and add the chicken mixture. Sauté until the chicken is nearly cooked through, about 5–10 minutes. Then add the tomatillos, roasted peppers, stock, and beans. Simmer, stirring occasionally, for 20 minutes or until the chicken is fully cooked and the tomatillos are soft.

PER SERVING Calories: 487 | Fat: 11 g | Protein: 47 g | Sodium: 189 mg | Fiber: 15 g | Carbohydrates: 53 g | Sugar: 14 g

Lemon Asparagus Soup

Use the last of winter's in-season lemons and spring's new asparagus and potatoes in this wholesome soup.

INGREDIENTS | SERVES 6

2½ pounds asparagus

1 onion, sliced

1 pound small red-skin potatoes

4 cups chicken or vegetable stock

¼ cup lemon juice

4 cloves garlic, minced

1 tablespoon tarragon vinegar

½ teaspoon sea salt

½ teaspoon white pepper

Parchment Paper Versus Waxed Paper

Parchment paper and waxed paper may look alike but their uses are very different. Parchment paper is coated, oven-safe paper. Waxed paper is paper that is coated in wax and is only suitable for wrapping cold items.

1. Preheat oven to 350°F. Line a baking sheet with parchment paper.

2. Arrange the asparagus, onion, and potatoes in a single layer on the baking sheet. Roast for about 30 minutes, flipping the vegetables occasionally to ensure even roasting, or until the asparagus and onion look caramelized.

3. Add the asparagus, onion, potatoes, stock, lemon juice, garlic, vinegar, salt, and pepper to Dutch oven and bring to a boil.

4. Remove from heat and purée using an immersion blender.

PER SERVING Calories: 157 | Fat: 2 g | Protein: 10 g | Sodium: 434 mg | Fiber: 6 g | Carbohydrates: 27 g | Sugar: 8 g

Cauliflower-Celeriac Soup

Just a hint of smoked paprika brings out the flavor of this earthy and amazingly creamy soup.

INGREDIENTS | SERVES 6–8

2 tablespoons olive oil

1 onion, chopped

2 heads cauliflower

1 bulb celeriac, peeled and diced

3 cups chicken or vegetable stock

1 cup 2% milk

½ teaspoon white pepper

½ teaspoon sea salt

½ teaspoon smoked paprika

Immersion Blender Tips

Immersion blenders can cause food to splatter so take care! Only use the blender in an up and down motion. Remove food from heat before blending. Blend in large bowls or pots to minimize splashing.

1. In a Dutch oven, heat the oil. Add the onion and sauté for 5 minutes, until the onion is softening but not browned.

2. Add the cauliflower, celeriac, and stock. Bring to a boil, then cover and reduce heat. Cook for 20 minutes or until the vegetables are fork-tender.

3. Use an immersion blender to purée the soup.

4. Stir in the milk, pepper, and sea salt. Divide among bowls and garnish with a sprinkle of smoked paprika.

PER SERVING Calories: 123 | Fat: 6 g | Protein: 6 g | Sodium: 336 mg | Fiber: 3 g | Carbohydrates: 13 g | Sugar: 6 g

Herbed Chicken and Rice Soup

The herbs add a lot of fresh flavor to this homey soup.

INGREDIENTS | SERVES 6

1 tablespoon olive oil

1 tablespoon unsalted butter

2 cloves garlic, minced

1 pound cubed, cooked chicken breast

1 bunch scallions, sliced

¾ cup uncooked jasmine rice

6 cups chicken stock

¼ cup lemon juice

1 teaspoon crushed rosemary

1 bay leaf

½ teaspoon sea salt

½ teaspoon freshly ground black pepper

2 tablespoons minced Italian parsley

2 tablespoons minced chives

1. In a Dutch oven, heat the olive oil and butter over medium heat. Add the garlic, chicken, and scallions. Sauté until the garlic is soft and fragrant, about 3–8 minutes.

2. Add the rice, stock, lemon juice, rosemary, bay leaf, salt, and pepper. Cover and cook until the rice is fully cooked, about 15 minutes. Stir in the parsley and chives.

PER SERVING Calories: 296 | Fat: 9 g | Protein: 24 g | Sodium: 629 mg | Fiber: 0 g | Carbohydrates: 28 g | Sugar: 4 g

What Is Jasmine Rice?

Jasmine rice is also known as Thai fragrant rice. It is a long-grain rice that is not as sticky as other Asian varieties. It has a nutty taste and almost floral aroma.

CHAPTER 12

Side Dishes

Black-Eyed Peas with Ham

This Southern classic is slow-cooked so the beans are extra creamy.

INGREDIENTS | SERVES 10

1 pound dried black-eyed peas

1 onion, diced

1 jalapeño, diced

1 stalk celery, diced

1 carrot, diced

6 cups ham stock or water

6 ounces diced ham

1 cup diced fresh tomato

1 tablespoon apple cider vinegar

1 tablespoon fresh thyme leaves

1 teaspoon cayenne

½ teaspoon salt

½ teaspoon freshly ground black pepper

1. The night before you want to serve the dish, place the black-eyed peas in a 4-quart slow cooker. Fill it with water. Cover and soak overnight.

2. The next day, drain the black-eyed peas then return them to the slow cooker and add the remaining ingredients. Stir. Cook on low 8–10 hours. Stir before serving.

PER SERVING Calories: 241 | Fat: 4 g | Protein: 18 g | Sodium: 555 mg | Fiber: 5 g | Carbohydrates: 35 g | Sugar: 7 g

Lucky Peas

Black-eyed peas (actually beans) are a traditional food to eat on New Year's Day. It is thought that they will bring prosperity in the coming year. That association occurred because they swell as they cook.

Summer Succotash

Look for fresh, creamy lima beans at farmers' markets during the summer.

INGREDIENTS | SERVES 6

2 tablespoons olive oil
1 pound fresh lima beans
Kernels from 5 ears of corn
1 zucchini, chopped
1 pint cherry tomatoes, halved
1 small red onion, diced
3 teaspoons tarragon vinegar
3 tablespoons minced basil
3 tablespoons minced Italian parsley
1 tablespoon thyme leaves
1 teaspoon salt
½ teaspoon white pepper

1. In a skillet, heat the oil. Add the lima beans, corn, and zucchini. Sauté until the vegetables are just warmed through, about 3–8 minutes.

2. Remove to a medium bowl and toss with the remaining ingredients.

PER SERVING Calories: 417 | Fat: 6 g | Protein: 20 g | Sodium: 418 mg | Fiber: 18 g | Carbohydrates: 77 g | Sugar: 13 g

Zucchini-Potato Latkes

Try using a mandolin to get the perfect, long thin strips of potato and zucchini.

INGREDIENTS | SERVES 8

2 pounds russet potatoes, cut into long, thin strips
2 medium zucchini, cut into long, thin strips
1 onion, grated
2 eggs, beaten
¼ cup matzo meal
Canola oil, for frying

1. In a large bowl, combine all ingredients. Form into flat fritters.

2. Meanwhile, heat ¼-inch of canola oil in a skillet over medium heat. Fry the latkes until golden, flipping once, about 3–8 minutes per side.

3. Drain on paper towel–lined plates.

PER SERVING Calories: 109 | Fat: 1.5 g | Protein: 4 g | Sodium: 29 mg | Fiber: 3 g | Carbohydrates: 21 g | Sugar: 3 g

Slow-Cooked Sauerkraut

In Baltimore, sauerkraut is served alongside turkey at every holiday meal.

INGREDIENTS | SERVES 8

28 ounces refrigerated or fresh sauerkraut

¼-pound pork loin

½ cup red wine vinegar

2 tablespoons yellow mustard seed

1 teaspoon dry mustard

1 teaspoon dill weed

½ teaspoon caraway seed

½ teaspoon prepared horseradish

3 tablespoons minced shallot

Place all ingredients in a 4-quart slow cooker. Stir. Cook on low for 8 hours. Stir and serve.

PER SERVING Calories: 71 | Fat: 4 g | Protein: 4 g | Sodium: 667 mg | Fiber: 3 g | Carbohydrates: 5 g | Sugar: 2 g

Cooking with Sauerkraut

If cooking with canned or bagged sauerkraut, it can be beneficial to rinse off the extra salt and brine. Do not dry the sauerkraut. This is less of an issue with fresh sauerkraut. Sauerkraut is a low-calorie food.

Fondant Potatoes and Pearl Onions

This twist on the classic French dish features nearly caramelized onions.

INGREDIENTS | SERVES 6

2 pounds unpeeled baby potatoes
1 pound pearl onions, peeled
1 tablespoon unsalted butter
1 tablespoon olive oil
½ teaspoon sea salt
½ teaspoon freshly ground black pepper
3 cups chicken stock
1 tablespoon Herbes de Provence

1. Arrange all of the potatoes and onions in the bottom of a large, nonstick pan in a single layer. Add the remaining ingredients. Bring to a boil.

2. Reduce heat and partially cover with a lid. Continue to boil until much of the stock has evaporated, about 20 minutes. The potatoes should still be about half submerged in the stock at this point.

3. Use a wooden spoon to press down on each potato, cracking the skin. Continue to cook until all of the stock has completely evaporated and the bottoms of the potatoes and onions are browned, about 10–25 minutes.

4. Flip the potatoes and onions and cook the other side for about 5 minutes. Use a large, flat spatula to remove the potatoes and onions from the pan.

PER SERVING Calories: 183 | Fat: 6 g | Protein: 6 g | Sodium: 377 mg | Fiber: 4 g | Carbohydrates: 28 g | Sugar: 4 g

Spring Onion Potato Cakes

These simple yet flavorful cakes are a wonderful way to use up leftover mashed potatoes.

INGREDIENTS | SERVES 6

1 tablespoon unsalted butter

1 bunch spring onions, white and green parts diced

1 egg, beaten

2 cups mashed potatoes

1 teaspoon salt

1 teaspoon minced chives

½ teaspoon minced sage

½ teaspoon chervil

2 tablespoons sour cream

Canola oil, for frying

Chives Tip

Chives easily bruise and then rot. However, they can be minced and frozen. Frozen chives can be used in equal amounts as fresh, without defrosting.

1. In a small pan, melt the butter. Add the spring onions and sauté until softened, about 3–5 minutes.

2. Allow the onions to cool slightly then remove them to a medium bowl. Add the remaining ingredients and mix until all ingredients are well incorporated. Form the mixture into 3–inch patties.

3. Heat ¼-inch canola oil in a large skillet. Pan-fry the patties until golden brown on each side, about 5–8 minutes. Drain on paper towel–lined plates and serve.

PER SERVING Calories: 105 | Fat: 5 g | Protein: 4 g | Sodium: 591 mg | Fiber: 0 g | Carbohydrates: 13 g | Sugar: 0 g

Roasted Beet Celeriac Mash

Roasting beets deepens their flavors and seems to sweeten them.

INGREDIENTS | SERVES 6

4 beets, peeled and cubed

2 pounds celeriac, cubed

¼ cup balsamic vinegar

⅓ cup plain Greek yogurt

1 tablespoon unsalted butter

¼ teaspoon celery seed

1 teaspoon sea salt

½ teaspoon freshly ground black pepper

Easy-Peel Beets

It is easy to remove the peels from beets. Simply place them in the middle of a large paper towel and rub them until the skin slides off. Gloves are optional but recommended because beets tend to stain everything they come in contact with.

1. Preheat oven to 375°F.

2. Arrange the beets in a single layer on a baking sheet. Roast the beets for 30 minutes or until fork-tender.

3. Meanwhile, bring a pot of water to a boil. Add the celeriac and boil until fork-tender, about 8–20 minutes.

4. Drain and place in a large bowl. Add the roasted beets and remaining ingredients. Mash until smooth.

PER SERVING Calories: 97 | Fat: 2 g | Protein: 4 g | Sodium: 550 mg | Fiber: 3 g | Carbohydrates: 16 g | Sugar: 4 g

Spicy Roasted Spaghetti Squash

Rather than pretend it is pasta, make this dish, which highlights its wonderful squash flavor.

INGREDIENTS | SERVES 4

1 (2-pound) spaghetti squash
2 tablespoons unsalted butter
1 shallot, minced
1 teaspoon salt
½ teaspoon freshly ground black pepper
1 teaspoon ground cayenne
½ teaspoon hot paprika
¼ teaspoon allspice
¼ teaspoon ground cloves

RDA?

RDA stands for recommended daily allowance. The RDA was developed in the 1930s to create standard recommendations of the daily allowance of each type of nutrient. It is meant to reflect the requirements of the majority of the population.

1. Preheat oven to 400°F.

2. Pierce the squash with the point of a knife multiple times. Place on a baking sheet. Roast for 1 hour or until the squash is easily pierced with a fork.

3. Halve the squash. Remove the seeds and discard. Scoop out the flesh. Shred with a fork. Set aside.

4. Melt the butter in a skillet. Add the shallot and sauté 2 minutes. Add the squash and spices. Sauté for an additional 5 minutes. Serve immediately.

PER SERVING Calories: 71 | Fat: 6 g | Protein: 1 g |
Sodium: 594 g | Fiber: 0 g | Carbohydrates: 5 g | Sugar: 0 g

Oyster Portobello Un-Stuffing

A twist on traditional stuffing, this stuffing is made into balls and cooks in the pan next to the turkey, not inside it.

INGREDIENTS | SERVES 10

3 tablespoons unsalted butter

1 pound celery, chopped

1 pound onions, chopped

4 portobello mushroom caps, diced

1 bunch parsley, minced

25 slices torn sandwich bread

2 eggs, beaten

1 teaspoon freshly ground black pepper

1 teaspoon sea salt

1 teaspoon celery seed

1 teaspoon paprika

16 ounces shucked oysters, liquid reserved

½ cup chicken stock

Turkey or chicken in the process of being roasted

1. Melt the butter in a large skillet. Add the celery, onions, and mushrooms and cook over very low heat until the onions are translucent but not browned, about 30–45 minutes. Allow to cool slightly. Sprinkle with parsley.

2. Scrape the mixture into a large bowl. Add the remaining ingredients. Using your hands, mix the ingredients together until all ingredients are evenly distributed.

3. Form the mixture into 3-inch balls that hold their shape. If the balls do not hold their shape, add the reserved oyster liquor until they can hold their shape.

4. Place balls in the bottom of the roasting pan under the rack and around the turkey (or chicken) and return to the oven for the last ½ hour of roasting.

PER SERVING Calories: 558 | Fat: 10 g | Protein: 60 g | Sodium: 1,042 mg | Fiber: 4 g | Carbohydrates: 54 g | Sugar: 6 g

Roasted Eggplant with Potato and Feta

Roasting eggplant gives it a silky texture without having to fry it.

INGREDIENTS | SERVES 6

1 eggplant, cubed
1 pound baby Yukon Gold potatoes
1 onion, sliced into rounds
2 tablespoons olive oil
2 tablespoons lemon juice
1 tablespoon minced mint
4 ounces crumbled feta cheese

1. Preheat oven to 375°F.

2. Arrange the eggplant and potatoes in a single layer on a baking sheet. Scatter the onions on top of the vegetables. Drizzle with olive oil. Roast for 40 minutes or until the potatoes are fork-tender.

3. Place the vegetables in a large bowl. Toss with the lemon juice, mint, and feta. Serve immediately.

PER SERVING Calories: 171 | Fat: 9 g | Protein: 5 g | Sodium: 216 mg | Fiber: 5 g | Carbohydrates: 20 g | Sugar: 4 g

What Is Fork-Tender?

Fork-tender is when a vegetable or meat is well-cooked enough to be poked with a fork or knife point and meet little to no resistance.

Roasted Asparagus

Asparagus really shines when roasted and dressed up with lemon and fancy vinegar.

INGREDIENTS | SERVES 4

1 pound asparagus
2 tablespoons olive oil
¼ cup lemon juice
2 tablespoons lemon zest
2 tablespoons champagne vinegar
1 teaspoon kosher salt
1 teaspoon freshly ground black pepper
1 tablespoon minced fresh dill

1. Preheat oven to 375°F.

2. Line a baking sheet with foil. Place the asparagus in a single layer on the sheet. Drizzle with olive oil. Roll the spears in the oil. Roast for 5–8 minutes or until the spears are tender but not browned.

3. Meanwhile, in a small bowl, whisk together the lemon juice, zest, vinegar, salt, pepper, and dill.

4. Arrange the asparagus on a platter and drizzle with the sauce.

PER SERVING Calories: 87 | Fat: 7 g | Protein: 3 g | Sodium: 595 mg | Fiber: 2 g | Carbohydrates: 5 g | Sugar: 2 g

Pickled Asparagus

This is a type of refrigerator pickling but this recipe is also safe for hot water bath canning. If you're familiar with hot water bath canning then follow proper safety procedures and process for 10 minutes.

INGREDIENTS | YIELDS 3 PINTS

3½ pounds asparagus, cut into 6-inch pieces
3 cloves garlic
1 shallot, minced
3 bay leaves
1½ teaspoons black peppercorns
1½ teaspoons dill seeds
1 tablespoon fresh dill
1½ teaspoons yellow mustard seed
2 cups water
2 cups white vinegar
¼ cup pickling salt

1. Evenly divide the asparagus, garlic, shallot, bay leaves, peppercorns, dill seeds, dill, and mustard seeds among 3 wide-mouth pint jars.

2. In a saucepan, bring the water, vinegar, and salt to a boil, stirring to dissolve the salt. Ladle over the asparagus. Close the jars. Allow them to come to room temperature and then refrigerate.

3. Wait 1 week before eating. Keep refrigerated at all times.

PER 1 CUP SERVING Calories: 82 | Fat: 0 g | Protein: 6 g | Sodium: 4,724 mg | Fiber: 6 g | Carbohydrates: 14 g | Sugar: 5 g

Canning

Canning fruits and vegetables is a great way to preserve food at its peak. Pickling is an easy place to start. Even unprocessed pickles keep for months in the refrigerator.

Herbed Wax Beans

If wax beans are unavailable, green beans are an acceptable substitute.

INGREDIENTS | SERVES 6

2 tablespoons olive oil

1¾ pounds wax beans

1 shallot, minced

2 cloves garlic, minced

2 tablespoons minced thyme

2 tablespoons minced oregano

2 tablespoons minced Italian parsley

1 tablespoon minced chives

½ teaspoon sea salt

1. Heat the oil in a skillet. Add the wax beans, shallot, and garlic. Sauté until the shallot is soft and the beans are fork-tender, about 5–10 minutes.

2. Sprinkle with herbs and salt. Serve hot or at room temperature.

PER SERVING Calories: 496 | Fat: 5 g | Protein: 29 g | Sodium: 222 mg | Fiber: 25 g | Carbohydrates: 86 g | Sugar: 11 g

Wax Beans

Similar in appearance and texture to green beans, wax beans come into season in early summer. They are a good source of vitamins C and A. They are also very low in calories.

Bubble and Squeak

This British dish is more frequently made with cabbage but Brussels sprouts make a wonderful variation.

INGREDIENTS | SERVES 6

3 pounds Yukon Gold potatoes

2 pounds Brussels sprouts, finely shredded

3 tablespoons olive oil

3 leeks, sliced

1 teaspoon sea salt

1 teaspoon freshly ground black pepper

Long Live the Brussels Sprout

Decried by many as foul smelling, Brussels sprouts can be quite delightful. The trick is not to overcook them. Roasting and sautéing yield the best results.

1. Bring a large pot of water to a boil. Boil the potatoes until fork-tender. For the last 5 minutes of cooking, place the Brussels sprouts in a metal sieve over the boiling potatoes to steam.

2. Drain the potatoes and place them in a large bowl. Mash the potatoes. Stir in the Brussels sprouts.

3. Meanwhile, heat the oil in a nonstick frying pan. Add leeks and sauté until softened but not browned, about 3–8 minutes. Add to the bowl. Add the salt and pepper. Stir to thoroughly combine.

4. Scrape the mixture back into the skillet. Use a spatula to pat it down. Cook, without stirring, until browned and cooked through.

PER SERVING Calories: 241 | Fat: 7 g | Protein: 4 g | Sodium: 415 mg | Fiber: 6 g | Carbohydrates: 41 g | Sugar: 4 g

Okra with Tomato and Black Beans

Try serving this over rice for an extra-hardy meal.

INGREDIENTS | SERVES 6

½ pound okra, sliced into coins

2 large tomatoes, diced

1 cup cooked black beans

½ red onion, chopped

1 tablespoon minced oregano

1 tablespoon minced basil

¼ cup red wine vinegar

1 teaspoon sea salt

1 teaspoon freshly ground black pepper

Toss all ingredients together in a medium bowl. Allow to marinate at room temperature 1 hour before serving.

PER SERVING Calories: 65 | Fat: 0 g | Protein: 4 g | Sodium: 527 mg | Fiber: 5 g | Carbohydrates: 12 g | Sugar: 3 g

Onion Types

The most common onions are yellow, red, and white. Yellow is the most commonly used and caramelizes well. Red onions are peppery and crisp and work well in salads or grilled. White onions are sweet and frequently used in Mexican dishes. Specialty onions like the Maui and Vidalia are super sweet and most often eaten raw.

Buttermilk Biscuits

What goes better with a Southern dinner than buttermilk biscuits?

INGREDIENTS | SERVES 10

1½ cups all-purpose flour
1½ teaspoons baking powder
1 teaspoon baking soda
1 teaspoon sugar
½ teaspoon salt
6 tablespoons cold unsalted butter, sliced
½ cup buttermilk
1 egg

1. Preheat oven to 350°F.

2. Pulse the flour, baking powder, baking soda, sugar, and salt in a food processor. Add the butter and pulse until just mixed.

3. In a small bowl, beat together the buttermilk and egg. Pour into the food processor and pulse until a dough forms.

4. Place the dough on a floured surface and knead briefly. Roll out into a ½-inch thickness. Cut with biscuit cutter. Place on a parchment paper–lined baking sheet.

5. Bake 10 minutes or until golden brown.

PER SERVING Calories: 239 | Fat: 13 g | Protein: 5 g | Sodium: 563 mg | Fiber: 1 g | Carbohydrates: 26 g | Sugar: 2 g

Grilled Corn with Spiced Butter

You can grill corn right alongside meats or fish, making it a perfect side dish for a cookout.

INGREDIENTS | SERVES 6

6 ears of corn, silks removed

¼ cup unsalted butter, at room temperature

½ teaspoon ground chipotle

½ teaspoon smoked paprika

¼ teaspoon salt

¼ teaspoon freshly ground black pepper

1. Prepare your grill according to manufacturer's instructions. Place the corn on the grill and roast, turning occasionally until fully cooked, about 5–10 minutes.

2. Meanwhile, in a small bowl, mash the spices into the butter with a fork. Serve over the hot corn.

PER SERVING Calories: 190 | Fat: 9 g | Protein: 4 g | Sodium: 106 mg | Fiber: 4 g | Carbohydrates: 29 g | Sugar: 5 g

Stir-Fried Gai Lan

Gai Lan, also known as Chinese broccoli, looks more like greens with thick stalks than broccoli.

INGREDIENTS | SERVES 8

2 tablespoons canola oil

1-inch knob ginger, minced

2 cloves garlic, minced

2 pounds chopped gai lan

¼ cup soy sauce

¼ cup oyster sauce

2 tablespoons black sesame oil

1. Heat the canola oil in a large wok. Add the ginger and garlic and stir-fry until fragrant, about 3–5 minutes. Add the gai lan and cook for 2 minutes or until it begins to wilt.

2. Add the remaining ingredients. Stir-fry 2 additional minutes or until the gai lan is fully cooked and coated in sauce. Serve immediately.

PER SERVING Calories: 73 | Fat: 7 g | Protein: 1 g | Sodium: 696 mg | Fiber: 0 g | Carbohydrates: 2 g | Sugar: 0 g

Meyer Lemon–Marinated Olives and Feta

Check out the deli counter for the best brine-cured olives.

INGREDIENTS | SERVES 12

1½ cups brine-cured green olives

1½ cups brine-cured Kalamata olives

1 cup olive oil

½ cup Meyer lemon juice

8 cloves garlic

2 tablespoons Meyer lemon zest

¼ cup chopped Italian parsley

1 tablespoon minced fresh rosemary

8 ounces cubed or crumbled feta cheese

Place all ingredients in a resealable plastic bag. Seal and shake to evenly distribute all ingredients without crushing the cheese. Refrigerate 24 hours before serving.

PER SERVING Calories: 496 | Fat: 47 g | Protein: 6 g | Sodium: 718 mg | Fiber: 2 g | Carbohydrates: 14 g | Sugar: 2 g

Kalamata Olive FYI

Kalamata olives are most often preserved in olive oil or wine vinegar. They are a protected variety and can only be picked when ripe and by hand in certain areas of Greece. If these conditions can not be met, those olives may not be called Kalamata.

Swiss Chard and Wild Mushroom Sauté

A wide assortment of wild mushrooms will add to the visual appeal and flavor of this dish.

INGREDIENTS | SERVES 6

3 tablespoons olive oil

1 onion, diced

3 cloves garlic, minced

8 ounces assorted wild mushrooms

2 pounds Swiss chard, chopped

¼ cup chopped hazelnuts

Hazy about Hazelnuts?

Hazelnuts are the nuts of the hazel tree. Hazelnuts are protein-rich and a good source of unsaturated fat. They are also full of vitamins B_6, E, and thiamine.

1. Heat the oil in a large skillet. Add the onion and garlic and sauté until the onion is soft, about 3–8 minutes.

2. Add the mushrooms. Sauté 2 minutes. Add half of the Swiss chard, sauté until it wilts, then add the remaining chard. Sauté until the Swiss chard is just tender.

3. Sprinkle with hazelnuts and serve.

PER SERVING Calories: 136 | Fat: 10 g | Protein: 5 g | Sodium: 321 mg | Fiber: 4 g | Carbohydrates: 10 g | Sugar: 3 g

CHAPTER 13

Grains and Rice

Farro with Rainbow Chard

The chewy texture of the farro contrasts with the more delicate tastes of the chard and fresh herbs.

INGREDIENTS | SERVES 4

4 cups water
1 cup farro
1 shallot, chopped
1 carrot, diced
1 stalk celery, diced
2 cloves garlic, minced
2 tablespoons olive oil
¼ cup chopped Italian parsley
1 bunch rainbow chard, roughly chopped
1½ tablespoons tarragon vinegar

1. Bring 4 cups water and the farro to a boil in a medium saucepan over high heat. Reduce heat to low and simmer until tender, stirring occasionally, about 25 minutes. Drain.

2. Meanwhile, sauté the shallot, carrot, celery, and garlic in olive oil until the shallots are transparent. Add the parsley and chard and sauté until they start to wilt, about 2–3 minutes. Remove from heat. Stir in the farro.

3. Drizzle with vinegar. Serve hot or at room temperature.

PER SERVING Calories: 259 | Fat: 7 g | Protein: 7 g | Sodium: 61 mg | Fiber: 3 g | Carbohydrates: 41 g | Sugar: 1 g

Viva Farro!

Farro is an ancient grain that is said to be the "mother" of all wheat. It has a nutty flavor and has been popular in Italy since the time when it sustained the Roman legions. Now it is commonly used as an alternative to pasta or rice.

Kimchi Fried Rice

This is a wonderful, new way to use up a surplus of kimchi and some leftover rice.

INGREDIENTS | SERVES 4

2 eggs, beaten
1½ tablespoons canola oil
4 cups leftover white or brown rice
2 heads cabbage kimchi, chopped

What Is Kimchi?

Kimchi is a spicy Korean fermented vegetable dish. It is most frequently made with cabbage but other varieties including radish and cucumber are also popular. Kimchi is loaded with vitamins A, B, and C and healthy bacteria.

1. Spray a nonstick skillet with cooking spray. Pour the eggs in. Allow to cook as a flat pancake until nearly set. Flip, cook fully. Remove to a plate and slice. Set aside.

2. Heat the oil in a wok or large pot. Add the rice and stir-fry until hot, about 3–10 minutes. Add the kimchi. Cook until cooked through, about 3–10 minutes, stirring occasionally. Stir in the sliced egg.

PER SERVING Calories: 412 | Fat: 10 g | Protein: 13 g | Sodium: 119 mg | Fiber: 15 g | Carbohydrates: 72 g | Sugar: 15 g

Ricotta Polenta

This amazingly creamy polenta is technically a side dish but so good, you might be tempted to have it as an entrée.

INGREDIENTS | SERVES 6

4 cups chicken stock or water
1 cup polenta
1 teaspoon sea salt
1 teaspoon freshly ground black pepper
1 tablespoon minced basil
1 tablespoon minced Italian parsley
½ cup ricotta

1. Bring the stock to a boil in a medium saucepan. Add the polenta and stir until it starts to thicken, 2–5 minutes. Simmer 30 minutes.

2. Stir in the salt, pepper, basil, parsley, and ricotta. Serve warm.

PER SERVING Calories: 120 | Fat: 3 g | Protein: 4 g | Sodium: 412 mg | Fiber: 1 g | Carbohydrates: 19 g | Sugar: 0 g

Rosemary Wild Rice Pilaf

Wild rice provides a nutty flavor and chewy texture to this pilaf.

INGREDIENTS | SERVES 10

3½ cups water
1 cup brown rice
½ cup wild rice
1 onion, chopped
2 stalks celery, chopped
2 carrots, diced
1 bulb fennel, diced
3 tablespoons chopped rosemary
½ teaspoon salt
½ teaspoon freshly ground black pepper

America's Grain

First harvested by Native Americans, wild rice is one of the very few grains native to North America. Despite the name, wild rice is actually a grain harvested from a type of grass, not rice. It grows in shallow lakes and streams. Wild rice is the state grain of Minnesota.

1. In a medium pot, bring the water to a boil. Add the brown rice and wild rice. Cook until tender, about 45 minutes.

2. Meanwhile, spray a skillet with nonstick cooking spray. Sauté the onion, celery, carrots, and fennel until softened.

3. Preheat oven to 350°F.

4. Drain the rice and wild rice. Pour into an 8" × 8" baking dish. Stir in the vegetable mixture. Cover and bake 1 hour. Add spices. Fluff with a fork prior to serving.

PER SERVING Calories: 73 | Fat: 1 g | Protein: 2 g | Sodium: 148 mg | Fiber: 3 g | Carbohydrates: 16 g | Sugar: 1 g

Hot Nectarine Quinoa Breakfast Cereal

The late addition of oats adds both additional fiber and creaminess to the final dish.

INGREDIENTS | SERVES 2

1½ cups water

¼ cup quinoa

2 nectarines, peeled and diced

½ cup milk

¼ cup old-fashioned rolled oats

1 tablespoon honey (optional)

1. Place the water, quinoa, and nectarines in a small saucepan over medium heat. Cook for 30 minutes. Stir.

2. Add the milk, oats, and honey. Stir to combine.

3. Cook, stirring occasionally, until the oats are fully cooked.

PER SERVING Calories: 247 | Fat: 4 g | Protein: 8 g | Sodium: 28 mg | Fiber: 5 g | Carbohydrates: 47 g | Sugar: 23 g

Keen on Quinoa

Quinoa is a seed that when cooked, has a slightly crunchy, nutty texture. As it contains all nine essential amino acids, quinoa is a complete protein. This makes it particularly appealing to people who are concerned about their protein intake.

Asiago-Cayenne Crackers

Homemade crackers are an impressive treat to serve guests.

INGREDIENTS | SERVES 12

1 cup white whole-wheat flour

5 tablespoons unsalted butter, melted and cooled

3 ounces finely grated Asiago cheese

2 tablespoons very cold water

½ teaspoon salt

1 teaspoon ground cayenne

1. Preheat oven to 325°F. Line a baking sheet with parchment paper. Set aside.

2. Place all ingredients in a food processor. Pulse until a thick dough forms. Roll the dough into a long, 1-inch thick log. Slice into ¼-inch thick slices and arrange on the baking sheet ½ inch apart.

3. Use the tines of a fork to dimple the top of each cracker. Bake for 20 minutes or until the bottoms are golden and the crackers are firm to the touch. Allow to cool completely before eating. Store in an airtight container.

PER SERVING Calories: 76 | Fat: 5 | Protein: 1 g | Sodium: 99 mg | Fiber: 1 g | Carbohydrates: 7 g | Sugar: 0 g

Sage-Parmesan Polenta

Try this creamy polenta at your next meal in place of potatoes, rice, or noodles.

INGREDIENTS | SERVES 4

1 cup polenta

2 cups water or chicken stock

2 cups 2% milk

1 tablespoon unsalted butter

3 ounces grated Parmesan cheese

1 tablespoon minced fresh sage

¼ teaspoon salt

¼ teaspoon freshly ground black pepper

1. Place the polenta, water, milk, and butter in a saucepan. Cook on medium heat, whisking occasionally, until thick, about 5–10 minutes.

2. Stir in the remaining ingredients. Serve hot.

PER SERVING Calories: 190 | Fat: 13 g | Protein: 12 g | Sodium: 374 mg | Fiber: 0 g | Carbohydrates: 6 g | Sugar: 7 g

The Creamy Cornmeal

Polenta is a boiled cornmeal dish. It has a thick, creamy texture. Once considered a peasant food, this whole grain has taken on gourmet tendencies. While it was once served plain, it is now common to see it dressed with sauces or enriched with cheese.

Kasha Varniskas

Try this classic Jewish dish as a side with roasted chicken.

INGREDIENTS | SERVES 6

1 large onion, chopped
1 tablespoon canola oil
1 egg
1 cup kasha (buckwheat groats)
2 cups chicken stock or water
½ pound cooked farfalle

The Lowdown on Kasha

Also known as buckwheat groats, kasha is a staple of both Eastern European and American Jewish cuisine. It has a chewy texture and robust flavor. Buckwheat is gluten-free, making it a good whole grain for those with celiac disease.

1. In a large skillet, sauté the onions in the oil until nearly blackened.

2. Meanwhile, mix the egg and kasha together in a small bowl. Add to the onions in the skillet. Sauté until the kernels begin to separate, about 10 minutes.

3. Add the stock and cover. Simmer over low heat until tender, about 10–25 minutes.

4. Remove from heat. Add the farfalle and toss to combine. Serve hot.

PER SERVING Calories: 272 | Fat: 4 g | Protein: 9 g | Sodium: 18 mg | Fiber: 4 g | Carbohydrates: 50 g | Sugar: 2 g

Quinoa with Andouille Sausage

Complete-protein quinoa gets a flavor boost from this spicy sausage.

INGREDIENTS | SERVES 4

2 tablespoons canola oil
1 onion, chopped
3 cloves garlic, minced
1 poblano pepper, diced
1 cubanelle pepper, diced
2 andouille sausages, sliced into coins
1 tomato, cubed
¾ cup quinoa
1½ cups chicken stock

1. Heat the oil in a large, lidded skillet over medium heat. Add the onion, garlic, and peppers and sauté until the onions are soft, about 5–10 minutes.

2. Add the sausage and tomatoes and sauté for 3–5 additional minutes. Add the quinoa and sauté 1 minute.

3. Add the stock and bring to a boil. Cover and simmer until the quinoa is tender, about 20 minutes.

PER SERVING Calories: 323 | Fat: 17 g | Protein: 12 g | Sodium: 313 mg | Fiber: 3 g | Carbohydrates: 30 g | Sugar: 5 g

Wild Rice Ricotta Fritters

These fritters make an excellent side dish or burger substitute.

INGREDIENTS | SERVES 8

2 eggs

½ cup ricotta

1½ cups cooked wild rice

¼ cup matzo meal

¼ cup chopped green onion

½ teaspoon sea salt

¼ teaspoon freshly ground black pepper

¼ teaspoon smoked paprika

⅛ teaspoon ground nutmeg

Canola oil, for frying

1. Beat the eggs in a medium bowl until fluffy.

2. Stir in the ricotta, wild rice, and matzo meal until a thick batter forms.

3. Stir in the green onion and spices.

4. Heat ¼-inch of canola oil in a large skillet. Place ¼-cup scoops of batter into the skillet. Cook for 3–5 minutes on each side or until the fritters are golden brown and heated through.

5. Drain on paper towel–lined plates. Serve hot.

PER SERVING Calories: 152 | Fat: 4 g | Protein: 8 g | Sodium: 180 mg | Fiber: 2 g | Carbohydrates: 23 g | Sugar: 1 g

Wild, Wild Rice

Wild rice is a nutritional powerhouse. A ½ cup serving has 30 of the 48 grams of the daily recommended requirement of whole grains. Wild rice is very high in protein and fiber and is virtually fat-free. Wild rice is gluten-free.

Bulgur Wheat with Mushrooms, Ham, and Peppers

Bulgur is a quick-cooking variety of whole wheat; its hardiness makes this suitable for a main dish.

INGREDIENTS | SERVES 4

2 tablespoons olive oil

1 onion, diced

4 cloves garlic, minced

2 portobello mushroom caps, diced

1 cup cubed smoked ham

1 poblano pepper, diced

1 cup bulgur wheat

1 cup ham or chicken stock

¼ teaspoon paprika

½ teaspoon salt

½ teaspoon freshly ground black pepper

1. Heat the oil in a large skillet over medium heat. Sauté the onion, garlic, mushrooms, ham, and peppers until the onions caramelize, about 20–40 minutes.

2. Meanwhile, bring the bulgur wheat and stock to a boil in a small saucepan. Reduce heat and simmer for 15 minutes or until tender.

3. Stir the mushroom mixture and spices into the bulgur wheat. Serve immediately.

PER SERVING Calories: 280 | Fat: 11 g | Protein: 13 g | Sodium: 838 mg | Fiber: 7 g | Carbohydrates: 34 g | Sugar: 3 g

Bulgur Wheat Facts

Bulgur wheat is sold parboiled then dried so it is quick to cook. It is a whole-grain, high-fiber food that can be served hot or cold. Common in pilafs and salads, it also can be used as an alternative to rice.

Buckwheat Crêpes

Traditionally, these crêpes are filled with savory ingredients like meat and vegetables and served as a main course.

INGREDIENTS | SERVES 6

¼ cup unsalted butter, melted and cooled
1⅓ cups whole milk
¾ cup buckwheat flour
½ cup flour
3 eggs
¼ teaspoon kosher salt

1. In a small bowl, whisk together butter, milk, flours, eggs, and salt. Allow to sit at room temperature 30 minutes.

2. Grease a crêpe pan. Heat the pan over medium-low heat. Add ½ cup batter to the center of the pan. Carefully tilt the pan to cover completely. Cook until it is beginning to brown, about 2 minutes. Flip. Repeat for remaining batter.

3. Stack the completed crêpes on a plate in a cool oven until ready to serve.

PER SERVING Calories: 224 | Fat: 12 g | Protein: 8 g | Sodium: 159 mg | Fiber: 2 g | Carbohydrates: 21 g | Sugar: 3 g

Pearl Couscous with Mixed Vegetables

Pearl couscous, sometimes labeled as "Israeli" couscous, looks like a jumbo version of traditional couscous and is especially delicious when cooked in stock rather than water.

INGREDIENTS | SERVES 8

1 tablespoon unsalted butter
1 tablespoon olive oil
1 small onion, chopped
2 cloves garlic, minced
2 zucchini, diced
½ head Savoy cabbage, sliced thinly
2 cups cooked pearl couscous

1. In a large skillet, heat the butter and oil. Add the onion, garlic, and zucchini and sauté until the zucchini is tender, about 5–10 minutes.

2. Add the cabbage and sauté until it begins to wilt, about 5–10 minutes.

3. Add the couscous and sauté 1 minute.

PER SERVING Calories: 219 | Fat: 4 g | Protein: 7 g | Sodium: 19 mg | Fiber: 4 g | Carbohydrates: 40 g | Sugar: 4 g

Arroz Rojo

Also known as Mexican rice, this is the perfect side dish to serve with your favorite Mexican dishes.

INGREDIENTS | SERVES 6

2 tablespoons canola oil

1½ cups medium-grain rice

1 small white onion, minced

1 clove garlic, minced

1 serrano pepper, minced

1 cup tomato purée

2 cups chicken stock

½ teaspoon sea salt

½ teaspoon freshly ground black pepper

1. Heat the oil in a medium saucepan over medium heat. Add the rice, onion, garlic, and pepper. Sauté until the rice is a nutty brown, about 8–10 minutes.

2. Add the remaining ingredients and bring to a boil. Reduce the heat to a simmer. Cover and cook for 25 minutes or until the rice is tender and has absorbed all of the liquids. Stir and serve immediately.

PER SERVING Calories: 272 | Fat: 6 g | Protein: 6 g | Sodium: 479 mg | Fiber: 2 g | Carbohydrates: 48 g | Sugar: 4 g

How to Season Cast Iron

Cast iron naturally becomes nonstick if a few simple rules are followed. Rub the surface with a small amount of canola oil then wipe it out so it looks "dry." Place the pan in a 500°F oven for 30 minutes.

Dirty Rice

Serve this as a main dish or as a side to another Louisianan specialty.

INGREDIENTS | SERVES 4–6

2 tablespoons canola oil

½ pound ground chicken

½ pound chicken livers, puréed

2 shallots, minced

1½ cups chicken stock (divided use)

2 teaspoons Cajun seasoning

2 stalks celery, diced

4 cloves garlic, minced

1 onion, chopped

2½ cups hot cooked rice

2 tablespoons minced Italian parsley

1 tablespoon minced oregano

Cast Iron Tips

Once your cast iron is seasoned, it is ready to use. However, there are some rules to follow. Never pour cold liquids into a hot pan. Preheat the pan before use. Do not soak the pan; briefly rinse it out.

1. Heat the oil in a 12-inch cast-iron skillet over medium heat. Add the meat and the shallots. Cook, stirring occasionally and breaking up any large chunks, until the meat is becoming caramelized and is starting to stick to the pan.

2. Add ⅓ cup of chicken stock and Cajun seasoning and cook until the stock evaporates. Add the celery, garlic, and onion, and cook until they are soft.

3. Stir in the rice, herbs, and remaining stock. Stir until the liquid is absorbed, then serve.

PER SERVING Calories: 431 | Fat: 19 g | Protein: 26 g | Sodium: 235 mg | Fiber: 1 g | Carbohydrates: 50 g | Sugar: 3 g

Eggplant Farro

This slightly brothy dish is delicious with crusty bread; serve it as an entrée or side.

INGREDIENTS | SERVES 4–6

¾ cup farro
2 tablespoons olive oil
1 onion, chopped
4 cloves garlic, minced
2 cups peeled and cubed eggplant
½ cup dry red wine
2¼ cups chicken stock
½ teaspoon salt
½ teaspoon freshly ground black pepper

1. Place the farro in a bowl. Cover with water and soak for 10 minutes.

2. In a Dutch oven over medium heat, heat the oil. Sauté the onion, garlic, and eggplant until the eggplant is softened, about 10 minutes.

3. Drain the farro and add it to the pan. Sauté for 2 minutes. Add the red wine and cook until the wine is absorbed. Add the stock, salt, and pepper and bring to a boil.

4. Reduce heat and simmer, covered, for 30 minutes. Stir before serving.

PER SERVING Calories: 186 | Fat: 6 g | Protein: 6 g | Sodium: 330 mg | Fiber: 2 g | Carbohydrates: 24 g | Sugar: 3 g

Wild Rice with Fennel and Chickpeas

Chickpeas provide texture interest in this chewy wild rice dish.

INGREDIENTS | SERVES 6

2½ cups cooked wild rice
1½ cups cooked chickpeas
2 heads fennel, sliced thinly
1 red onion, sliced thinly
1 avocado, cubed
¼ cup white wine vinegar
3 tablespoons avocado oil
1 tablespoon minced fresh dill
1 tablespoon Dijon mustard
1 teaspoon yellow mustard seed
1 teaspoon sea salt
1 teaspoon freshly ground black pepper

1. In a large bowl, toss together the wild rice, chickpeas, fennel, and onion. Stir in the avocado.

2. In a small bowl, whisk together the vinegar, avocado oil, dill, mustard, mustard seed, sea salt, and pepper. Pour over the wild rice mixture. Toss lightly. Serve immediately.

PER SERVING Calories: 377 | Fat: 15 g | Protein: 13 g | Sodium: 440 mg | Fiber: 13 g | Carbohydrates: 50 g | Sugar: 7 g

Savory Grits

Grits can be made with heavy cream and lots of cheese, but these are made with lots of vegetables instead.

INGREDIENTS | SERVES 6

2 tablespoons olive oil

2 stalks celery, diced

2 shallots, minced

2 cloves garlic, minced

1 carrot, diced

1 parsnip, peeled and diced

2¼ cups chicken or vegetable stock

½ cup old-fashioned grits

2 tablespoons tarragon vinegar

1 tablespoon thyme leaves

½ teaspoon sea salt

1. Heat the oil in a skillet. Add the celery, shallots, garlic, carrot, and parsnip and sauté until the carrot and parsnip are softened, about 5–15 minutes.

2. Meanwhile, bring the stock to boil in a medium pot. Add the grits and stir continuously for 10 minutes or until all of the liquid is absorbed.

3. Remove from heat and stir in the cooked vegetables, vinegar, thyme, and salt.

PER SERVING Calories: 148 | Fat: 5 g | Protein: 4 g | Sodium: 293 mg | Fiber: 2 g | Carbohydrates: 22 g | Sugar: 2 g

How to Sauté

Sautéing is a method of cooking when food is cooked in a small amount of fat and is kept moving by using a spatula or spoon or even by flipping the pans. This makes the food cook evenly and quickly. When sautéing, the food should all be able to fit in the pan in a single layer.

Blackberry-Flax Muffins

Flax adds a buttery flavor to these muffins without using butter.

INGREDIENTS | SERVES 12

1½ cups white whole-wheat flour
¼ cup flaxseed meal
1 teaspoon baking powder
1 teaspoon baking soda
½ teaspoon ground ginger
½ cup dark brown sugar
½ cup buttermilk
½ cup canola oil
1 teaspoon vanilla
1¾ cups fresh blackberries

Limiting Pesticide Exposure

Some fruits absorb pesticides more easily than others. Buy organic versions of these fruits to cut your consumption of pesticides. Peaches, nectarines, apples, strawberries, cherries, grapes, plums, and pears all have soft, edible skins that soak up pesticides.

1. Preheat oven to 350°F. Line or grease and flour 12 wells in a muffin tin.

2. In a medium bowl, whisk together flour, flaxseed meal, baking powder, baking soda, ginger, and brown sugar.

3. In a small bowl, whisk together buttermilk, oil, and vanilla until well combined. Pour into the dry ingredients and stir until just mixed. Fold in blackberries.

4. Evenly divide the batter among the wells in the muffin tin. Bake 20 minutes or until a toothpick inserted in the center of the center muffin comes out clean.

PER SERVING Calories: 198 | Fat: 10 g | Protein: 3 g | Sodium: 159 mg | Fiber: 2 g | Carbohydrates: 24 g | Sugar: 10 g

Brooklyn Roll

This twist on the classic kasha knish is attractive and festive enough to serve at a party; when cut it looks like a pinwheel.

INGREDIENTS | SERVES 16

5 tablespoons unsalted butter or schmaltz, divided use

1 large onion, chopped

1¼ cups chopped crimini mushrooms

4 eggs, divided use

1 cup kasha

2 cups beef stock

1 cup mashed potatoes

1½ teaspoons salt, divided use

1 teaspoon freshly ground black pepper

2½ cups all-purpose flour

1 cup white whole-wheat flour

1 teaspoon baking powder

½ cup low-fat plain Greek yogurt

Using Stocks

Always use or make unsalted stocks. This will help cut down on the sodium content of the final dish. Instead of salt, simmer the stock with spices and herbs that will complement the meal before using.

1. Melt 2 tablespoons butter in a skillet over medium heat. Leave the remaining 3 tablespoons on the counter to soften. Sauté the onion and mushrooms until browned, about 5–15 minutes.

2. In a small bowl, mix 1 egg into the kasha. Add the kasha to the mushroom mixture and sauté until the kernels start to separate, about 5–15 minutes. Add the stock. Cover and cook until the stock is absorbed.

3. Stir in the mashed potato, 1 teaspoon salt, and pepper. Remove from heat and stir in 2 eggs.

4. Preheat oven to 350°F. Line a baking sheet with parchment paper. Set aside. In a large bowl, whisk together the flours, baking powder, and remaining ½ teaspoon salt. Set aside.

5. In a medium bowl, whisk together the yogurt and remaining 3 tablespoons softened butter. Add the flour and yogurt mixtures to the bowl of a stand mixer. Using the dough hook, mix them together until a uniform dough forms. Split the dough in half.

6. Roll out each half of the dough on a floured surface until it is ⅛-inch thick. Evenly divide the kasha mixture and spread it on the dough, leaving a 1-inch margin on each side. Use a spatula to smooth the mixture to a uniform thickness. Roll the dough from the long side into a tight spiral. Pinch the ends shut.

7. Beat the last egg in a small bowl. Brush the tops of both rolls. Bake 30 minutes or until fully cooked and golden brown. Slice and serve.

PER SERVING Calories: 207 | Fat: 6 g | Protein: 7 g | Sodium: 368 mg | Fiber: 2 g | Carbohydrates: 32 g | Sugar: 1 g

CHAPTER 14

Snacks and Appetizers

Sour Cherry Granola

Dried sour cherries are a great way to bring the summer home any time of the year.

INGREDIENTS | SERVES 8

5 cups old-fashioned rolled oats
5 ounces dried sour cherries
⅔ cup slivered almonds
¼ cup hulled sunflower seeds
⅓ cup agave nectar
¼ cup unsalted butter, melted and cooled slightly

Dry Your Own Cherries

Dried sour cherries are a great way to bring the flavors of summer home any time of the year. Dehydrators are about $40 but it is worth the investment if one is a dried fruit fan. To dry cherries, de-stem and pit the cherries. Place the cherries on the dehydrator tray, leaving a ¼-inch space between them. Dehydrate for about 6 hours.

1. Preheat oven to 300°F. Line a baking sheet with parchment paper.

2. Place all of the dry ingredients in a large bowl.

3. Whisk together the agave nectar and butter in a small bowl. Drizzle over the dry ingredients. Stir to coat.

4. Arrange the mixture in a thin layer on the pan. Bake 25–35 minutes or until lightly golden, stirring every 10 minutes. Cool completely. Eat immediately or store in an airtight container.

PER SERVING Calories: 368 | Fat: 15 g | Protein: 10 g | Sodium: 5 mg | Fiber: 7 g | Carbohydrates: 51 g | Sugar: 15 g

Sweet and Spicy Almonds

. Tastes like dessert but it is actually an excellent source of good fats and protein.

INGREDIENTS | SERVES 8

1 tablespoon olive oil
2 cups whole almonds
1 tablespoon sugar
1 teaspoon cayenne pepper
1 teaspoon chipotle powder
½ teaspoon chili powder

Awesome Almonds

Almonds are an excellent source of vitamin E, a powerful antioxidant that helps protect the skin from oxygen free radicals. Almonds are also a good source of fiber. 100 grams of almonds also contains 25 percent of the daily recommended dose of calcium.

1. Preheat the oven to 250°F. Line two baking sheets with parchment paper.

2. Toss all ingredients together. Make sure the nuts are evenly coated.

3. Arrange in a single layer on 1 of the baking sheets and bake for 25 minutes, or until the almonds look mostly dry, stirring every 5 minutes.

4. Remove from the oven. Pour onto the remaining lined baking sheet to cool.

PER SERVING Calories: 158 | Fat: 13 g | Protein: 5 g | Sodium: 0.3 mg | Fiber: 3 g | Carbohydrates: 7 g | Sugar: 3 g

Boiled Peanuts

Protein-rich hot boiled peanuts have been a staple snack in the South for decades.

INGREDIENTS | SERVES 8

8 cups water

1 pound green (raw) peanuts, in shells

2 tablespoons kosher salt

What Is Kosher Salt?

Kosher salt is a coarse, flaky salt. Its name came from its use in the koshering of meat. It does not contain added iodine. Many cooks prefer to use it because it is easier to take pinches of it to add to a dish than table salt.

1. Bring the water to a boil in a large, lidded stockpot over medium heat. Add the peanuts and salt. Bring to a boil again. Cover. Cook for 2–5 hours or until desired softness is reached, checking periodically to make sure the water has not evaporated. Add additional water as needed.

2. Drain. Eat within 48 hours.

PER SERVING Calories: 315 | Fat: 27 g | Protein: 14 g | Sodium: 1,774 mg | Fiber: 5 g | Carbohydrates: 9 g | Sugar: 2 g

Fresh Ricotta–Topped Crostini

Peppery radishes top creamy, calcium-rich ricotta for this easy appetizer.

INGREDIENTS | SERVES 8

1 baguette, sliced

10 ounces fresh ricotta

12 red radishes, thinly sliced

½ cup chopped chives

Viva Ricotta

Ricotta is an Italian cheese-like product traditionally made from the whey leftover from cheese making. Technically it is not a true cheese because it is not produced by coagulation of casein, but it is treated as such in recipes. It can also be made at home using whole milk and buttermilk.

1. Preheat oven to 300°F.

2. Place the baguette slices in a single layer on a baking sheet. Bake for 5 minutes or until lightly toasted. Remove from oven and allow to cool.

3. Spread the baguette slices with fresh ricotta. Top with radish slices. Sprinkle with chives.

PER SERVING Calories: 103 | Fat: 5 g | Protein: 6 g | Sodium: 123 mg | Fiber: 1 g | Carbohydrates: 9 g | Sugar: 1 g

Perfect Popcorn

High in fiber, low in fat, popcorn is the perfect whole-grain snack.
Making it at home is a breeze. No microwave required!

INGREDIENTS | SERVES 4

3 tablespoons canola oil
⅓ cup popcorn kernels

Popcorn Suggestions

Popcorn can be flavored with nearly anything! If using air-popped popcorn, a drizzle of butter will help the spices adhere. Try topping it with Chesapeake Bay Seasoning; Parmesan; popcorn salt; chopped chives; chile powder and lime zest; or brewer's yeast.

1. Heat the oil in a 3-quart lidded saucepan. Test the temperature by tossing a few kernels in. If they pop, the oil is ready. Add the rest of the popcorn. Cover.

2. Once the popcorn starts to pop, carefully shake the pan by sliding it back and forth over the burner.

3. Once the popcorn stops popping in earnest, and there are several seconds between pops, remove from heat and pour into a bowl. Add desired toppings.

PER SERVING Calories: 125 | Fat: 11 g | Protein: 1 g | Sodium: 1 mg | Fiber: 1 g | Carbohydrates: 7 g | Sugar: 0 g

Goat Cheese–Stuffed Dates

Gooey dates are the perfect foil for the zesty, savory filling.

INGREDIENTS | SERVES 6–8

½ pound pitted Medjool dates

4 ounces soft goat cheese, at room temperature

2 tablespoons lemon zest

¼ teaspoon salt

¼ teaspoon ground culinary lavender

Darling Dates

One serving of Medjool dates contains 3 grams of fiber and is a great source of potassium, iron, magnesium, and calcium. Despite their sweetness, their glycemic index is only a 9. They also contain the anti-oxidants zeaxanthin, lutein, and beta carotene.

1. Slice each date lengthwise to make an opening without cutting all the way through. Set aside.

2. In a small bowl, stir together the cheese, zest, salt, and lavender. Spoon an equal amount into each date. Serve immediately or refrigerate.

PER SERVING Calories: 142 | Fat: 5 g | Protein: 5 g | Sodium: 123 mg | Fiber: 2 g | Carbohydrates: 21 g | Sugar: 18 g

Classic Hummus

Try this protein-rich spread as a dip for raw vegetables at your next party.

INGREDIENTS | SERVES 20

20 ounces warm, cooked chickpeas

3 cloves garlic

¼ cup lemon juice

3½ tablespoons tahini

3 tablespoons olive oil

¼ teaspoon cumin

¼ teaspoon smoked paprika

¼ teaspoon garlic powder

Place all ingredients in a food processor and purée. Add water or additional lemon juice as needed to create a smooth mixture.

PER SERVING Calories: 135 | Fat: 5 g | Protein: 6 g | Sodium: 10 mg | Fiber: 5 g | Carbohydrates: 18 g | Sugar: 3 g

Homemade Tahini

The sesame paste tahini is fairly easy to find in stores but can be quite expensive. However, it can be made at home if one has a powerful food processor or blender. Simply blend together 1½ cups toasted sesame seeds (look for them in bulk) and ¼ cup olive oil until as smooth as possible. Refrigerate.

Watermelon-Mozzarella Skewers

This simple summer recipe is surprisingly complex tasting.

INGREDIENTS | SERVES 20

20 (1-inch) cubes seedless watermelon
20 small balls fresh mozzarella
20 slices speck
20 large basil leaves

1. On a small skewer, thread 1 watermelon cube on then 1 mozzarella ball. Fold the speck in half and thread that on as well. Fold the basil leaf and attach to the end of the skewer.

2. Repeat for remaining skewers.

PER SERVING Calories: 133 | Fat: 9 g | Protein: 11 g | Sodium: 534 mg | Fiber: 0 g | Carbohydrates: 2 g | Sugar: 1 g

Homemade Pita Chips

Tastier and more affordable than store-bought, these chips are great with hummus and many dips.

INGREDIENTS | SERVES 24

12 pitas, each cut into 8 triangles
⅓ cup olive oil
½ teaspoon sea salt
½ teaspoon freshly ground black pepper
½ teaspoon dried parsley
½ teaspoon dried basil
¼ teaspoon hot paprika

1. Preheat oven to 400°F. Line 2 baking sheets with parchment paper.

2. Arrange the pita wedges in a single layer on the sheets. Set aside.

3. Stir together the oil and spices. Brush the top of each triangle with the seasoned oil. Bake for 5–8 minutes or until crispy.

PER SERVING Calories: 109 | Fat: 3 g | Protein: 3 g | Sodium: 210 mg | Fiber: 1 g | Carbohydrates: 17 g | Sugar: 0 g

White Bean Artichoke Dip

No one would believe this protein-packed dip is so low in fat.

INGREDIENTS | SERVES 20

1 pound cooked cannellini beans

14 ounces fresh or defrosted frozen artichoke hearts

2 cloves garlic, minced

1 tablespoon plain Greek yogurt

¼ cup lemon juice

¼ cup feta cheese

2 tablespoons minced fresh dill

1. Place all ingredients in a food processor. Pulse until slightly chunky.

2. To serve cold: refrigerate 1 hour prior to serving. To serve warm: preheat oven to 350°F. Grease or spray with cooking spray a small casserole pan. Bake for 15 minutes or until warmed through. Serve immediately.

PER SERVING Calories: 32 | Fat: 1 g | Protein: 2 g | Sodium: 97 mg | Fiber: 2 g | Carbohydrates: 5 g | Sugar: 1 g

Food Processor FYI

If one is looking just to chop an occasional onion, a small capacity processor would be fine. If one wanted to make large batches of dips or use it for dough and crusts, a larger 12–14 cup capacity is a better choice. Some processors come with special features like a juicer or slicer attachment.

Shrimp Shiitake Pot Stickers

Homemade pot stickers are easier to make than one might think and unlike their supermarket counterparts, are full of fresh ingredients and preservative free.

INGREDIENTS | SERVES 25

1 egg

1 bunch scallions, minced

4 fresh shiitake mushrooms, minced

2 heads baby bok choy, finely chopped

1 pound raw shrimp, deveined and minced

2 tablespoons sesame oil

2 tablespoons soy sauce

2 tablespoons grated fresh ginger

1½ tablespoons grated garlic

1½ tablespoons cornstarch

1 teaspoon finely ground fresh black pepper

50 round dumpling wrappers

5 cups water

Easy Dumpling Dipping Sauce

Wow guests with this homemade sauce. Simply whisk together ¼ cup soy sauce, ¼ cup rice wine vinegar, 1½ teaspoon sesame oil, and ½ teaspoon chile garlic sauce. Garnish with chopped scallions if desired.

1. In a large bowl, combine the egg, scallions, mushrooms, bok choy, shrimp, sesame oil, soy sauce, ginger, garlic, cornstarch, and pepper to form a uniform mixture.

2. Place a dumpling wrapper on a plate or clean, dry surface. Place a teaspoon of filling in the center of the dumpling wrapper. Fold the wrapper in half to form a half-moon shape, pinching the wrapper tightly together. Press the "fold" side gently down on the plate so it can stand alone, seam side up. Repeat until all of the filling and wrappers are gone.

3. Heat a small amount of canola oil in a large saucepan over medium heat. Place about 10 pot stickers flat side down and fry until the bottom is browned. Add 1 cup of water, cover immediately. Allow dumplings to steam for about 5–10 minutes.

4. Once the dumplings are fully cooked the water will have fully evaporated and the bottoms will be crisp. Repeat for remaining dumplings.

PER SERVING Calories: 89 | Fat: 2 g | Protein: 7 g | Sodium: 237 mg | Fiber: 1 g | Carbohydrates: 12 g | Sugar: 1 g

Shrimp Cocktail

Making your own cocktail sauce is easy to do and is free of the sugar, preservatives, and high fructose corn syrup found in most commercial brands.

INGREDIENTS | SERVES 12

6 ounces tomato paste

¼ cup white wine vinegar

¼ cup fresh lemon juice

2 cloves garlic

1 shallot

1½ tablespoons Worcestershire sauce

½ teaspoon salt

½ teaspoon freshly ground black pepper

⅓ cup prepared horseradish

2 pounds jumbo shrimp

1. Place the tomato paste, vinegar, lemon juice, garlic, shallot, Worcestershire sauce, salt, and pepper into a food processor. Blend until mostly smooth.

2. Scrape into a small bowl and stir in the horseradish. Refrigerate.

3. Add the shrimp to a lidded saucepan. Add ½ inch of water. Cover and bring to a boil. Cook until the shrimp is pink and cooked through. Peel and devein the shrimp if necessary. Chill.

4. Serve the shrimp and cocktail sauce together.

PER SERVING Calories: 101 | Fat: 1 g | Protein: 16 g | Sodium: 342 mg | Fiber: 0.5 g | Carbohydrates: 5 g | Sugar: 2 g

Smoky, Spicy Deviled Eggs

Deviled eggs get a makeover with yogurt filling in for mayonnaise.

INGREDIENTS | SERVES 24

1 dozen hardboiled eggs

¼ cup plain Greek yogurt

1 tablespoon Dijon mustard

½ teaspoon smoked paprika

¼ teaspoon ground chipotle

⅛ teaspoon white pepper

⅛ teaspoon sea salt

Paprika, for garnish

Did You Know?

Dijon mustard was originally produced in Dijon, France? It was a less acidic mustard made with verjuice, a type of juice made from the unripe grapes of the region, not the harsher vinegars common at the time. Now it is made all over the world, but still must adhere to certain standards in order to be called "Dijon."

1. Peel the eggs. Halve them lengthwise. Place all of the yolks in a small bowl. Set the whites aside. Mash the yolks with a potato masher until fluffy.

2. In a small bowl, whisk together the yogurt, mustard, and spices. Scrape the mixture into the bowl of yolks. Use a fork to beat it into the yolks until smooth.

3. Pipe or spoon the mixture into the whites. Sprinkle with paprika.

PER SERVING Calories: 38 | Fat: 3 g | Protein: 3 g | Sodium: 56 mg | Fiber: 0 g | Carbohydrates: 0 g | Sugar: 0.3 g

Cinnamon Toasted Pumpkin Seeds

A twist on the classic salted pumpkin seeds of yesteryear.

INGREDIENTS | SERVES 12

2 cups fresh pumpkin seeds

¼ cup sea salt

3 tablespoons olive oil

2 tablespoons Saigon Cinnamon

1 teaspoon ground ginger

½ teaspoon ground cloves

¼ teaspoon ground allspice

Pumpkin Power!

Pumpkin seeds are more than something to throw away prior to carving a jack-o'-lantern. Also known as pepitas, they are a low-calorie snack that is high in manganese, magnesium, iron, zinc, and protein. Omega-3 fats, (healthy fat), are also found in pumpkin seeds.

1. Preheat oven to 350°F.

2. Place the pumpkin seeds in a large pot. Fill halfway with water. Add salt. Bring to a boil. Boil for 10 minutes. Drain thoroughly.

3. Drizzle the seeds with olive oil, toss to coat. Sprinkle with spices. Toss again to distribute the spices.

4. Line a baking sheet with parchment paper. Arrange the seeds in a single layer on the baking sheet. Bake for 15 minutes. Stir the seeds. Bake an additional 5 minutes or until they are toasted. Cool prior to serving.

PER SERVING Calories: 162 | Fat: 15 g | Protein: 7 g | Sodium: 2,359 mg | Fiber: 2 g | Carbohydrates: 3 g | Sugar: 0.3 g

Texas Caviar

Don't let the name fool you; this regional specialty isn't caviar, it is a black-eyed pea salad that is eaten with a fork or scooped up with a tortilla chip.

INGREDIENTS | SERVES 12

4 cups cooked black-eyed peas

4 stalks celery, diced

3 cubanelle peppers, diced

1 red bell pepper, diced

1 red onion, diced

2 cloves garlic, minced

1 tomato, diced

1 bunch green onion, chopped

¼ cup chopped Italian parsley

½ cup olive oil

⅓ cup lime juice

1 tablespoon red hot sauce

3 tablespoons minced cilantro

1 tablespoon Worcestershire sauce

1 tablespoon minced oregano

½ teaspoon sea salt

½ teaspoon freshly ground black pepper

1. In a large bowl, toss together the black-eyed peas, celery, peppers, red onion, garlic, tomato, green onion, and parsley. Set aside.

2. Whisk together the remaining ingredients in a small bowl. Pour over the salad. Toss to distribute the dressing. Refrigerate 3–5 hours before serving.

PER SERVING Calories: 162 | Fat: 9 g | Protein: 5 g | Sodium: 293 mg | Fiber: 5 g | Carbohydrates: 16 g | Sugar: 4 g

Give Cubanelles a Chance

Technically a sweet pepper, cubanelle peppers have a spicy kick to them. You can identify them by their yellow-green color and slightly wrinkled appearance. They are about the same size as poblano peppers. Use them instead of bland bell peppers.

Stilton-Stuffed Endive

Belgian endive is rich in folate as well vitamins A and K, making this elegant appetizer a healthful choice.

INGREDIENTS | SERVES 10

4 endives
½ cup roasted almonds
½ cup dried tart cherries
1½ cups crumbled Stilton cheese
½ tablespoon minced fresh rosemary
¼ teaspoon sea salt
¼ teaspoon freshly ground black pepper

1. Cut the ends off the endive. Separate out the leaves and arrange them on a platter.

2. In a small bowl, gently mix together the almonds, cherries, Stilton, rosemary, salt, and pepper.

3. Evenly distribute the mixture among the leaves, placing it on the wider end. Serve immediately.

PER SERVING Calories: 108 | Fat: 8 g | Protein: 6 g | Sodium: 342 mg | Fiber: 1 g | Carbohydrates: 4 g | Sugar: 1 g

Tomato-Pea Crostini

Try to make this crostini during that brief, shining moment in summer when both fresh peas and tomatoes are in-season.

INGREDIENTS | SERVES 12

12 slices of baguette bread
1 cup fresh peas
¼ cup minced fresh basil
½ teaspoon sea salt
½ teaspoon freshly ground black pepper
12 plum tomatoes, sliced
¼ cup shaved Parmesan

1. Preheat oven to 300°F. Place the baguette slices in a single layer on a baking sheet. Bake for 5 minutes or until lightly toasted. Remove from oven and allow to fully cool.

2. In a small bowl, mash together the peas, basil, salt, and pepper. Spread on each of the toasts.

3. Top with tomato slices and a bit of shaved Parmesan.

PER SERVING Calories: 129 | Fat: 1 g | Protein: 6 g | Sodium: 331 mg | Fiber: 3 g | Carbohydrates: 25 g | Sugar: 5 g

Citrus Scallop Crudo

Thai-influenced flavors give this classic Italian dish new life.

INGREDIENTS | SERVES 6

¼ cup fresh blood orange juice

¼ cup fresh lemon juice

2 tablespoons lime juice

1 tablespoon ginger juice

1 tablespoon cane vinegar

1 tablespoon extra-virgin olive oil

½ teaspoon salt

1 Thai Bird's Eye pepper, sliced

¾ pound sea scallops, thinly sliced

¼ cup sliced Thai basil

¼ cup diced scallions

1. Whisk together the orange juice, lemon juice, lime juice, ginger juice, cane vinegar, oil, salt, and pepper in a small bowl. Pour into a large, shallow, rimmed platter.

2. Arrange the scallop slices over the dressing. Sprinkle with basil and scallions. Serve immediately.

PER SERVING Calories: 81 | Fat: 3 g | Protein: 10 g | Sodium: 290 mg | Fiber: 0 g | Carbohydrates: 4 g | Sugar: 2 g

What Is Crudo?

Crudo is the general term for an Italian raw fish dish. It typically contains sea salt, olive oil and citrus juice. When making crudo take care to use the freshest fish possible from a reputable fishmonger. Although the fish "cooks" slightly in the acidic juice, it is better to be safe than sorry.

Grilled Soy-Glazed Tofu

Grilling tofu leaves it with a crispy outside and a creamy center.

INGREDIENTS | SERVES 8

16 ounces firm tofu, cut into 8 planks

⅓ cup soy sauce

1 tablespoon chile garlic sauce

⅓ cup rice vinegar

⅓ cup mirin

2 tablespoons sesame oil

4 cloves minced garlic

2 tablespoons minced fresh ginger

2 tablespoons lime juice

2 tablespoons minced shallot

Chef Anthony Bourdain on Shallots

In his memoir *Kitchen Confidential,* Anthony Bourdain called the shallot a necessary food item. "You almost never see this item in a home kitchen, but out in the world they're an essential ingredient. Shallots are one of the things—a basic prep item in every mise-en-place—that make restaurant food taste different from your food. In my kitchen, we use nearly twenty pounds a day." Use shallots!

1. Place the tofu in a resealable container. Set aside.

2. Whisk together the soy sauce, chile garlic sauce, rice vinegar, mirin, sesame oil, garlic, ginger, lime juice, and shallot in a small bowl. Pour over the tofu. Seal the container and marinate at least 2 hours or up to 3 hours.

3. Prep grill to manufacturer's directions. Place each plank of tofu on its own skewer. Grill, turning once, until golden brown, about 3–10 minutes.

4. Use the leftover marinade as a dipping sauce if desired.

PER SERVING Calories: 79 | Fat: 5 g | Protein: 5 g | Sodium: 621 mg | Fiber: 0 g | Carbohydrates: 4 g | Sugar: 1 g

Raw Oysters with Mignonette Sauce

This is the classic way to serve raw oysters.

INGREDIENTS | SERVES 12

24 raw, in-shell oysters

½ cup red wine vinegar

1 large shallot, minced

1 tablespoon freshly ground coarse black pepper

⅛ teaspoon salt

Oh, the Oyster!

More than just a rumored aphrodisiac, oysters are a healthy choice. Oysters are an excellent source of calcium, zinc, iron, and vitamins A and B_{12}. To receive the maximum health benefits, oysters are best consumed raw.

1. Line a plate with ice. Shuck the oysters and arrange them on the half shell on the ice.

2. In a small bowl, whisk together the vinegar, shallot, pepper, and salt. Pour into a ramekin and place it beside the oysters.

PER SERVING Calories: 28 | Fat: 1 g | Protein: 2 g | Sodium: 86 mg | Fiber: 0 g | Carbohydrates: 3 g | Sugar: 0 g

CHAPTER 15

Ice Pops, Granitas, and Sorbets

Blackberry-Yogurt Pops

These ice pops are attractive and nutritious. Blackberries are an excellent source of fiber, vitamin C, vitamin K, and folic acid.

INGREDIENTS | SERVES 6

2 cups plain yogurt
½ cup sugar
½ cup puréed blackberries

Crack the Ice Pop Code

The secret to a good ice pop is simple: sugar. Sugar lowers the freezing point of the pop so it stays soft and smooth, not brittle like an ice cube. So resist the urge to fully eliminate sugar from ice pop recipes that call for it.

1. In a medium bowl, whisk together the sugar and yogurt until the sugar dissolves.

2. Divide half of the yogurt mixture between 6 ice pop molds. Evenly divide all of the blackberry purée between the six ice pop molds. Top with remaining yogurt mixture.

3. Insert pop sticks and freeze until solid.

PER SERVING Calories: 120 | Fat: 3 g | Protein: 3 g | Sodium: 37 mg | Fiber: 1 g | Carbohydrates: 22 g | Sugar: 21 g

Watermelon-Lime Ice Pops

Lime tempers the super sweetness of watermelon without overpowering it.

INGREDIENTS | SERVES 6

2 pounds seedless watermelon, puréed
½ cup lime juice
1½ tablespoons lime zest
⅓ cup sugar

1. Whisk together all ingredients in a medium bowl until the sugar dissolves.

2. Evenly divide the mixture between 6 (3-ounce) ice pop molds.

3. Insert the pop sticks. Freeze until solid.

PER SERVING Calories: 92 | Fat: 0 g | Protein: 1 g | Sodium: 6 mg | Fiber: 1 g | Carbohydrates: 24 g | Sugar: 21 g

Pineapple Ice Pops

Fruity, tropical pineapple gets a savory, spicy touch from Chinese five spice powder.

INGREDIENTS | SERVES 6

3 cups fresh pineapple chunks
½ teaspoon Chinese five-spice powder
¼ cup sugar
¼ cup pineapple juice

Easy Ice Pops
Depending on the ice pop, it can take from 2–6 hours for them to freeze completely. Resist the urge to unmold the pops before fully frozen. To unmold ice pops, run the outside of the container under warm water for 2–5 seconds.

1. Place all ingredients in a blender and blend until smooth.

2. Evenly divide among 6 (3-ounce) ice pop molds.

3. Freeze until solid.

PER SERVING Calories: 79 | Fat: 0 g | Protein: 0 g | Sodium: 1 mg | Fiber: 1 g | Carbohydrates: 21 g | Sugar: 18 g

Pomegranate-Grape Pops

Fresh pomegranate juice is a sweet-tart no-sugar-added delight! Combined with the pop of the grapes, this is an uncommon treat.

INGREDIENTS | SERVES 6

2½ cups fresh pomegranate juice
1 cup sugar
2 cups water
1 cup halved red grapes

1. In a large bowl, stir together the juice, sugar, and water until the sugar fully dissolves. Stir in the grapes.

2. Pour into 6 (3-ounce) ice pop molds.

3. Freeze until solid.

PER SERVING Calories: 203 | Fat: 0 g | Protein: 0 g | Sodium: 10 mg | Fiber: 0 g | Carbohydrates: 51 g | Sugar: 51 g

Tropical Fruit Bowl Ice Pops

These ice pops are as pretty as they are tasty. The fruit looks like it is floating in ice.

INGREDIENTS | SERVES 6

1 Alphonso mango, peeled and cut into ½-inch slices

2 kiwis, peeled and cut into thin rounds

2 starfruit, cut into ¼-inch thick slices

⅓ cup diced papaya

2 cups coconut water

What Is Coconut Water?

Not to be confused with coconut milk or cream of coconut, coconut water is the thin liquid that is found in the center of a fresh young coconut. It has a very high potassium content and is full of electrolytes. In countries where coconuts are native it is often served, with a straw, still in the coconut. Alternatively, look for it in bottles or pouches at the grocery store.

1. Arrange the fruit snugly into 6 (3-ounce) ice pop molds. No fruit should extend above the fill line.

2. Pour the coconut water into each mold to cover the fruit.

3. Freeze until solid.

PER SERVING Calories: 66 | Fat: 0 g | Protein: 1 g | Sodium: 87 mg | Fiber: 3 g | Carbohydrates: 15 g | Sugar: 9 g

Mango-Chile Paletas

Paletas are a Latin American ice pop. They are made with fresh fruit and often include spices.

INGREDIENTS | SERVES 6

1 pound diced mango
1 dried chile guajillo, freshly ground
¾ cup lime juice
1 teaspoon ground cayenne
2 tablespoons sugar

Using Dried Peppers

Although it may seem that fresh is better, dried peppers have their place. They can have a richer, deeper flavor than their fresh counterparts. You can grind them into spice or rehydrate them in hot water for use in many recipes.

1. Add ¾ of the mango, chile guajillo, lime juice, cayenne, and sugar in blender and pulse until almost smooth.

2. Stir in the mango chunks. Divide among 6 (3-ounce) ice pop molds.

3. Freeze until solid.

PER SERVING Calories: 68 | Fat: 0 g | Protein: 1 g | Sodium: 2 mg | Fiber: 1 g | Carbohydrates: 17 g | Sugar: 16 g

Mexican Chocolate Sorbet

Sorbet is the perfect guilt-free alternative to ice cream.

INGREDIENTS | SERVES 4

½ cup cocoa powder
1 cup sugar
¼ teaspoon Mexican cinnamon
¼ teaspoon ground cayenne
2 cups water
¼ teaspoon vanilla

1. In a small bowl, whisk together the cocoa powder, sugar, Mexican cinnamon, and cayenne. Pour into a heavy-bottomed saucepan. Add the water and vanilla.

2. Cook over medium heat, stirring continuously until the cocoa and sugar are fully dissolved. Refrigerate until cold.

3. Pour the mixture into an ice cream or sorbet maker and churn according to manufacturer's instructions.

PER SERVING Calories: 220 | Fat: 1 g | Protein: 2 g | Sodium: 3 mg | Fiber: 4 g | Carbohydrates: 56 g | Sugar: 50 g

Strawberry Granita

Fresh strawberries add flavor, fiber, and a beautiful pink color to this granita.

INGREDIENTS | SERVES 4

1 cup water
1 cup sugar
4 cups whole strawberries

What Is a Granita?

Originally from Sicily, granitas are a popular Italian treat. Similar to Italian ices, granitas are also made from sugar, water and flavorings. Unlike Italian ices, however, they are made with flavored liquid, rather than plain ice simply doused with flavoring. Their texture should be flaky and granular, not too chunky or icy.

1. Bring the water and sugar to a boil in a medium saucepan. Boil, stirring occasionally, until it reduces and thickens into a light syrup, about 10–20 minutes. Remove from heat and allow to fully cool.

2. Pour the syrup into a blender. Add the strawberries. Pulse until smooth.

3. Pour the mixture into a 13" × 9" metal pan. Freeze for 20 minutes.

4. Remove from the freezer and rake any frozen bits with a fork. Return to the freezer for 20 additional minutes.

5. Remove from the freezer and rake any frozen bits with a fork. Freeze for an additional 30 minutes.

6. Remove from the freezer and rake again. Serve.

PER SERVING Calories: 198 | Fat: 0 g | Protein: 0 g | Sodium: 1 mg | Fiber: 0 g | Carbohydrates: 51 g | Sugar: 51 g

Espresso Granita

*On hot summer days in Italy, coffee granitas are sold in cafés at breakfast
time as a change of pace from the regular hot espresso.*

INGREDIENTS | SERVES 6

2 cups cooled espresso
⅓ cup sugar
½ tablespoon cocoa powder

1. In a medium bowl, whisk together all of the ingredients until the sugar and cocoa power are fully dissolved.

2. Pour the mixture into a 13" × 9" metal pan. Freeze for 20 minutes.

3. Remove from the freezer and rake any frozen bits with a fork. Return to the freezer for 20 additional minutes.

4. Remove from the freezer and rake any frozen bits with a fork. Freeze for an additional 30 minutes.

5. Remove from the freezer and rake again. Serve.

PER SERVING Calories: 46 | Fat: 0 g | Protein: 0 g | Sodium: 11 mg | Fiber: 0 g | Carbohydrates: 11 g | Sugar: 11 g

Coconut-Lime Granita

Coconut milk adds rich creaminess to this granita.

INGREDIENTS | SERVES 4

1 cup water
1 cup sugar
14 ounces coconut milk
¼ cup fresh lime juice
2 tablespoons lime zest

1. Bring the water and sugar to a boil in a medium saucepan. Boil, stirring occasionally, until it reduces and thickens into light syrup. Remove from heat and allow to fully cool.

2. Whisk the coconut milk, lime juice, and zest into the syrup until smooth.

3. Pour the mixture into a 13" × 9" metal pan. Freeze for 20 minutes.

4. Remove from the freezer and rake any frozen bits with a fork. Return to the freezer for 20 additional minutes.

5. Remove from the freezer and rake any frozen bits with a fork. Freeze for an additional 30 minutes.

6. Remove from the freezer and rake again. Serve.

PER SERVING Calories: 391 | Fat: 21 g | Protein: 2 g | Sodium: 16 mg | Fiber: 0 g | Carbohydrates: 54 g | Sugar: 51 g

Blood Orange Granita

There are many varieties of blood oranges available in the market today. Use your favorite to make this granita.

INGREDIENTS | SERVES 4

2 cups fresh blood orange juice

2 tablespoons blood orange zest

¼ cup sugar

2 tablespoons orange liquor

Choosing an Ice Cream Maker

Ice cream makers can vary greatly in price and features. The simplest are the old-fashioned crank models. Mid-range machines generally have a removable insert that has to be frozen in the freezer prior to use. High-end models have a compressor that cools the ice cream quickly in the machine itself.

1. In a medium bowl, whisk together all of the ingredients until the sugar is fully dissolved.

2. Pour the mixture into a 13" × 9" metal pan. Freeze for 20 minutes.

3. Remove from the freezer and rake any frozen bits with a fork.

4. Return to the freezer for 20 additional minutes. Remove from the freezer and rake any frozen bits with a fork.

5. Freeze for an additional 30 minutes. Remove from the freezer and rake again. Serve.

PER SERVING Calories: 126 | Fat: 0 g | Protein: 1 g | Sodium: 3 mg | Fiber: 0 g | Carbohydrates: 27 g | Sugar: 23 g

Ginger Granita

Think of this as an icy, dessert version of ginger beer.

Fresh Ginger Made Easy

Cut off the desired amount of ginger. Cut off any dried-out ends. Press the edge of a spoon on the top edge of the ginger and rake along the root to the bottom to peel. Use a serrated knife to slice.

1. Bring 1 cup water, sugar, and ginger to a boil in a medium saucepan. Boil, stirring occasionally, until it reduces and thickens into light syrup, about 5–20 minutes. Remove from heat and allow to fully cool. Discard the ginger slices. Stir in remaining water.

2. Pour the mixture into a 13" × 9" metal pan. Freeze for 20 minutes.

3. Remove from the freezer and rake any frozen bits with a fork. Return to the freezer for 20 additional minutes.

4. Remove from the freezer and rake any frozen bits with a fork. Freeze for an additional 30 minutes.

5. Remove from the freezer and rake again. Serve.

PER SERVING Calories: 211 | Fat: 0 g | Protein: 0 g | Sodium: 3 mg | Fiber: 0 g | Carbohydrates: 54 g | Sugar: 51 g

Kiwi Granita

Kiwis are easy to peel. Just slice them in half and pop the insides out with a spoon!

INGREDIENTS | SERVES 6

2 cups water, divided use
1 cup sugar
2 tablespoons lime juice
6 kiwi, peeled

1. Bring 1 cup water and sugar to a boil in a medium saucepan. Boil, stirring occasionally, until it reduces and thickens into a light syrup, about 5–20 minutes. Remove from heat and allow to fully cool. Stir in the remaining water.

2. Pour the mixture into a blender. Add the lime juice and kiwi. Pulse until very, very smooth. If desired, whisk the mixture through a mesh metal sieve to remove the seeds.

3. Pour the mixture into a 13" × 9" metal pan. Freeze for 20 minutes.

4. Remove from the freezer and rake any frozen bits with a fork. Return to the freezer for 20 additional minutes.

5. Remove from the freezer and rake any frozen bits with a fork. Freeze for an additional 30 minutes.

6. Remove from the freezer and rake again. Serve.

PER SERVING Calories: 177 | Fat: 0 g | Protein: 1 g | Sodium: 5 mg | Fiber: 3 g | Carbohydrates: 45 g | Sugar: 34 g

Blueberry-Mint Granita

Mint has natural breath freshening properties that your dining companions are sure to appreciate!

INGREDIENTS | SERVES 6

2⅓ cups fresh blueberries
½ cup sugar
¾ cup water
2 teaspoons lemon juice
1 tablespoon minced fresh mint

1. Place the blueberries in a food processor. Purée until smooth. Scrape into a metal mesh sieve and whisk the blueberries into a bowl. Discard the skins left in the sieve. Set the blueberry purée aside.

2. In a small bowl, whisk the sugar into the water until it dissolves. Pour the mixture into the blender.

3. Add the blueberry purée, lemon juice, and mint. Pulse until smooth.

4. Pour the mixture into a 13" × 9" metal pan. Freeze for 20 minutes.

5. Remove from the freezer and rake any frozen bits with a fork. Return to the freezer for 20 additional minutes.

6. Remove from the freezer and rake any frozen bits with a fork. Freeze for an additional 30 minutes.

7. Remove from the freezer and rake again. Serve.

PER SERVING Calories: 117 | Fat: 1 g | Protein: 1 g | Sodium: 6 mg | Fiber: 2 g | Carbohydrates: 27 g | Sugar: 22 g

Basil Sorbet

Try this herby sorbet as a palate cleanser or as dessert.

INGREDIENTS | SERVES 4

¾ cup water

⅔ cup chopped basil

3 tablespoons agave nectar

1 tablespoon ground lemon peel

Sweet Facts about Agave Nectar

Agave nectar, also known as agave syrup, is a sweetener made from the agave plant. It is about 1.5 times sweeter than sugar. Since it is available in liquid form it can dissolve faster than sugar, making it a popular choice for sweetening beverages. Light agave has the mildest flavor while amber and dark agave have a more pronounced caramel flavor.

1. Place all ingredients in a food processor and pulse until smooth.

2. Pour into an ice cream or sorbet maker and churn according to manufacturer's instructions.

PER SERVING Calories: 51 | Fat: 0 g | Protein: 0 g | Sodium: 1 mg | Fiber: 0 g | Carbohydrates: 14 g | Sugar: 13 g

Raspberry Sorbet

Try this sorbet using red, yellow, or purple raspberries or a combination of all three.

INGREDIENTS | SERVES 6

2 cups water

2 cups sugar

8 cups fresh raspberries

¼ cup lemon juice

1 tablespoon lemon zest

1. Bring the water and sugar to a boil in a medium saucepan. Boil, stirring occasionally, until it reduces and thickens into light syrup, about 5–20 minutes. Remove from heat and allow to fully cool.

2. Place the raspberries, lemon juice, and zest in a food processor. Purée. While the machine is running, stream in the syrup.

3. Pour the mixture into an ice cream or sorbet maker and churn according to manufacturer's instructions.

PER SERVING Calories: 262 | Fat: 0 g | Protein: 0 g | Sodium: 3 mg | Fiber: 0 g | Carbohydrates: 68 g | Sugar: 67 g

Beet Sorbet

This is the ultimate in adult sorbets; rich, creamy, and earthy.

INGREDIENTS | SERVES 6

2 pounds red beets

¼ cup sugar

½ cup balsamic vinegar

1 tablespoon lemon juice

1. Place the beets in a saucepan. Add water and bring to a boil. Boil until the beets are tender, about 20–40 minutes. Remove the beets and allow them to cool. Reserve the beet water. Rub the skins off of the beets with a paper towel.

2. Place the peeled beets, sugar, vinegar, and lemon juice in a food processor. Add some of the beet water as needed to ensure a smooth purée.

3. Pour the mixture into an ice cream or sorbet maker and churn according to manufacturer's instructions.

PER SERVING Calories: 116 | Fat: 0 g | Protein: 3 g | Sodium: 122 mg | Fiber: 4 g | Carbohydrates: 26 g | Sugar: 22 g

Grapefruit Sorbet

Sweet-tart and refreshing, this sorbet is full of vitamin C.

INGREDIENTS | SERVES 6

3 cups fresh pink grapefruit juice

⅔ cup sugar

2 tablespoons water

2 tablespoons gin (optional)

1. In a large bowl, stir all of the ingredients together until the sugar fully dissolves.

2. Pour the mixture into an ice cream or sorbet maker and churn according to manufacturer's instructions.

PER SERVING Calories: 134 | Fat: 0 g | Protein: 1 g | Sodium: 1 mg | Fiber: 0 g | Carbohydrates: 33 g | Sugar: 33 g

Cranberry Sorbet

This is a light, refreshing dessert for the holidays.

INGREDIENTS | SERVES 6

12 ounces fresh cranberries

1 cup sugar

2 cups cranberry juice

¾ cup water

1. Place the cranberries, sugar, juice, and water into a medium saucepan. Bring to a boil. Reduce heat and simmer for 20 minutes. Allow to cool slightly.

2. Whisk through a metal mesh sieve into a large bowl. Refrigerate until cold.

3. Pour the mixture into an ice cream or sorbet maker and churn according to manufacturer's instructions.

PER SERVING Calories: 194 | Fat: 0 g | Protein: 1 g | Sodium: 3 mg | Fiber: 3 g | Carbohydrates: 51 g | Sugar: 46 g

Pluot Sorbet

Bergamot extract gives this sorbet an slightly musky, citrus note.

INGREDIENTS | SERVES 6

⅔ cup sugar

¾ cup water

2½ pounds pluots, stones removed

3 tablespoons lemon juice

¼ tablespoon bergamot extract

Pluot Power

Pluots are a hybrid of plums and apricots. More plum-like than the similar aprium, they feature sweet, juicy flesh and crisp skin. Visually, they look very similar in size, skin, and color to plums. Pluots are an excellent source of vitamin A.

1. Bring the sugar and water to a boil in a medium saucepan. Add the pluots and cook until they are soft, about 10 minutes. Remove from heat and allow to cool to room temperature. Add remaining ingredients.

2. Pour the mixture into a food processor and blend until smooth. Refrigerate until cold.

3. Pour the mixture into an ice cream or sorbet maker and churn according to manufacturer's instructions.

PER SERVING Calories: 174 | Fat: 1 g | Protein: 1 g | Sodium: 2 mg | Fiber: 3 g | Carbohydrates: 44 g | Sugar: 16 g

Desserts

Classic Chocolate Chip Cookies

The addition of white whole-wheat flour adds extra fiber, but these cookies taste like the original.

INGREDIENTS | YIELDS 2 DOZEN

6 tablespoons unsalted butter, at room temperature

¾ cup sugar

1 egg, at room temperature

1 teaspoon vanilla

1 cup white whole-wheat flour

⅓ cup all-purpose flour

½ teaspoon baking powder

¼ teaspoon salt

6 ounces dark chocolate chips

1. Preheat oven to 350°F. Line 2 cookie sheets with parchment paper.

2. In a large bowl, cream together the butter and sugar.

3. Beat in the egg and the vanilla.

4. In a separate bowl, whisk together the flours, baking powder, and salt. Add to the butter mixture and mix until well combined. Fold in chips.

5. Place tablespoons of dough 2 inches apart on the cookie sheets. Bake for 12 minutes or until the top of the cookie is mostly set and the bottoms are golden. Carefully remove to a wire rack and cool completely.

PER SERVING Calories: 114 | Fat: 5 g | Protein: 1 g | Sodium: 38 mg | Fiber: 1 g | Carbohydrates: 16 g | Sugar: 10 g

Blackberry Oatmeal Crisp

Oats get wonderfully crisp and toasty when baked.

INGREDIENTS | SERVES 8

4 cups blackberries

⅓ cup sugar

⅓ cup all-purpose flour

⅓ cup old-fashioned rolled oats

¼ cup unsalted butter, melted and cooled

¼ teaspoon ground cinnamon

¼ teaspoon ground lemon peel

¼ teaspoon nutmeg

¼ teaspoon ground ginger

Bold Blackberries

Blackberries are very high in fiber, vitamins C and K, and folic acid. Blackberries are also high in antioxidants. The seed of the blackberry has fiber and omega-3 oils.

1. Preheat oven to 350°F. Grease an 8" × 8" baking dish.

2. In a medium bowl, toss the berries together with the sugar. Pour into the bottom of the dish.

3. In a separate bowl, whisk together the flour, oats, butter, and spices. Sprinkle over the berries.

4. Bake 35 minutes or until the top is crisp and the berries are bubbling.

PER SERVING Calories: 127 | Fat: 6 g | Protein: 2 g | Sodium: 2 mg | Fiber: 4 g | Carbohydrates: 18 g | Sugar: 12 g

Greek Yogurt Cake

Greek yogurt not only makes this cake moist, it adds a pleasant tang.

INGREDIENTS | SERVES 16

3 eggs, at room temperature

1¼ cups light brown sugar

½ cup unsalted butter, at room temperature

8 ounces low-fat plain Greek yogurt

1 teaspoon vanilla

½ cup milk

2 teaspoons baking powder

¼ teaspoon salt

3 cups all-purpose flour

¼ teaspoon nutmeg

1. Preheat oven to 350°F. Grease and flour a bundt pan.

2. In a large bowl, beat together the eggs, brown sugar, and butter until creamy. Mix in the yogurt, vanilla, and milk.

3. In a separate bowl, whisk together the dry ingredients. Slowly beat them into the wet ingredients.

4. Pour into the prepared pan. Bake 55 minutes or until a knife comes out clean.

5. Cool in the pan on a wire rack for 5 minutes before removing from the pan to cool completely.

PER SERVING Calories: 228 | Fat: 7 g | Protein: 5 g | Sodium: 126 mg | Fiber: 1 g | Carbohydrates: 36 g | Sugar: 18 g

Jelly Roll

The simple sponge jelly roll is a great way to showcase homemade jam.

INGREDIENTS | SERVES 10

⅔ cup all-purpose flour
1 teaspoon baking powder
¼ teaspoon salt
4 eggs, separated
¾ cup sugar, divided use
1½ teaspoons vanilla
8 ounces jam

1. Preheat oven to 375°F. Grease a jelly-roll pan. Line the pan with parchment paper and grease again.

2. Whisk together the flour, baking powder, and salt in a medium bowl. Set aside.

3. In a separate bowl, whisk the yolks together until yellow and creamy. Add ½ cup sugar in a steady stream and beat until well mixed. Stir in the vanilla. Slowly stream into the flour mixture until incorporated.

4. In another large mixing bowl, beat the egg whites with an electric mixer until soft peaks form. Gradually add the remaining sugar. Continue beating until stiff peaks form. Fold the egg whites into the batter.

5. Pour the batter into the prepared pan. Bake for 12–15 minutes or until golden and spongy to the touch.

6. Turn the cake over onto a towel. Peel off the parchment paper then roll the cake and towel together tightly, starting with the narrow end. Allow to cool to room temperature.

7. Unroll and spread with jam. Re-roll and slice with a bread or serrated cake knife.

PER SERVING Calories: 180 | Fat: 2 g | Protein: 3 g | Sodium: 143 mg | Fiber: 0 g | Carbohydrates: 37 g | Sugar: 26 g

Nectarine Upside-Down Cake

The sugars in the nectarines caramelize, forming a sort of sauce.

INGREDIENTS | SERVES 10

½ cup unsalted butter, at room temperature, divided use

½ cup light brown sugar

1 egg, at room temperature

1 teaspoon vanilla

1 cup flour

1 teaspoon baking powder

¼ teaspoon salt

⅓ cup buttermilk

¼ cup demerara sugar

2 cups sliced nectarines

Demerara Sugar Facts

Demerara sugar is a type of natural brown sugar. It is made by partially refining sugar cane extract rather than by adding molasses. It is easily recognizable by its dry, large, light brown crystals.

1. Preheat oven to 350°F.

2. In a large bowl, cream together 7 tablespoons of butter and the brown sugar. Once combined, add the egg and vanilla; beat thoroughly.

3. In a medium bowl, whisk together the flour, baking powder, and salt.

4. Add the buttermilk and the flour mixture to the butter mixture alternately, beginning and ending with the flour mixture. The batter should be very fluffy.

5. Use the remaining tablespoon of butter to coat the bottom and sides of an 8" × 8" baking pan. Sprinkle the demerara sugar over the butter, top with nectarine slices. Pour the batter over the mixture.

6. Bake for 40 minutes or until a toothpick inserted in the middle comes out with a few moist but not wet crumbs.

7. Cool completely on a wire rack. Invert onto a platter to serve upside down.

PER SERVING Calories: 203 | Fat: 10 g | Protein: 2 g | Sodium: 79 mg | Fiber: 1 g | Carbohydrates: 27 g | Sugar: 17 g

Raspberry Icebox Pie

Icebox pies are perfect for summer because they require no baking; they set up in the refrigerator.

INGREDIENTS | SERVES 8

¼ cup cornstarch

¼ cup water

5 cups raspberries, divided use

2 tablespoons lemon juice

¼ cup sugar

¼ teaspoon minced fresh mint

1 tablespoon unsalted butter

1 (10-inch) graham cracker pie crust

Graham Cracker Crust

You can buy a graham cracker crust or make your own: Mix 2 cups of finely crushed graham crackers, 3 tablespoons sugar and 3–4 tablespoons of butter until the crumbs are dampened. Press the mixture into a pie plate. Use the bottom of a measuring spoon to flatten until well packed.

1. Whisk together the cornstarch and water; set aside.

2. In a medium saucepan, bring 3 cups of the raspberries, lemon juice, and sugar to a boil. After the raspberries come to a boil, stir in the cornstarch mixture and mint.

3. Continue to cook for 2 minutes. Remove from heat and stir in the remaining 2 cups of raspberries and the butter.

4. Pour into the pie shell. Refrigerate for 4–6 hours before serving.

PER SERVING Calories: 222 | Fat: 7 g | Protein: 2 g | Sodium: 89 mg | Fiber: 5 g | Carbohydrates: 39 g | Sugar: 20 g

Key Lime Bars

Look for diminutive Key limes at your local store during winter months.

INGREDIENTS | SERVES 12

2 cups graham cracker crumbs

¼ cup unsalted butter, melted and cooled slightly

4 eggs, at room temperature

1¾ cups sugar

¾ cup freshly squeezed Key lime juice

¾ cup flour

1½ tablespoons Key lime zest

1. Preheat oven to 350°F.

2. In a small bowl, mix together the graham cracker crumbs and melted butter with a fork. Press into the bottom of an 8" × 8" baking pan. Bake for 5 minutes. Set aside.

3. Meanwhile, in a medium bowl, whisk together eggs, sugar, Key lime juice, flour, and zest. Pour over the graham cracker crust.

4. Return the pan to the oven and bake for 35 minutes or until the bars are fully set. Cool completely before slicing.

PER SERVING Calories: 303 | Fat: 6 g | Protein: 6 g | Sodium: 28 mg | Fiber: 1 g | Carbohydrates: 58 g | Sugar: 30 g

Oatmeal-Jam Bars

If available, homemade jam really takes these bars to the next level.

INGREDIENTS | SERVES 12

¾ cup unsalted butter, at room temperature

¾ cup light brown sugar

2 cups old-fashioned rolled oats

1 cup all-purpose flour

¾ teaspoon baking powder

½ teaspoon cinnamon

½ teaspoon ground ginger

¼ teaspoon freshly ground nutmeg

½ cup chopped hazelnuts

¾ cup jam

The Healthful Oat

Oats have been credited with having cholesterol-lowering properties. They are an excellent source of soluble fiber. Oats have the highest protein levels of any of the cereal grains.

1. Preheat oven to 350°F.

2. In a large bowl, cream together the butter and brown sugar.

3. In a separate bowl, whisk together oats, flour, baking powder, and spices. Add to the butter mixture and stir to combine. Fold in hazelnuts.

4. Grease an 8" × 8" baking dish. Press 2 cups of the oat mixture into the pan. Spread with jam. Sprinkle the remaining oat mixture over the jam to coat.

5. Bake 25 minutes. Cool completely before cutting into squares.

PER SERVING Calories: 290 | Fat: 15 g | Protein: 3 g | Sodium: 43 mg | Fiber: 2 g | Carbohydrates: 37 g | Sugar: 23 g

Boysenberry Custard Pie

Boysenberries are a cross between raspberries, blackberries, and loganberries.

INGREDIENTS | SERVES 8

1¼ cups sugar
1 cup water
1 cup boysenberry juice
⅓ cup cornstarch
2 tablespoons unsalted butter
4 egg yolks, beaten
1 prepared pie crust

DIY Berry Juice

Make your own berry juice by mashing the berries through a sieve into a bowl. Use a whisk to press any extra juice out of the pulp left in the sieve. Refrigerate the juice until ready to use.

1. Preheat oven to 350°F.

2. In a medium saucepan, whisk together the sugar, water, juice, and cornstarch. Bring the mixture to a boil. Stir in butter. Reduce heat to low.

3. Place the egg yolks in a bowl. Take ½ cup of the boysenberry mixture and gradually whisk it into the egg yolks.

4. Whisk the egg mixture into the boysenberry mixture on the stove. Bring it to a boil and cook, whisking continuously until very thick, about 5–20 minutes.

5. Pour into pie crust. Bake 10 minutes. Cool completely before slicing.

PER SERVING Calories: 209 | Fat: 5 g | Protein: 1 g | Sodium: 7 mg | Fiber: 0 g | Carbohydrates: 40 g | Sugar: 37 g

Pomegranate Chiffon Cake

Garnish this cake with fresh pomegranate arils or a drizzle of pomegranate molasses.

INGREDIENTS | SERVES 12

2¼ cups cake flour

1½ cups sugar, divided use

1 tablespoon baking powder

½ teaspoon salt

6 eggs, separated

¾ cup fresh pomegranate juice

2 tablespoons lime zest

½ cup canola oil

1 teaspoon cream of tartar

Tube Pan Versus Bundt

It is important to use the pan called for in the recipe. Tube pans have straight sides so delicate cakes can be removed easily. Bundt pans often have designs that the cake sticks to, and are better suited to sturdier cakes.

1. Preheat oven to 325°F.

2. In a large bowl, whisk together the flour, 1¼ cups sugar, baking powder, and salt. Beat in the egg yolks, juice, zest, and oil. Mix until well combined. Set aside.

3. In a separate bowl, beat the egg whites until frothy. Add the cream of tartar and beat into soft peaks. Gradually stream the remaining ¼ cup sugar and beat into stiff peaks.

4. Gently fold the egg whites into the batter using a spoon.

5. Pour the batter into a footed tube pan and bake 1 hour. Invert the pan and cool completely before releasing the cake.

PER SERVING Calories: 316 | Fat: 12 g | Protein: 5 g | Sodium: 257 mg | Fiber: 0 g | Carbohydrates: 48 g | Sugar: 27 g

Cranberry-Walnut Cake

This is a festive addition to any holiday table.

To Toast or Not to Toast?

Toasting nuts can bring out their flavor. If a pronounced nutty flavor is desired, toasting is a good idea. Toasted nuts can be used interchangeably with untoasted.

1. Preheat oven to 350°F. Grease a bundt pan.

2. In a large bowl, cream together the butter and brown sugar. Once combined, add the milk, eggs, sour cream, and vanilla paste. Beat until smooth.

3. In a medium bowl, whisk together the flours, baking soda, baking powder, and salt. Slowly stream it into the wet ingredients until well incorporated. Fold in walnuts, and cranberries.

4. Pour into the prepared pan. Bake 55 minutes or until a thin knife inserted into the middle of the cake comes out clean.

5. Cool for 5 minutes in the pan then remove and cool completely on a wire rack.

PER SERVING Calories: 324 | Fat: 14 g | Protein: 5 g | Sodium: 206 mg | Fiber: 1 g | Carbohydrates: 45 g | Sugar: 24 g

Lime Sparkle Cookies

These cookies sparkle on the outside and have a chewy, soft, lime-packing interior.

INGREDIENTS | SERVES 8

Demerara sugar, for rolling

½ cup unsalted butter, at room temperature

⅔ cup sugar

1 egg, at room temperature

2½ tablespoons golden syrup

2 tablespoons lime juice

¾ cup all-purpose flour

¾ cup white whole-wheat flour

1 teaspoon baking powder

2 tablespoons lime zest

1. Preheat oven to 350°F. Line 2 cookie sheets with parchment paper. Set aside.

2. Sprinkle some demerara sugar on a plate. Set aside.

3. In a large bowl, cream together the butter and sugar. Once combined, beat in the egg, golden syrup, and lime juice until well incorporated.

4. Mix in the flours, baking powder, and lime zest until smooth.

5. Roll into 1-inch balls, then lightly roll in the demerara sugar.

6. Place on the baking sheet 2 inches apart. Flatten the balls slightly with a spatula.

7. Bake 8 minutes. Cool on a wire rack.

PER SERVING Calories: 264 | Fat: 12 g | Protein: 3 g | Sodium: 72 mg | Fiber: 1 g | Carbohydrates: 36 g | Sugar: 17 g

Fresh Cherry Oatmeal Cookies

Wait until these cookies are fully cool before eating; the cherry juice gets molten hot!

INGREDIENTS | YIELDS 2 DOZEN COOKIES

¼ cup unsalted butter, at room temperature

¾ cup light brown sugar

1 egg, at room temperature

1 teaspoon vanilla

¾ cup all-purpose flour

½ cup old-fashioned rolled oats

1 teaspoon baking powder

¼ teaspoon salt

1½ cups chopped fresh cherries

1. Preheat oven to 350°F. Line 2 cookie sheets with parchment paper.

2. In a large bowl, cream together the butter and brown sugar. Once combined, beat in the egg and the vanilla.

3. In a separate bowl, whisk together the flour, oats, baking powder, and salt. Add to the butter mixture and mix until well combined. Fold in cherries.

4. Place tablespoons of dough 2 inches apart on the cookie sheets.

5. Bake for 12 minutes or until the top of the cookie is mostly set and the bottoms are golden.

6. Carefully remove to a wire rack and cool completely.

PER SERVING Calories: 81 | Fat: 2 g | Protein: 1 g | Sodium: 51 mg | Fiber: 0 g | Carbohydrates: 15 g | Sugar: 10 g

Spiced Pear Pie

An alternative to the more traditional apple pie, pear pie is an autumnal treat.

INGREDIENTS | SERVES 10

2½ pounds Anjou pears, cored, peeled, and sliced

½ cup light brown sugar

1½ tablespoons unsalted butter, cubed

½ teaspoon cinnamon

½ teaspoon ground ginger

¼ teaspoon allspice

¼ teaspoon ground cloves

⅛ teaspoon freshly ground nutmeg

1 double pie crust

Cheddar Pie Crust

Try this crust instead of a plain pie crust. In a food processor, pulse 2 cups flour, ½ cup cold unsalted butter, ½ cup grated sharp Cheddar cheese, and ½ teaspoon salt. Slowly add 5 tablespoons cold water to form a ball. Divide in two and roll out on a floured surface to form two crusts. Place one in the pie plate, reserving the second for the top crust.

1. Preheat oven to 350°F. Line a pie plate with 1 pie crust.

2. Place all of the pie ingredients in a large bowl and stir to evenly distribute all ingredients.

3. Pour into the pie plate. Use the back of a spoon to spread the mixture evenly. Cover with the remaining pie crust and press shut. Pierce the top with the tines of a fork.

4. Bake for 30 minutes or until the filling is bubbly and the crust is golden. Cool before slicing.

PER SERVING Calories: 326 | Fat: 14 g | Protein: 2 g | Sodium: 192 mg | Fiber: 4 g | Carbohydrates: 51 g | Sugar: 22 g

Zesty Hamantaschen

Hamantaschen are the official cookie of Purim. They are supposed to resemble the ears of Haman, the enemy of the Jewish people.

INGREDIENTS | YIELDS 2 DOZEN COOKIES

¾ cup unsalted butter, at room temperature

½ cup sugar

3 eggs, at room temperature

3 cups all-purpose flour

2½ teaspoons baking powder

1 teaspoon orange zest

1 teaspoon lemon zest

½ teaspoon lime zest

8 ounces jam

1. Preheat oven to 375°F. Line 2 cookie sheets with parchment paper. Set aside.

2. Cream together the butter and sugar. Once combined, beat in the eggs.

3. In a separate bowl, whisk together the flour, baking powder, and zests. Add to the butter mixture and mix until a thick dough forms.

4. Place the dough on a flat, floured surface. Roll the dough out to ¼-inch thick.

5. Use a 2½-inch round cookie cutter to cut out rounds. Place on cookie sheets 2 inches apart.

6. Spoon a small amount of jam into the center of every cookie. Fold the top and both sides toward the middle and press the corners shut, forming a triangle with a small window of jam in the center. Repeat for each cookie.

7. Bake for 12 minutes or until golden. Cool on wire rack.

PER SERVING Calories: 159 | Fat: 7 g | Protein: 2 g | Sodium: 21 mg | Fiber: 1 g | Carbohydrates: 23 g | Sugar: 9 g

Star Anise Pears

Poaching pears makes them incredibly tender. Serve these as is or with ice cream.

INGREDIENTS | SERVES 4

4 pears, halved lengthwise
1 teaspoon ground star anise
⅓ cup sugar
½ cup water

1. Use a small spoon or melon baller to scoop out the seeds of each pear. Heat a large nonstick skillet over medium heat.

2. In a small bowl, whisk together the star anise and sugar. Pour onto a plate.

3. Press the cut side of each pear into the sugar.

4. Place the pear halves, sugar side down, into the skillet and cook 5–8 minutes or until the pears begin to brown. Add the water. Cover and simmer for 5 more minutes or until the pears are tender.

5. Remove the pears to a platter. Reduce the water-sugar mixture remaining in the skillet until syrupy, about 2 minutes, and pour over pears. Serve.

PER SERVING Calories: 161 | Fat: 0 g | Protein: 1 g | Sodium: 2 mg | Fiber: 5 g | Carbohydrates: 42 g | Sugar: 33 g

Peach Coffee Cake

Coffee cake gets a fruity twist when peaches are added. Make this at the height of peach season.

INGREDIENTS | SERVES 10

½ cup unsalted butter, at room temperature, divided use
¾ cup light brown sugar
¾ cup buttermilk, at room temperature
1 teaspoon vanilla bean paste
1 egg, at room temperature
2 cups white whole-wheat flour
1 teaspoon baking powder
1 teaspoon baking soda
½ teaspoon sea salt
2 peaches, peeled and sliced thinly
½ cup sugar
⅓ cup all-purpose flour

1. Preheat oven to 350°F. Grease a 9-inch springform pan.

2. In a large bowl, cream together ¼ cup butter and light brown sugar. Once combined, beat in the buttermilk, vanilla paste, and egg until well incorporated.

3. Add the white whole-wheat flour, baking powder, baking soda, and salt. Mix until a batter forms.

4. Pour into the pan. Top with a single layer of peach slices.

5. In a small bowl, use a fork to mix together the remaining butter, sugar, and flour until it forms coarse crumbs. Sprinkle over the peaches.

6. Bake for 50 minutes or until a toothpick inserted in the middle of the cake comes out clean. Cool for at least 15 minutes before releasing the cake and serving.

PER SERVING Calories: 315 | Fat: 10 g | Protein: 5 g | Sodium: 325 mg | Fiber: 1 g | Carbohydrates: 52 g | Sugar: 30 g

Vanilla Bean Frozen Yogurt

A healthier dessert or smoothie ingredient; no preservatives and only three ingredients!

INGREDIENTS | SERVES 6

4 cups plain 2% Greek yogurt

¾ cup sugar

1 tablespoon vanilla bean paste

What Is Vanilla Bean Paste?

Vanilla bean paste is a thick vanilla extract that is flecked with vanilla bean specks. It is a cheaper alternative than using and scraping out whole beans, but more flavorful than regular extract.

1. In a medium bowl, stir together all of the ingredients until the sugar dissolves.

2. Pour the mixture into an ice cream maker and churn until thick. Freeze in a freezer-safe container.

PER SERVING Calories: 186 | Fat: 0 g | Protein: 16 g | Sodium: 62 mg | Fiber: 0 g | Carbohydrates: 31 g | Sugar: 31 g

Recommended Online Resources

Whole Living
The online version of the popular magazine of the same name, wholeliving.com is an invaluable resource of tips, videos, and recipes focusing on whole foods and healthy living.
www.wholeliving.com

Slow Food
Slow Food is a worldwide organization that champions local food traditions, whole foods, and an awareness of where food comes from.
www.slowfood.com

Farmers' Market Search
Search engine for U.S. farmers' market locations.
http://search.ams.usda.gov/farmersmarkets

Locavore
Free iPhone and Android application for finding local, in-season foods and farmers' markets.
www.getlocavore.com

Epicurious: Seasonal Ingredient Map
Map showing which foods are in-season in every state, by month.
www.epicurious.com/articlesguides/seasonal cooking/farmtotable/seasonalingredientmap

Coopdirectory.org
Directory of food co-op locations in the United States.
www.coopdirectory.org

Food on the Table
A free meal planning and grocery list generating site.
www.foodonthetable.com

LocalHarvest
Locator service for family farms, CSAs, pick-your-own farms and farm stands.
www.localharvest.org

Sustainable Table
Online resource for learning more, and teaching others about, sustainable home cooking.
www.sustainabletable.org

FoodRoutes
A nonprofit organization dedicated to "reintroducing Americans to their food."
www.foodroutes.org

Whole Foods Shopping List

Meats and Seafood

- Pork
- Beef
- Chicken
- Turkey
- Duck
- Bison
- Venison
- Sablefish
- Salmon
- Tuna
- Sea and bay scallops
- Shrimp
- Oysters

Fruits and Vegetables

- Cherries
- Strawberries
- Rhubarb
- Watermelon
- Cucumber
- Swiss and rainbow chard
- Tomato
- Eggplant
- Zucchini
- Lettuces

- Red, white, and yellow onions
- Spring onions, scallions, green onions
- Sweet potatoes, Yukon Gold potatoes, and russet potatoes
- Apples
- Pears

Dairy

- Milk
- Buttermilk
- Plain and Greek yogurt
- Eggs
- Sour cream

Dry Goods

- du Puy lentils
- Black, white, and kidney beans
- Bulgur wheat
- Farro
- All-purpose, white whole-wheat, whole-wheat, and buckwheat flours
- Brown and white rice
- Walnuts, black walnuts, pinenuts, almonds, hazelnuts

Weekly Meal Plan

▼ ONE WEEK OF WHOLE FOODS

Day	Breakfast	Lunch	Dinner
Sunday	Banana Black Walnut Muffin	Summer Salad with Poached Egg	Chicken Pot Pie
Monday	Power Green Smoothie	Peach and Chevre Panino	Spicy Peanut Noodles
Tuesday	Breakfast Tacos	Beet and Grapefruit Salad	Sausage and Rapini with White Beans
Wednesday	Berry-Oatmeal Smoothie	Hummus and Tofu Sandwich	Black Bean Tacos
Thursday	Milk and Oat Bars	Tuna Cannellini Sandwich	Maryland Crab Soup
Friday	Crab Scramble	Dilled Shrimp on Rye Crisp Bread	Buddha Bowl
Saturday	Raspberry Waffles	Chicken-Sage Burgers	Shrimp Drunken Noodles

Whole Foods for Healing

Allergies

- Cranberries
- Pineapples
- Cherries
- Mango
- Lamb

High Cholesterol

- Oatmeal
- Wheat berries
- Buckwheat
- Walnuts
- Lentils

Breast Cancer

- Whole Grains
- Soybeans
- Kiwi
- Lentils
- Flaxseed

Osteoporosis

- Kale
- Spinach
- Swiss chard
- Soy
- Yogurt

Inflammation

- Pineapple
- Cabbage
- Papaya
- Olives
- Cucumbers

Standard U.S./Metric Measurement Conversions

VOLUME CONVERSIONS

U.S. Volume Measure	Metric Equivalent
⅛ teaspoon	0.5 milliliters
¼ teaspoon	1 milliliters
½ teaspoon	2 milliliters
1 teaspoon	5 milliliters
½ tablespoon	7 milliliters
1 tablespoon (3 teaspoons)	15 milliliters
2 tablespoons (1 fluid ounce)	30 milliliters
¼ cup (4 tablespoons)	60 milliliters
⅓ cup	90 milliliters
½ cup (4 fluid ounces)	125 milliliters
⅔ cup	160 milliliters
¾ cup (6 fluid ounces)	180 milliliters
1 cup (16 tablespoons)	250 milliliters
1 pint (2 cups)	500 milliliters
1 quart (4 cups)	1 liter (about)

WEIGHT CONVERSIONS

U.S. Weight Measure	Metric Equivalent
½ ounce	15 grams
1 ounce	30 grams
2 ounces	60 grams
3 ounces	85 grams
¼ pound (4 ounces)	115 grams
½ pound (8 ounces)	225 grams
¾ pound (12 ounces)	340 grams
1 pound (16 ounces)	454 grams

Standard U.S./Metric Measurement Conversions (continued)

OVEN TEMPERATURE CONVERSIONS

Degrees Fahrenheit	Degrees Celsius
200 degrees F	95 degrees C
250 degrees F	120 degrees C
275 degrees F	135 degrees C
300 degrees F	150 degrees C
325 degrees F	160 degrees C
350 degrees F	180 degrees C
375 degrees F	190 degrees C
400 degrees F	205 degrees C
425 degrees F	220 degrees C
450 degrees F	230 degrees C

BAKING PAN SIZES

American	Metric
8 x 1½ inch round baking pan	20 x 4 cm cake tin
9 x 1½ inch round baking pan	23 x 3.5 cm cake tin
11 x 7 x 1½ inch baking pan	28 x 18 x 4 cm baking tin
13 x 9 x 2 inch baking pan	30 x 20 x 5 cm baking tin
2 quart rectangular baking dish	30 x 20 x 3 cm baking tin
15 x 10 x 2 inch baking pan	30 x 25 x 2 cm baking tin (Swiss roll tin)
9 inch pie plate	22 x 4 or 23 x 4 cm pie plate
7 or 8 inch springform pan	18 or 20 cm springform or loose bottom cake tin
9 x 5 x 3 inch loaf pan	23 x 13 x 7 cm or 2 lb narrow loaf or pate tin
1½ quart casserole	1.5 liter casserole
2 quart casserole	2 liter casserole

Index

We Have

EVERYTHING®
on Anything!

With more than 19 million copies sold, the Everything® series has become one of America's favorite resources for solving problems, learning new skills, and organizing lives. Our brand is not only recognizable—it's also welcomed.

The series is a hand-in-hand partner for people who are ready to tackle new subjects—like you!

For more information on the Everything® series, please visit *www.adamsmedia.com*

The Everything® list spans a wide range of subjects, with more than 500 titles covering 25 different categories:

Business	History	Reference
Careers	Home Improvement	Religion
Children's Storybooks	Everything Kids	Self-Help
Computers	Languages	Sports & Fitness
Cooking	Music	Travel
Crafts and Hobbies	New Age	Wedding
Education/Schools	Parenting	Writing
Games and Puzzles	Personal Finance	
Health	Pets	